W9-DAA-277

BBC

DOCTOR WHO

THE TWELFTH DOCTOR

VOL 5: THE TWIST

"A hefty dose of style!"
NEWSARAMA

"The art and coloring is terrific!"
DOCTOR WHO NEWS

"Nails the tone of the show."
COMIC BOOK

"Gives me the same sort of feeling I get settling in to watch an episode..."
WE THE NERDY

"Absolutely delightful."
THE GEEK GIRL PROJECT

"A fun, engaging, and gorgeous reading experience"
THE FANDOM POST

"The latest from Titan Comics is touching, heartfelt and visually spectacular."
BLOGTOR WHO

"A smart, funny romp through the world of comic books. Absolutely recommended."
SCI FI PULSE

"Exciting, fast-moving, funny and mysterious."
GEEK MOM

"The Doctor is back and better than ever!"
KABOOOOOM

"Perfect, enjoyable and intriguing!"
MCM BUZZ

"The Twelfth Doctor's comic adventures are something insanely special!"
WARPED FACTOR

"Titan's Twelfth Doctor Who comics are everything that's good about comic books."
FANBOY NATION

TITAN COMICS

SENIOR COMICS EDITOR
Andrew James

ASSISTANT EDITORS
Jessica Burton, Amoona Saohin

COLLECTION DESIGNER
Andrew Leung

TITAN COMICS EDITORIAL
Tom Williams

PRODUCTION ASSISTANT
Peter James

PRODUCTION SUPERVISORS
Maria Pearson, Jackie Flook

PRODUCTION MANAGER
Obi Onuora

ART DIRECTOR
Oz Browne

SENIOR SALES MANAGER
Steve Tothill

PRESS OFFICER
Will O'Mullane

COMICS BRAND MANAGER
Chris Thompson

DIRECT SALES & MARKETING MANAGER
Ricky Claydon

COMMERCIAL MANAGER
Michelle Fairlamb

HEAD OF RIGHTS
Jenny Boyce

PUBLISHING MANAGER
Darryl Tothill

PUBLISHING DIRECTOR
Chris Teather

OPERATIONS DIRECTOR
Leigh Baulch

EXECUTIVE DIRECTOR
Vivian Cheung

PUBLISHER
Nick Landau

Special thanks to Steven Moffat, Brian Minchin, Mandy Thwaites, Matt Nicholls, James Dudley, Edward Russell, Derek Ritchie, Scott Handcock, Kirsty Mullan, Kate Bush, Julia Nocciolino and Ed Casey for their invaluable assistance.

BBC WORLDWIDE

DIRECTOR OF EDITORIAL GOVERNANCE
Nicholas Brett

HEAD OF UK PUBLISHING
Chris Kerwin

DIRECTOR OF CONSUMER PRODUCTS AND PUBLISHING
Andrew Moultrie

PUBLISHER
Mandy Thwaites

PUBLISHING CO-ORDINATOR
Eva Abramik

For rights information
contact Jenny Boyce
jenny.boyce@titanemail.com

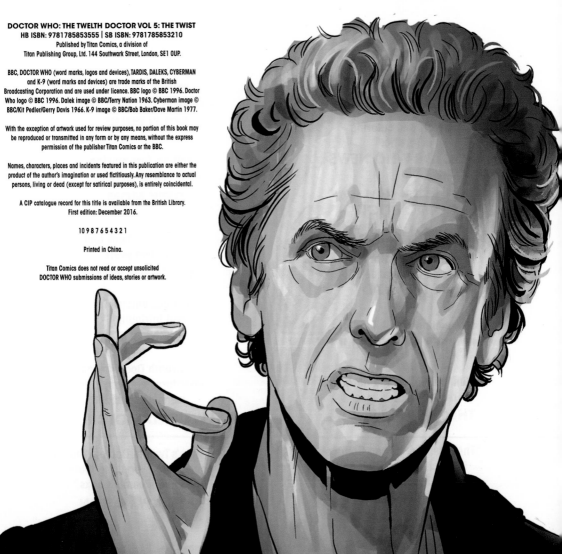

DOCTOR WHO: THE TWELFTH DOCTOR VOL 5: THE TWIST
HB ISBN: 9781785853555 | SB ISBN: 9781785853210
Published by Titan Comics, a division of
Titan Publishing Group, Ltd. 144 Southwark Street, London, SE1 0UP.

A CIP catalogue record for this title is available from the British Library.
First edition: December 2016.

10 9 8 7 6 5 4 3 2 1

Printed in China.

Titan Comics does not read or accept unsolicited
DOCTOR WHO submissions of ideas, stories or artwork.

DOCTOR WHO

THE TWELFTH DOCTOR

VOL 5: THE TWIST

WRITER:
GEORGE MANN

ARTISTS:
MARIANO LACLAUSTRA
& RACHAEL STOTT

WITH AGUS CALCAGNO
& FER CENTURION

COLORISTS:
CARLOS CABRERA,
ALEXANDRE SIQUIERA
& RODRIGO FERNANDES

WITH THIAGO RIBIERO
& JUAN MANUEL TUMBURUS

LETTERS: RICHARD STARKINGS
AND COMICRAFT'S
JIMMY BETANCOURT

TITAN
COMICS

BBC

DOCTOR WHO

THE TWELFTH DOCTOR

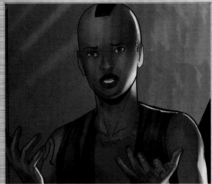

THE DOCTOR

Last of the Time Lords of Gallifrey. Never cruel or cowardly, he champions the oppressed across time and space. Even without a regular companion to show off to, the Doctor still manages to find adventure – and danger – wherever he goes!

HATTIE

Since the departure of Clara Oswald, the Doctor has been adventuring alone. Will he offer a spot on the TARDIS to anyone else? Who knows what kind of exciting people he will next meet on his travels...

THE TARDIS

'Time and Relative Dimension in Space'. Bigger on the inside, this unassuming blue box is your ticket to unforgettable adventure!
The Doctor likes to think he's in control, but more often than not, the TARDIS takes him where and when he needs to be...

PREVIOUSLY...

The Doctor and Clara Oswald saved the universe together for the last time.

Now traveling alone, the Doctor is expanding his horizons, catching up on his favorite music from all across history...

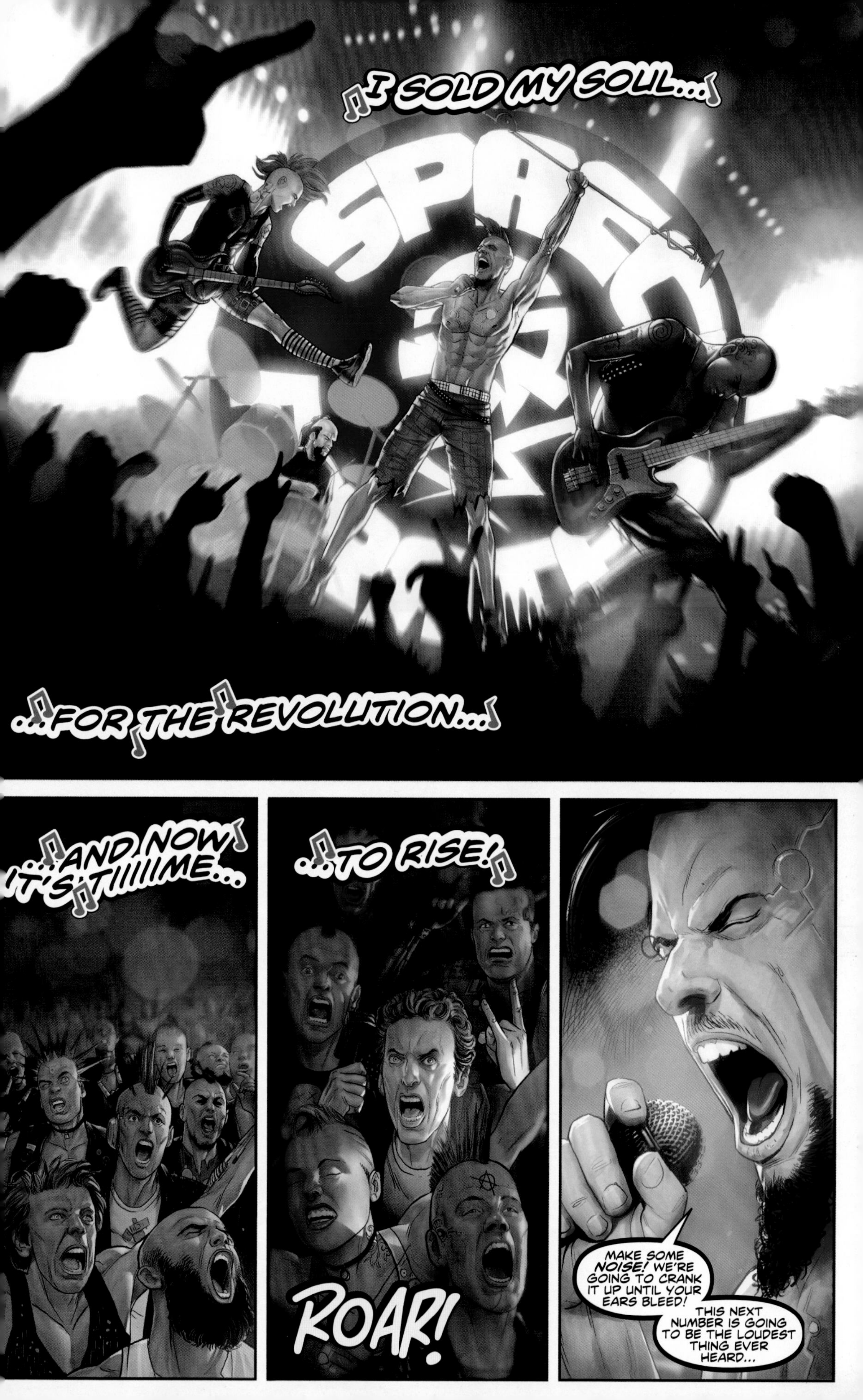

I SOLD MY SOUL...
...FOR THE REVOLUTION...
...AND NOW IT'S TIIIIIIME...
...TO RISE!
ROAR!
MAKE SOME NOISE! WE'RE GOING TO CRANK IT UP UNTIL YOUR EARS BLEED!
THIS NEXT NUMBER IS GOING TO BE THE LOUDEST THING EVER HEARD...

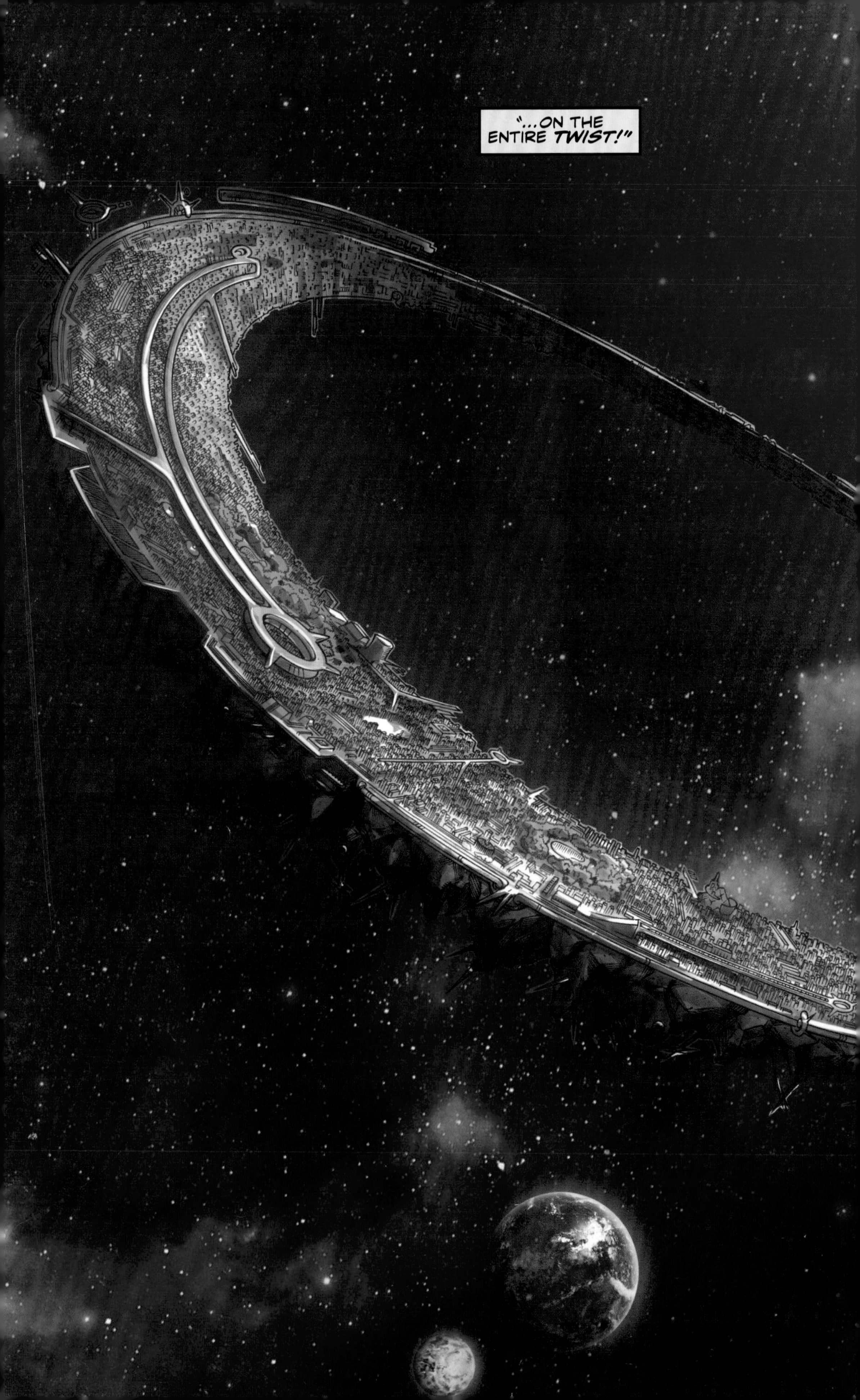
"...ON THE ENTIRE TWIST!"

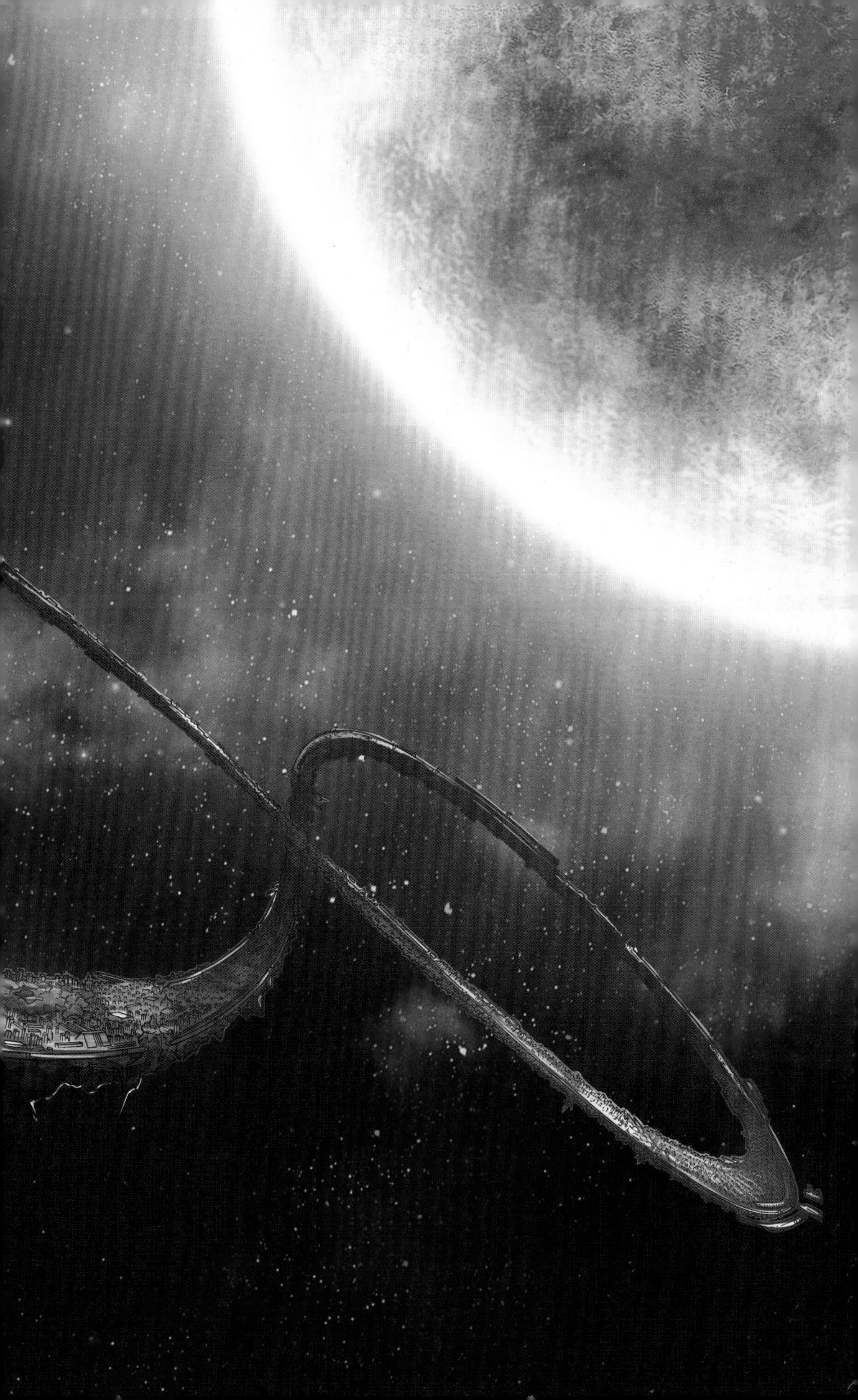

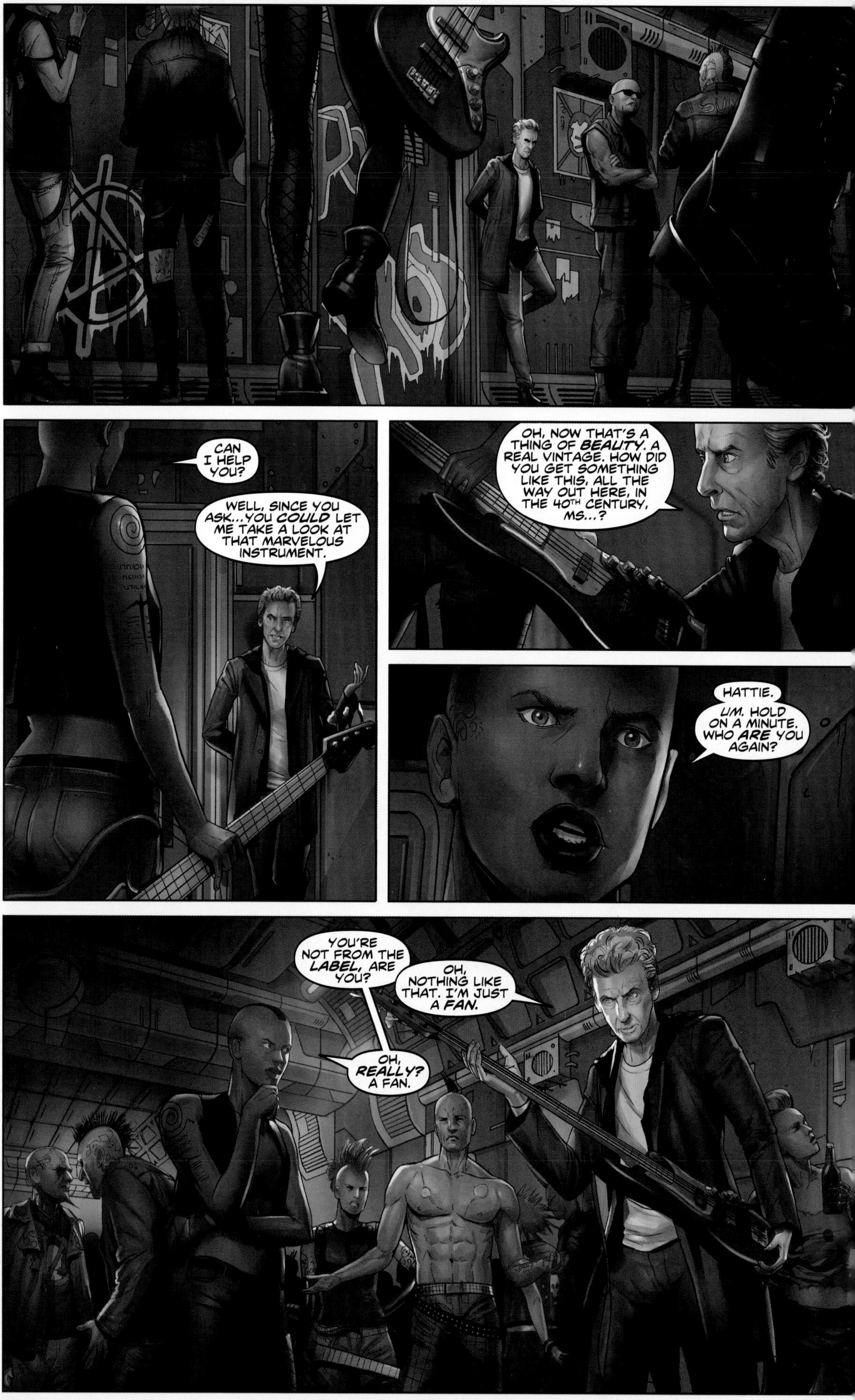
CAN I HELP YOU?
WELL, SINCE YOU ASK...YOU COULD LET ME TAKE A LOOK AT THAT MARVELOUS INSTRUMENT.
OH, NOW THAT'S A THING OF BEAUTY. A REAL VINTAGE. HOW DID YOU GET SOMETHING LIKE THIS, ALL THE WAY OUT HERE, IN THE 40TH CENTURY, MS...?
HATTIE.
UM. HOLD ON A MINUTE. WHO ARE YOU AGAIN?
YOU'RE NOT FROM THE LABEL, ARE YOU?
OH, NOTHING LIKE THAT. I'M JUST A FAN.
OH, REALLY? A FAN.

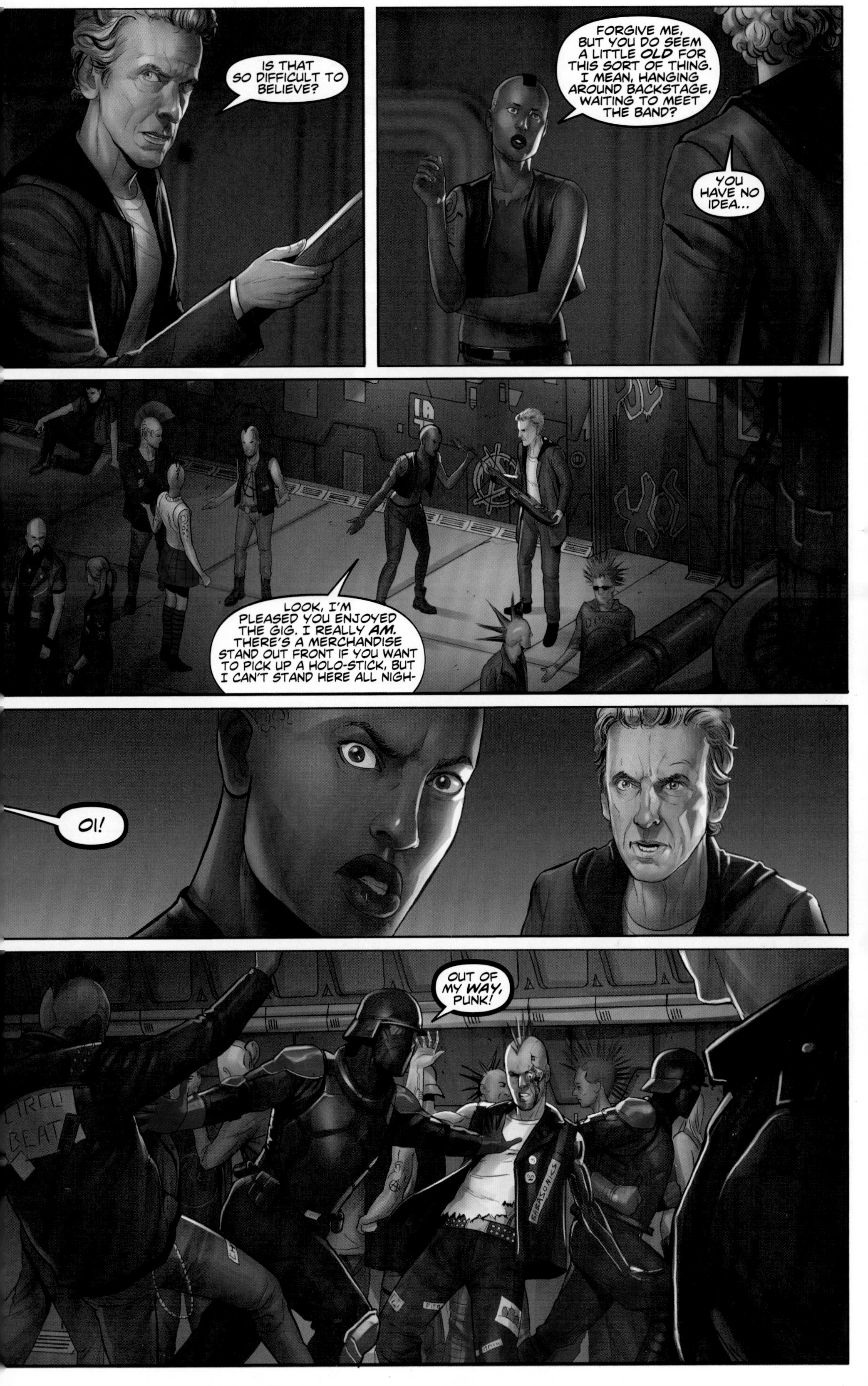
IS THAT SO DIFFICULT TO BELIEVE?
FORGIVE ME, BUT YOU DO SEEM A LITTLE OLD FOR THIS SORT OF THING. I MEAN, HANGING AROUND BACKSTAGE, WAITING TO MEET THE BAND?
YOU HAVE NO IDEA...
LOOK, I'M PLEASED YOU ENJOYED THE GIG. I REALLY AM. THERE'S A MERCHANDISE STAND OUT FRONT IF YOU WANT TO PICK UP A HOLO-STICK, BUT I CAN'T STAND HERE ALL NIGH-
OI!
OUT OF MY WAY, PUNK!

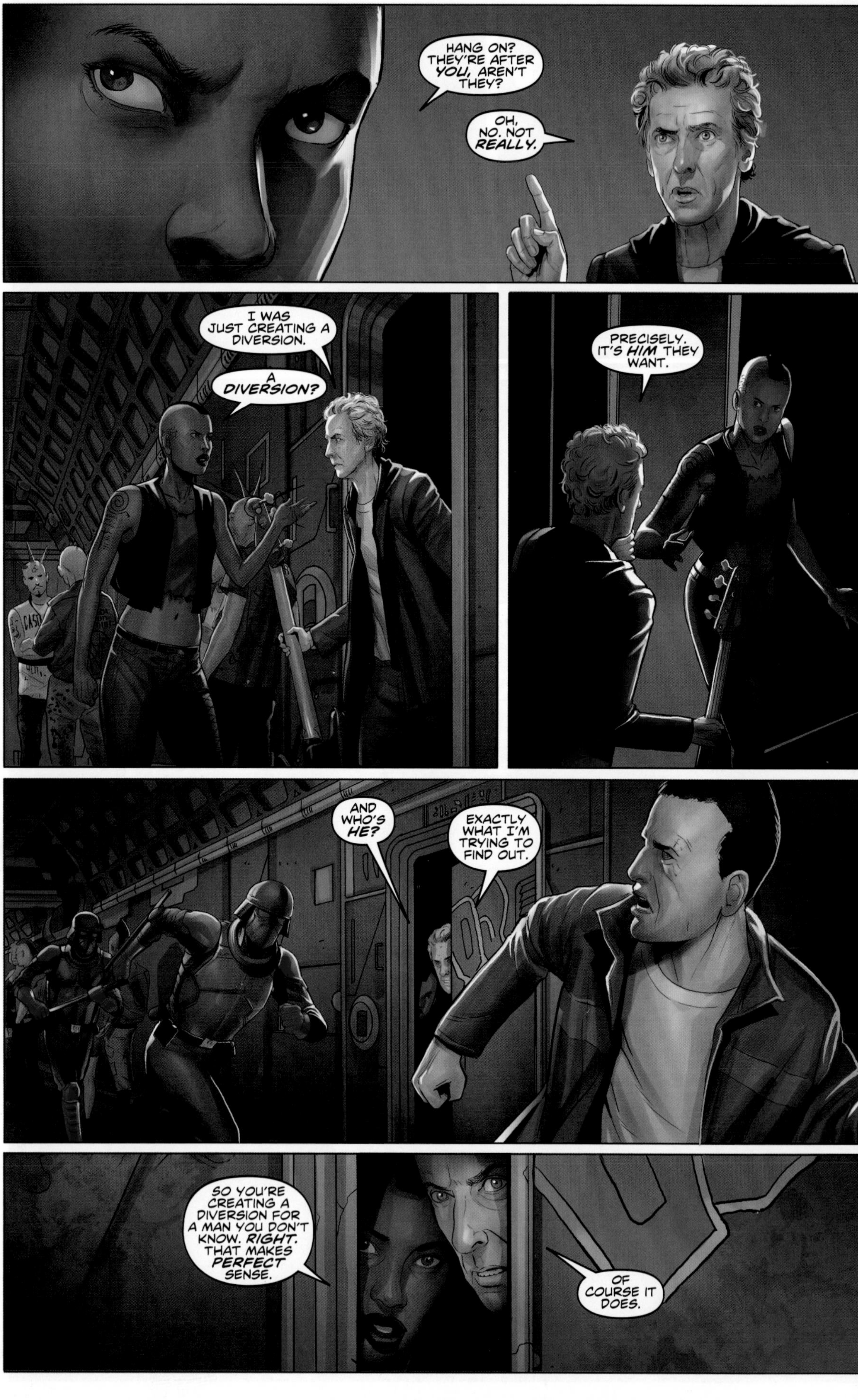
HANG ON? THEY'RE AFTER YOU, AREN'T THEY?
OH, NO. NOT REALLY.
I WAS JUST CREATING A DIVERSION.
A DIVERSION?
PRECISELY. IT'S HIM THEY WANT.
AND WHO'S HE?
EXACTLY WHAT I'M TRYING TO FIND OUT.
SO YOU'RE CREATING A DIVERSION FOR A MAN YOU DON'T KNOW. RIGHT. THAT MAKES PERFECT SENSE.
OF COURSE IT DOES.

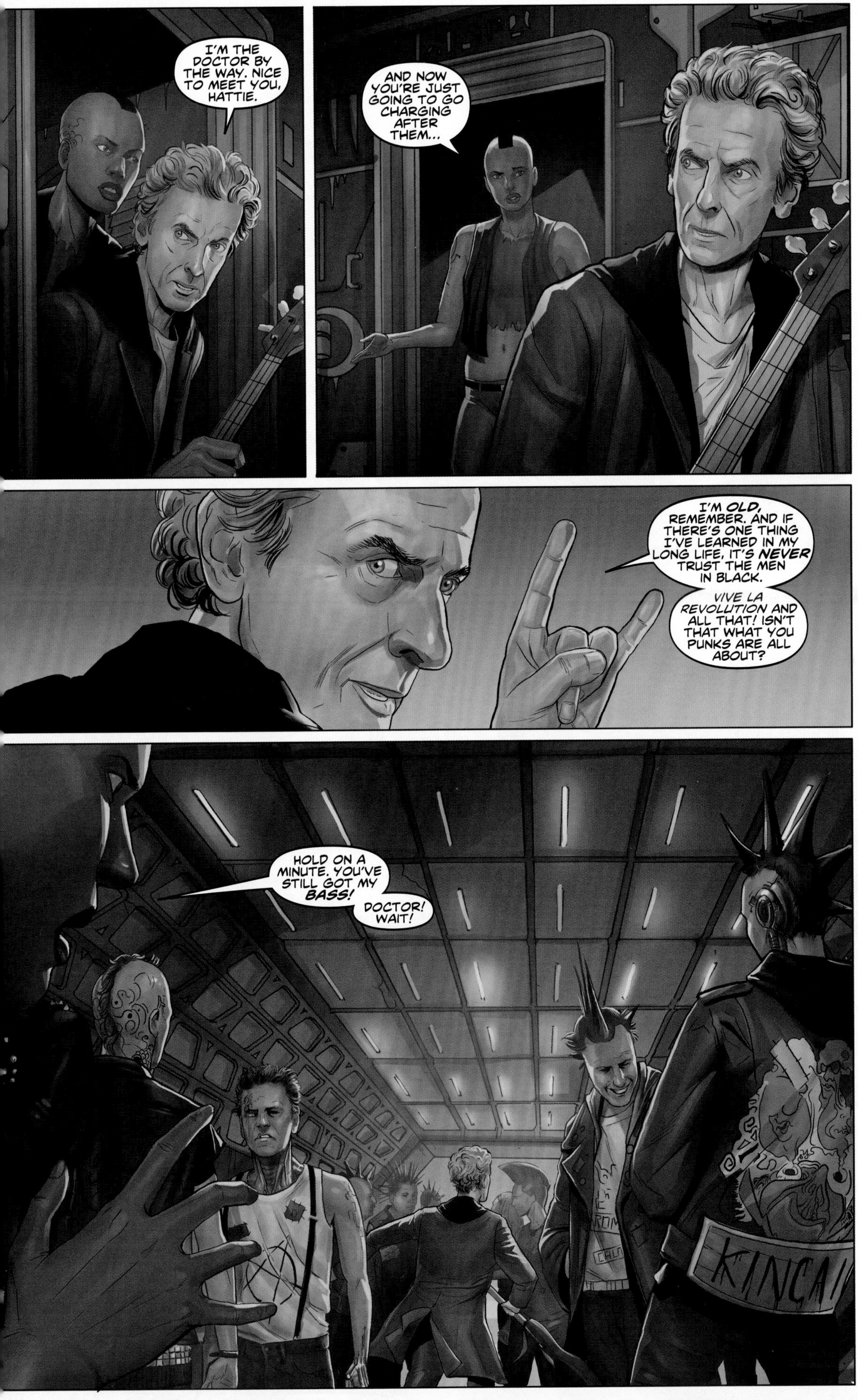
I'M THE DOCTOR BY THE WAY. NICE TO MEET YOU, HATTIE.
AND NOW YOU'RE JUST GOING TO GO CHARGING AFTER THEM...
I'M **OLD**, REMEMBER. AND IF THERE'S ONE THING I'VE LEARNED IN MY LONG LIFE, IT'S **NEVER** TRUST THE MEN IN BLACK.
VIVE LA REVOLUTION AND ALL THAT! ISN'T THAT WHAT YOU PUNKS ARE ALL ABOUT?
HOLD ON A MINUTE. YOU'VE STILL GOT MY **BASS!**
DOCTOR! WAIT!

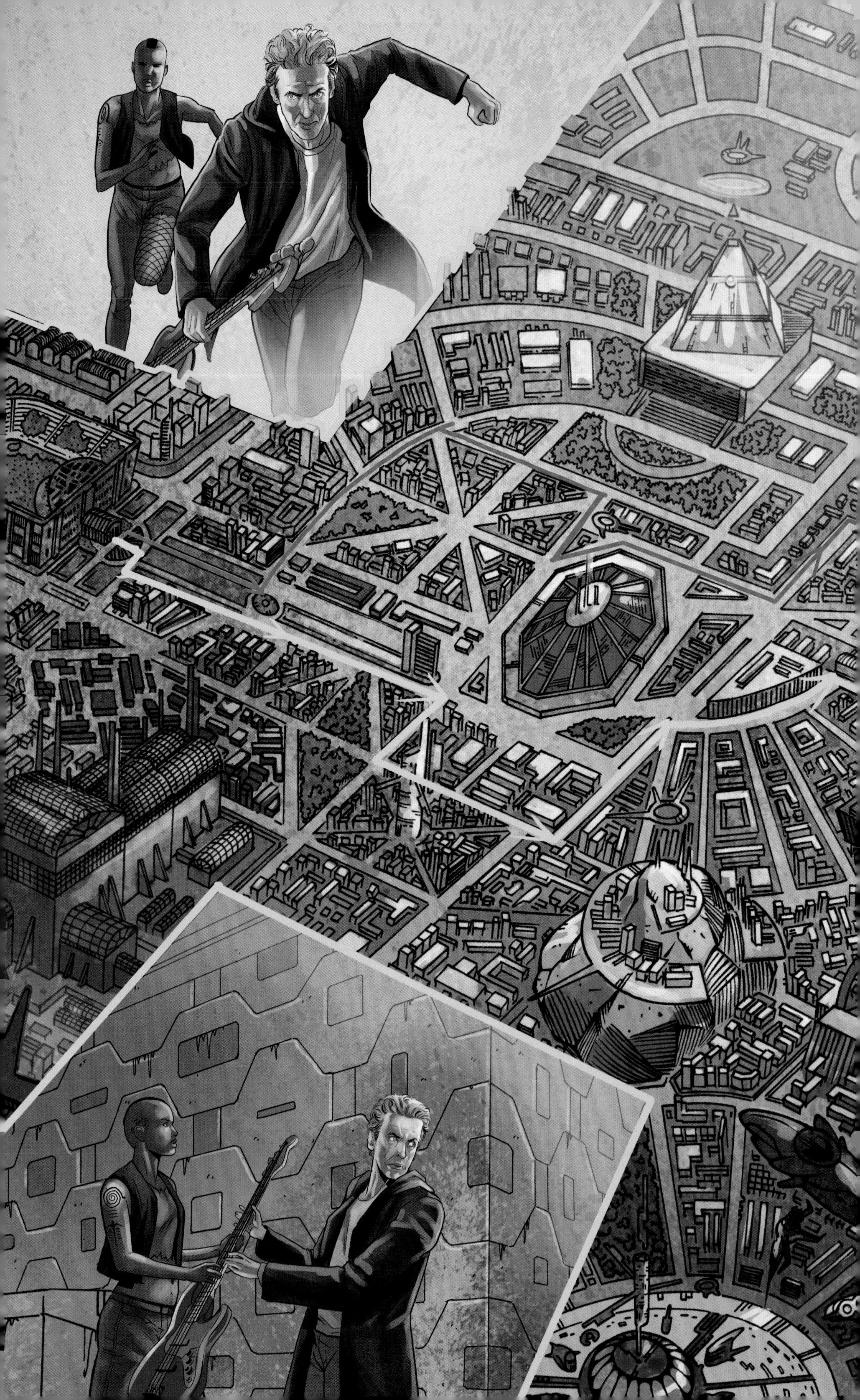

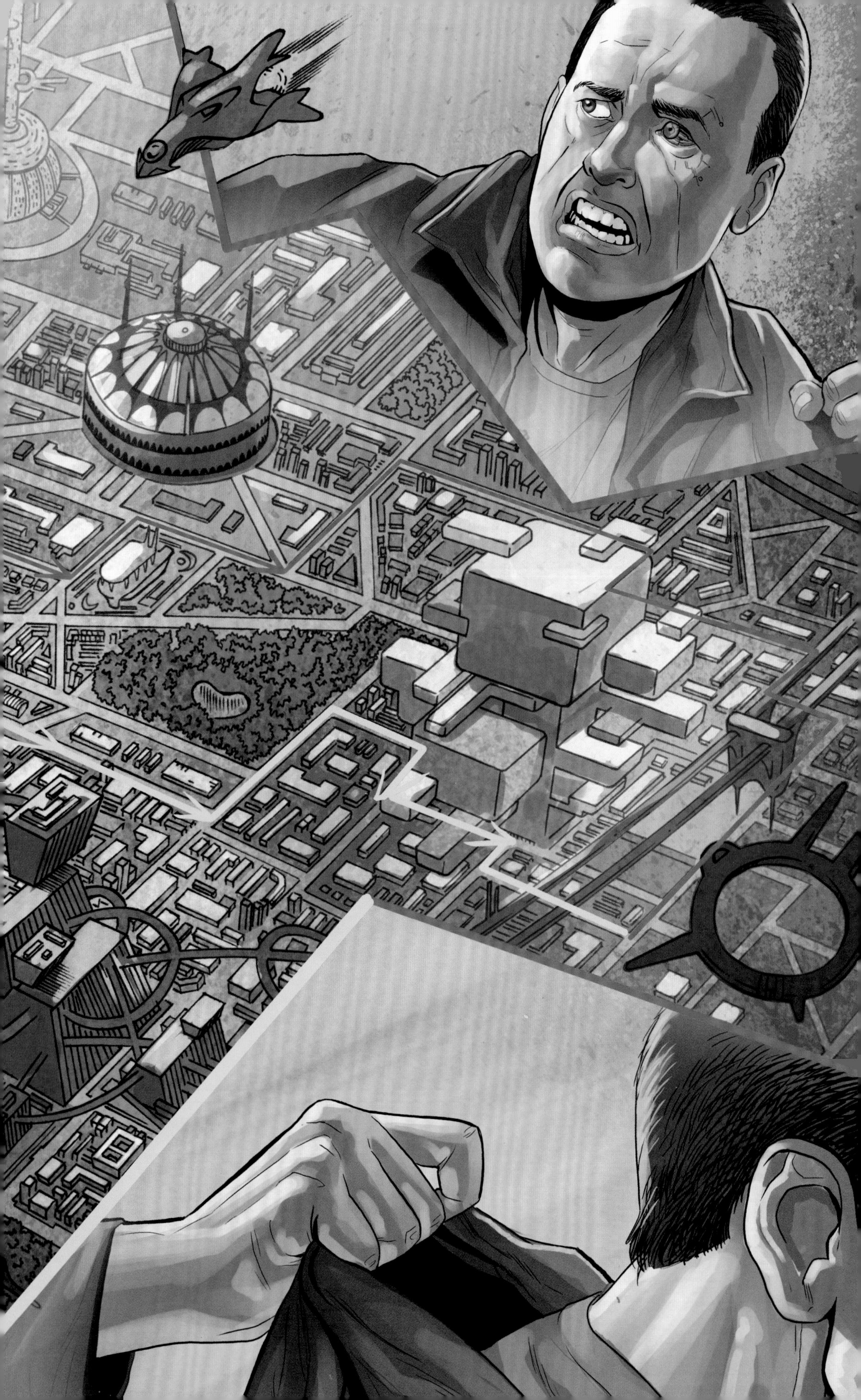

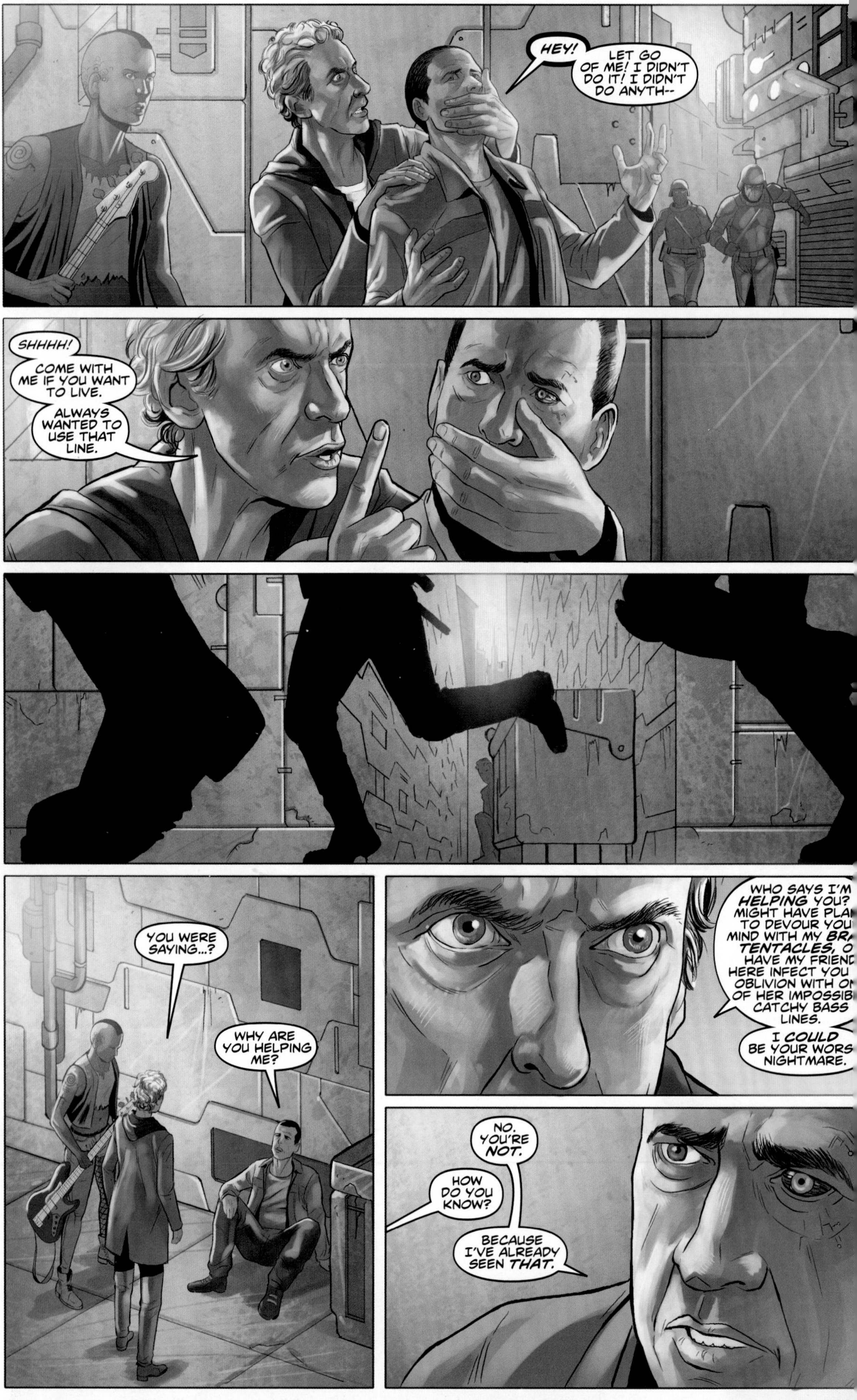
HEY!
LET GO OF ME! I DIDN'T DO IT! I DIDN'T DO ANYTH--
SHHHH!
COME WITH ME IF YOU WANT TO LIVE.
ALWAYS WANTED TO USE THAT LINE.
YOU WERE SAYING...?
WHY ARE YOU HELPING ME?
WHO SAYS I'M HELPING YOU? MIGHT HAVE PLA TO DEVOUR YOU MIND WITH MY BR TENTACLES, O HAVE MY FRIEND HERE INFECT YOU OBLIVION WITH O OF HER IMPOSSIB CATCHY BASS LINES.
I COULD BE YOUR WORS NIGHTMARE.
NO. YOU'RE NOT.
HOW DO YOU KNOW?
BECAUSE I'VE ALREADY SEEN THAT.

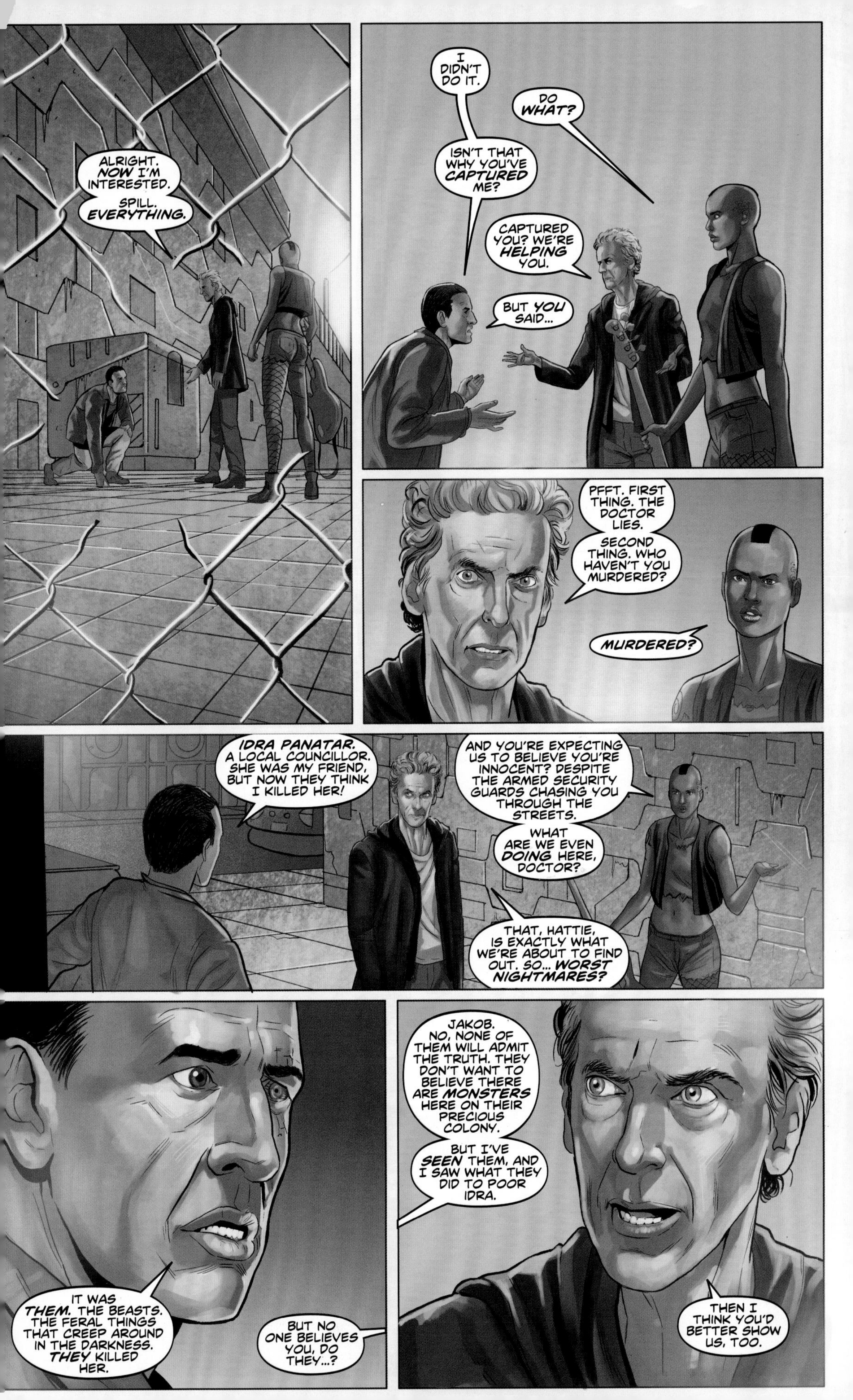
ALRIGHT. NOW I'M INTERESTED.
SPILL. EVERYTHING.
I DIDN'T DO IT.
DO WHAT?
ISN'T THAT WHY YOU'VE CAPTURED ME?
CAPTURED YOU? WE'RE HELPING YOU.
BUT YOU SAID...
PFFT. FIRST THING. THE DOCTOR LIES.
SECOND THING. WHO HAVEN'T YOU MURDERED?
MURDERED?
IDRA PANATAR. A LOCAL COUNCILLOR. SHE WAS MY FRIEND, BUT NOW THEY THINK I KILLED HER!
AND YOU'RE EXPECTING US TO BELIEVE YOU'RE INNOCENT? DESPITE THE ARMED SECURITY GUARDS CHASING YOU THROUGH THE STREETS.
WHAT ARE WE EVEN DOING HERE, DOCTOR?
THAT, HATTIE, IS EXACTLY WHAT WE'RE ABOUT TO FIND OUT. SO... WORST NIGHTMARES?
IT WAS THEM. THE BEASTS. THE FERAL THINGS THAT CREEP AROUND IN THE DARKNESS. THEY KILLED HER.
BUT NO ONE BELIEVES YOU, DO THEY...?
JAKOB. NO, NONE OF THEM WILL ADMIT THE TRUTH. THEY DON'T WANT TO BELIEVE THERE ARE MONSTERS HERE ON THEIR PRECIOUS COLONY.
BUT I'VE SEEN THEM, AND I SAW WHAT THEY DID TO POOR IDRA.
THEN I THINK YOU'D BETTER SHOW US, TOO.

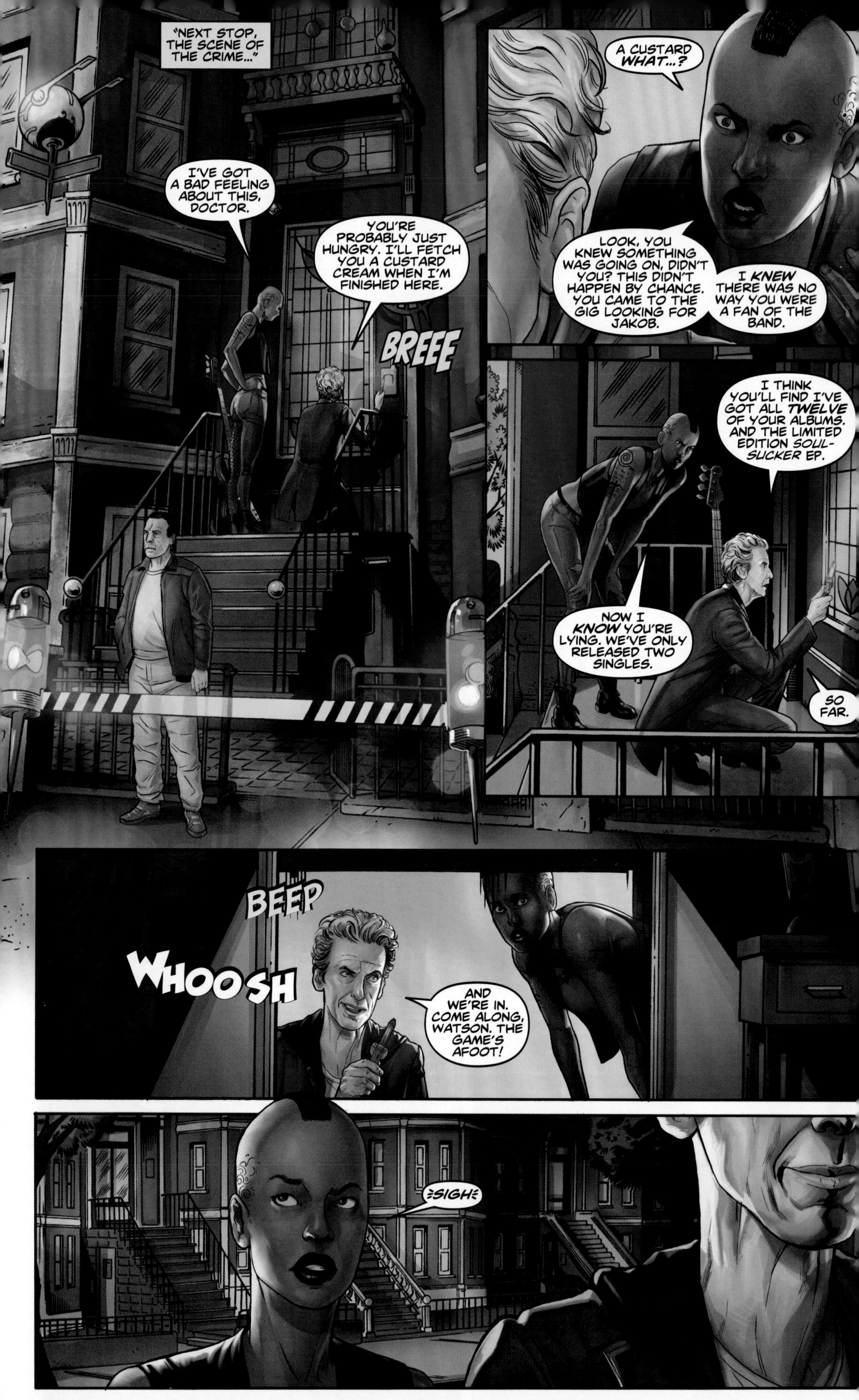
"NEXT STOP, THE SCENE OF THE CRIME..."
I'VE GOT A BAD FEELING ABOUT THIS, DOCTOR.
YOU'RE PROBABLY JUST HUNGRY. I'LL FETCH YOU A CUSTARD CREAM WHEN I'M FINISHED HERE.
BREEE
A CUSTARD WHAT...?
LOOK, YOU KNEW SOMETHING WAS GOING ON, DIDN'T YOU? THIS DIDN'T HAPPEN BY CHANCE. YOU CAME TO THE GIG LOOKING FOR JAKOB.
I KNEW THERE WAS NO WAY YOU WERE A FAN OF THE BAND.
I THINK YOU'LL FIND I'VE GOT ALL TWELVE OF YOUR ALBUMS. AND THE LIMITED EDITION SOUL-SUCKER EP.
NOW I KNOW YOU'RE LYING. WE'VE ONLY RELEASED TWO SINGLES.
SO FAR.
BEEP
WHOOSH
AND WE'RE IN. COME ALONG, WATSON. THE GAME'S AFOOT!
SIGH

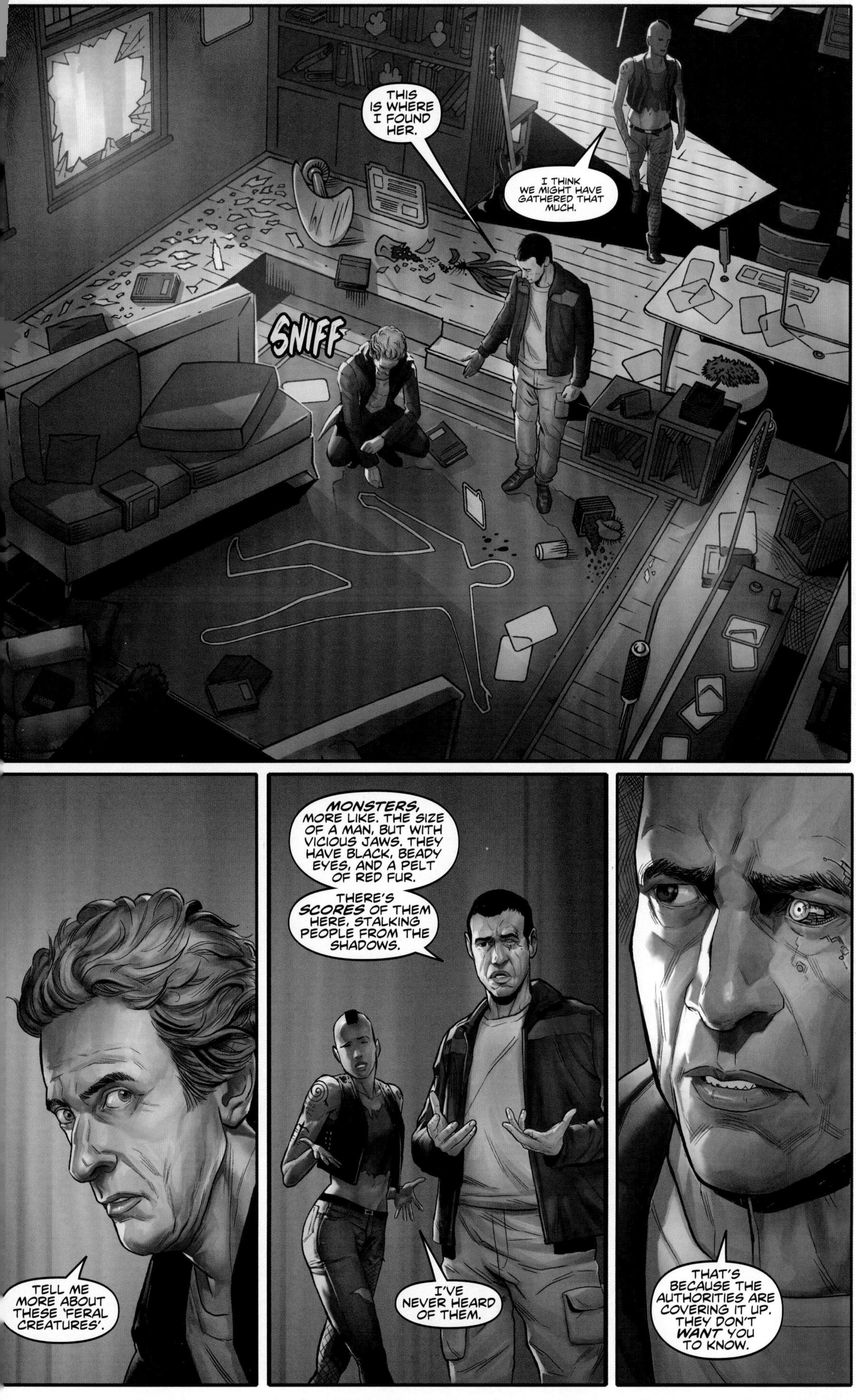
THIS IS WHERE I FOUND HER.
I THINK WE MIGHT HAVE GATHERED THAT MUCH.
SNIFF
TELL ME MORE ABOUT THESE 'FERAL CREATURES'.
I'VE NEVER HEARD OF THEM.
MONSTERS, MORE LIKE. THE SIZE OF A MAN, BUT WITH VICIOUS JAWS. THEY HAVE BLACK, BEADY EYES, AND A PELT OF RED FUR.
THERE'S SCORES OF THEM HERE, STALKING PEOPLE FROM THE SHADOWS.
THAT'S BECAUSE THE AUTHORITIES ARE COVERING IT UP. THEY DON'T WANT YOU TO KNOW.

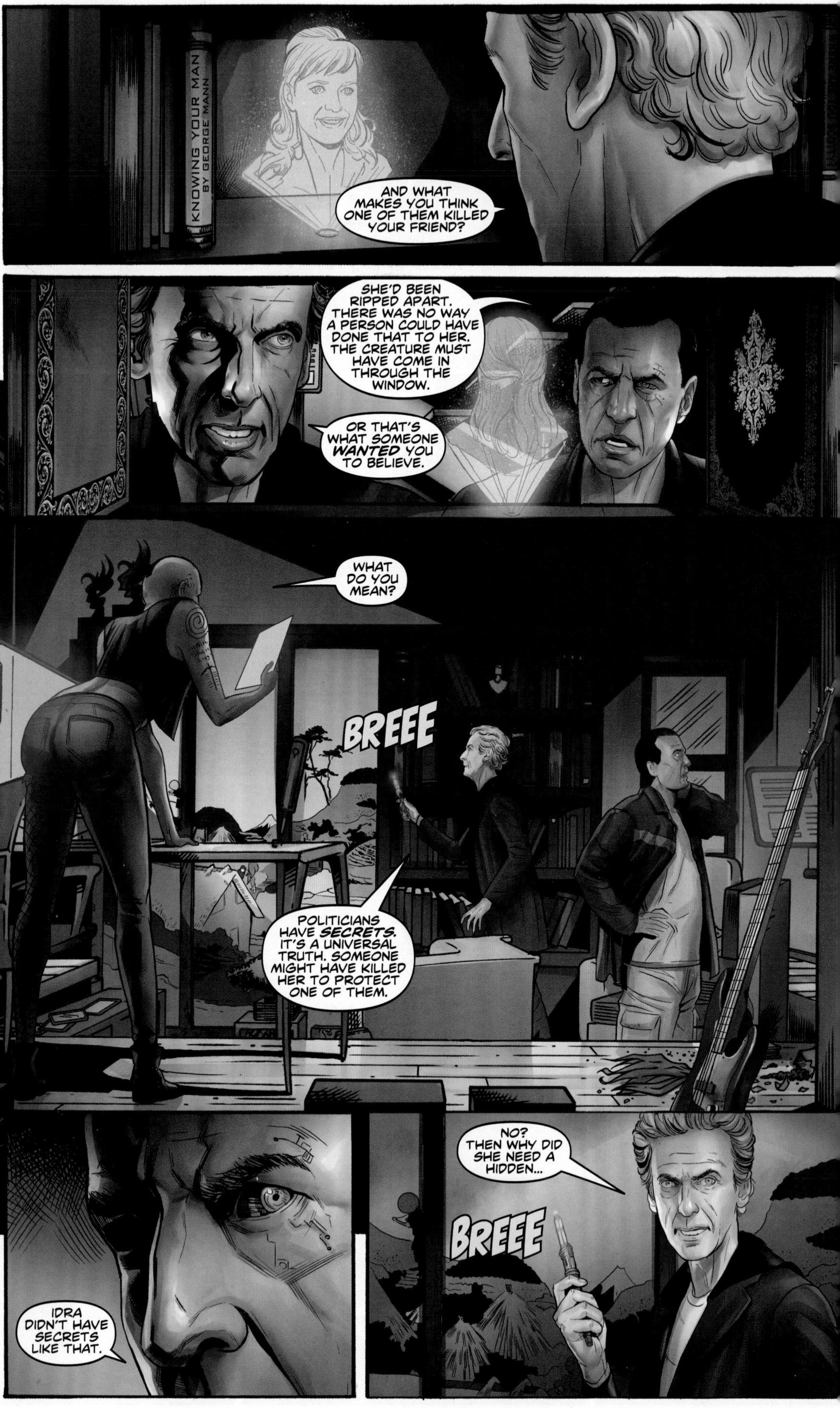
KNOWING YOUR MAN BY GEORGE MANN
AND WHAT MAKES YOU THINK ONE OF THEM KILLED YOUR FRIEND?
SHE'D BEEN RIPPED APART. THERE WAS NO WAY A PERSON COULD HAVE DONE THAT TO HER. THE CREATURE MUST HAVE COME IN THROUGH THE WINDOW.
OR THAT'S WHAT SOMEONE WANTED YOU TO BELIEVE.
WHAT DO YOU MEAN?
BREEE
POLITICIANS HAVE SECRETS. IT'S A UNIVERSAL TRUTH. SOMEONE MIGHT HAVE KILLED HER TO PROTECT ONE OF THEM.
IDRA DIDN'T HAVE SECRETS LIKE THAT.
NO? THEN WHY DID SHE NEED A HIDDEN...
BREEE

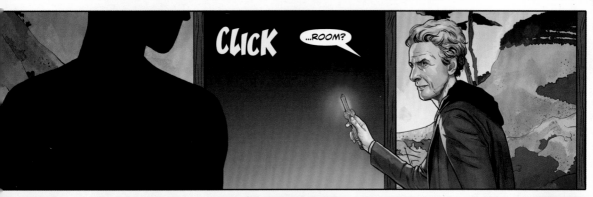

CLICK

...ROOM?

SECRETS, SECRETS, SECRETS...

THESE PICTURES... THEY'RE FROM ALL OVER THE TWIST.

AND THEY'RE ALL SHOTS OF THE CREATURES. THIS IS THE PROOF I'VE BEEN LOOKING FOR.

SO EITHER YOUR FRIEND WAS INVOLVED IN KEEPING THIS A SECRET, OR SOMEONE WAS TRYING TO STOP HER FROM REVEALING IT TO THE WORLD.

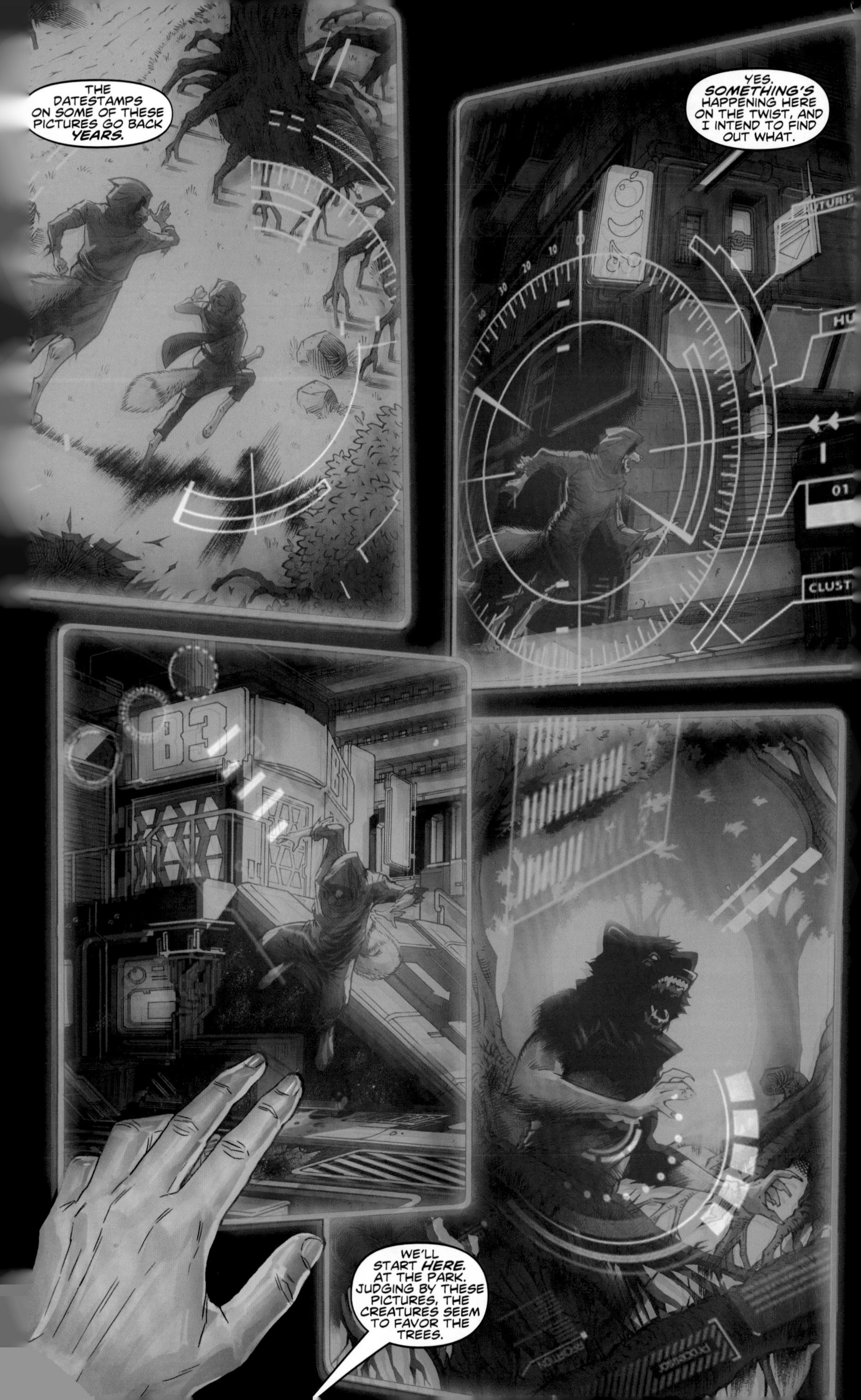
THE DATESTAMPS ON SOME OF THESE PICTURES GO BACK *YEARS.*
YES. *SOMETHING'S* HAPPENING HERE ON THE TWIST, AND I INTEND TO FIND OUT WHAT.
B3
01
WE'LL START *HERE.* AT THE PARK. JUDGING BY THESE PICTURES, THE CREATURES SEEM TO FAVOR THE TREES.

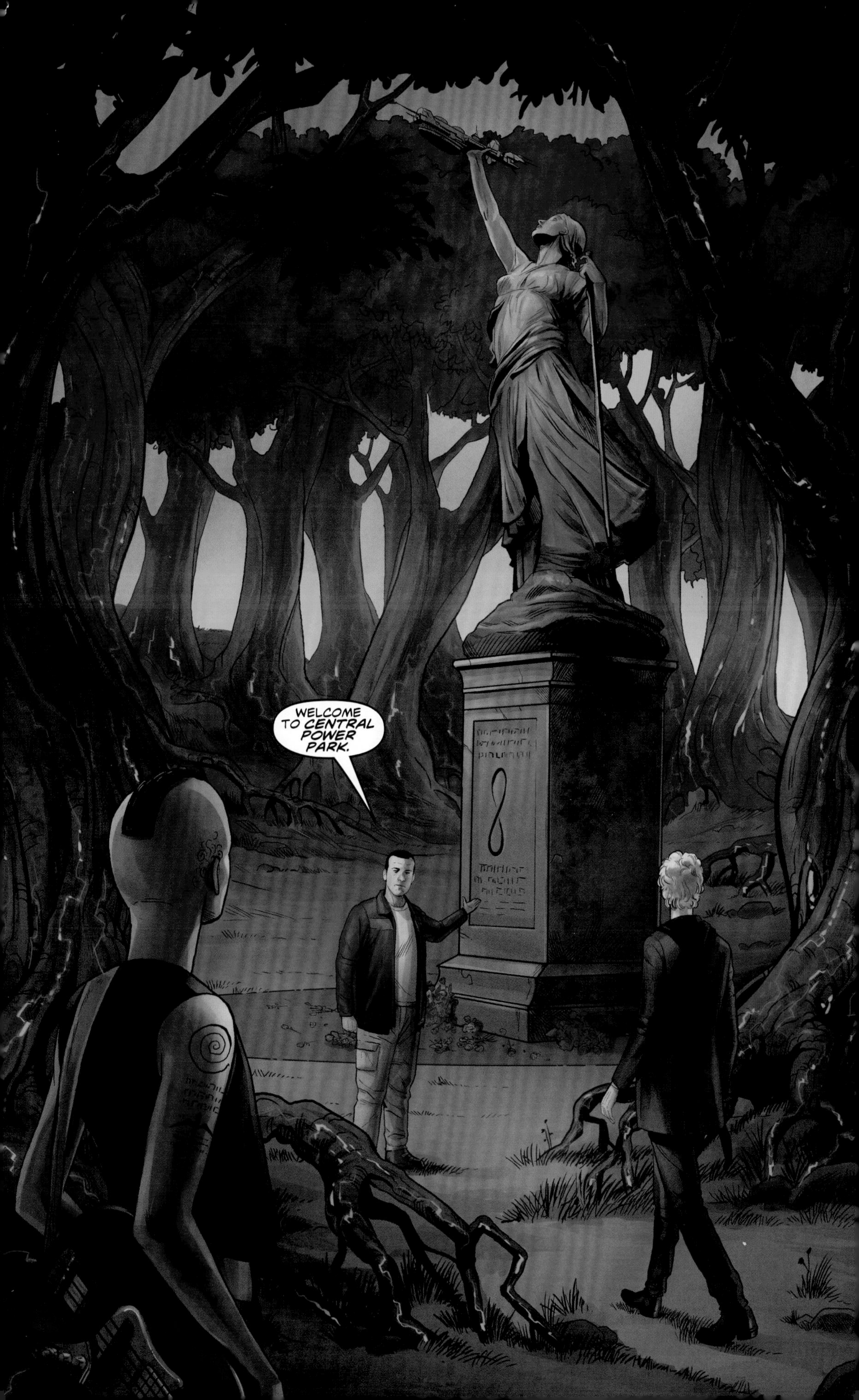
WELCOME TO CENTRAL POWER PARK.

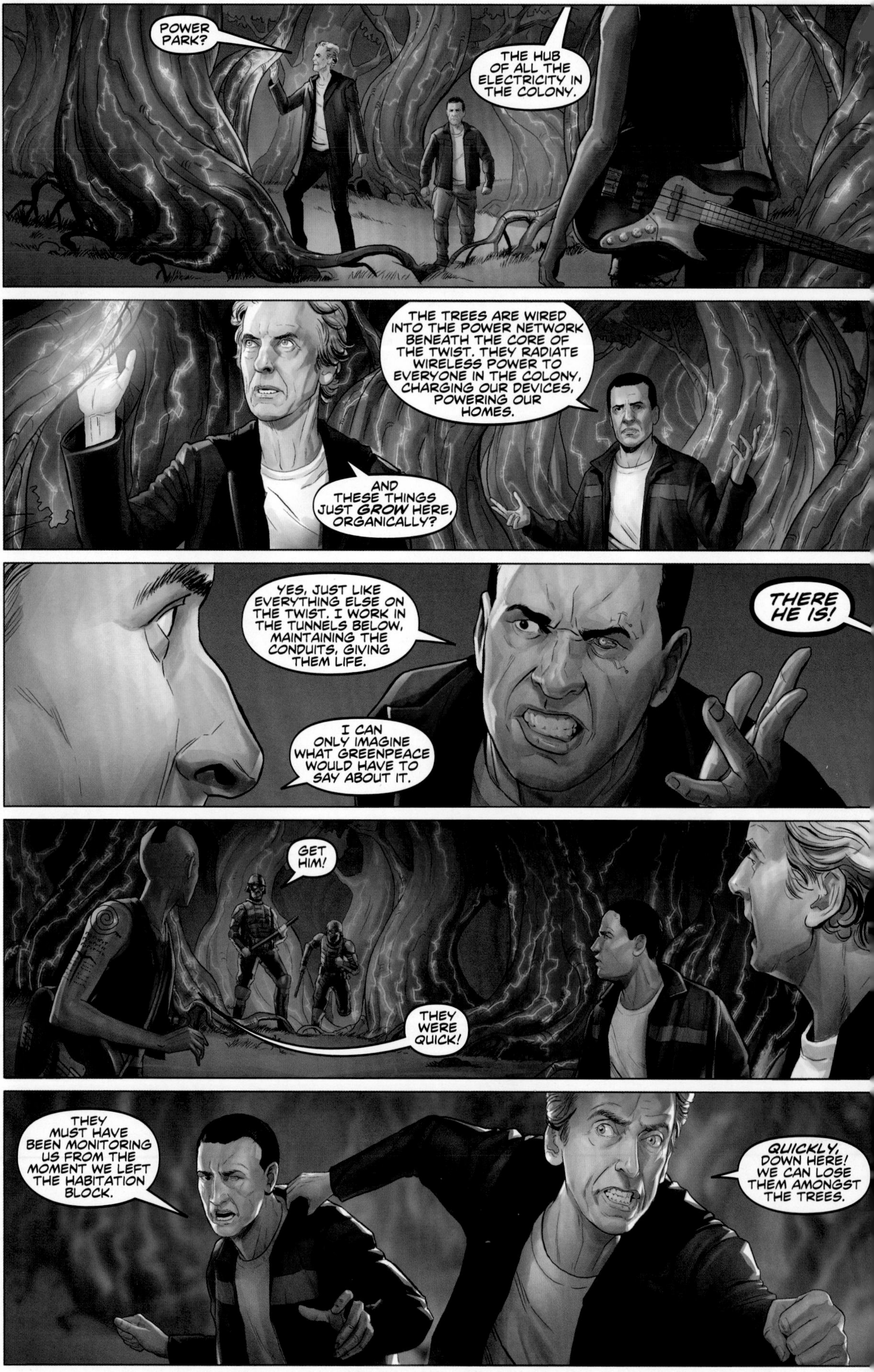
POWER PARK?
THE HUB OF ALL THE ELECTRICITY IN THE COLONY.
THE TREES ARE WIRED INTO THE POWER NETWORK BENEATH THE CORE OF THE TWIST. THEY RADIATE WIRELESS POWER TO EVERYONE IN THE COLONY, CHARGING OUR DEVICES, POWERING OUR HOMES.
AND THESE THINGS JUST GROW HERE, ORGANICALLY?
YES, JUST LIKE EVERYTHING ELSE ON THE TWIST. I WORK IN THE TUNNELS BELOW, MAINTAINING THE CONDUITS, GIVING THEM LIFE.
I CAN ONLY IMAGINE WHAT GREENPEACE WOULD HAVE TO SAY ABOUT IT.
THERE HE IS!
GET HIM!
THEY WERE QUICK!
THEY MUST HAVE BEEN MONITORING US FROM THE MOMENT WE LEFT THE HABITATION BLOCK.
QUICKLY, DOWN HERE! WE CAN LOSE THEM AMONGST THE TREES.

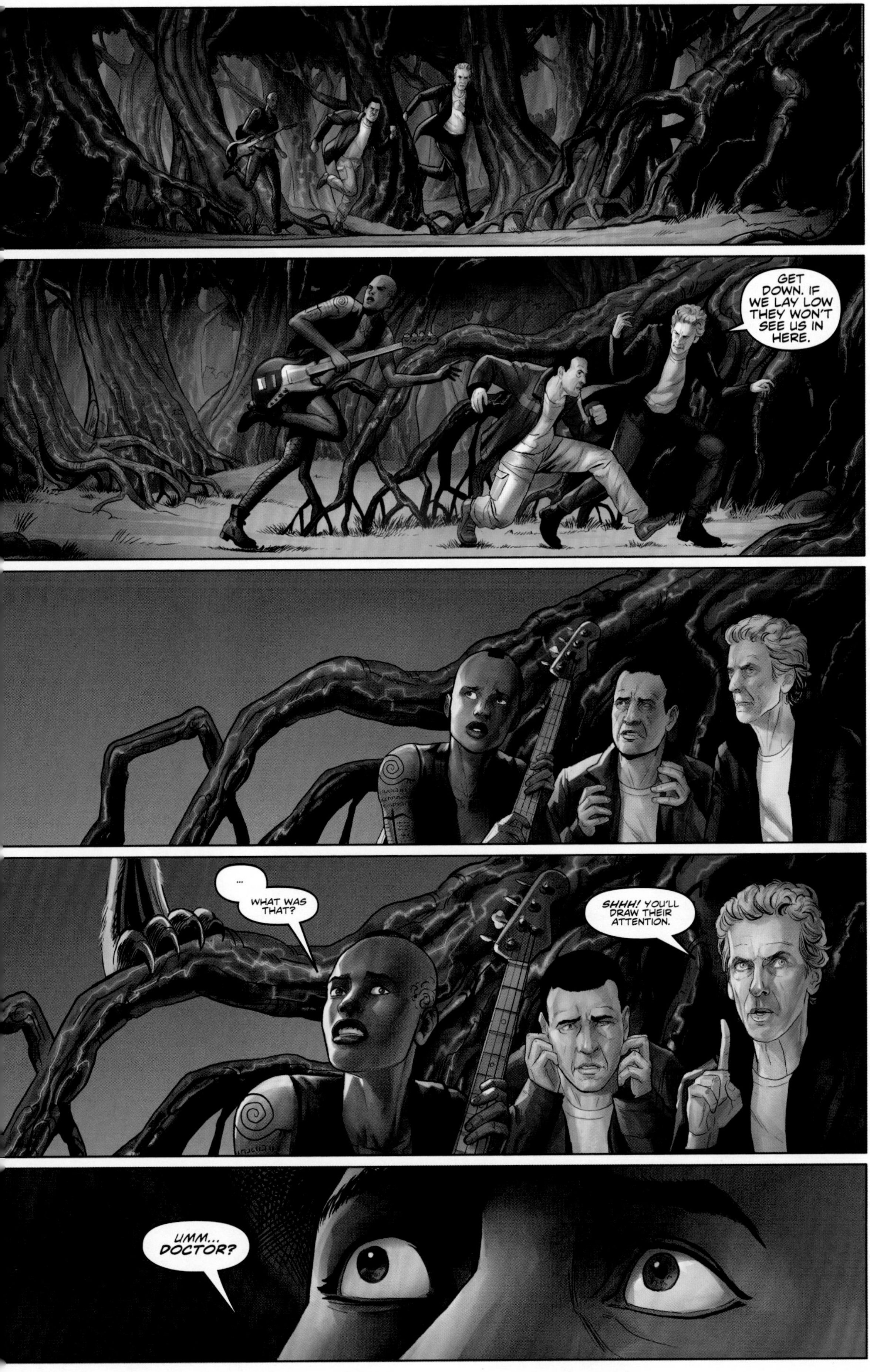
GET DOWN. IF WE LAY LOW THEY WON'T SEE US IN HERE.
... WHAT WAS THAT?
SHHH! YOU'LL DRAW THEIR ATTENTION.
UMM... DOCTOR?

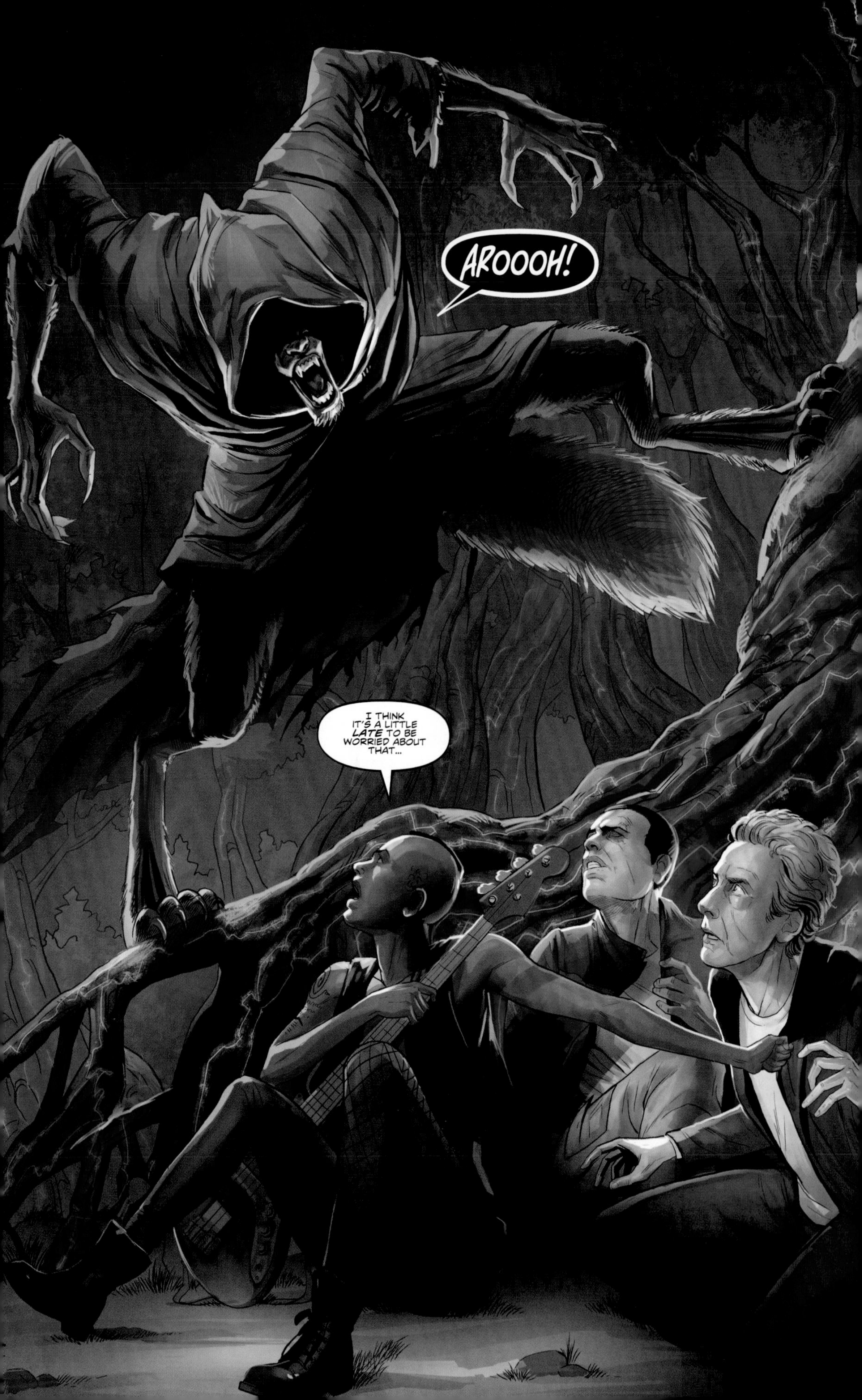
AROOOH!
I THINK IT'S A LITTLE *LATE* TO BE WORRIED ABOUT THAT...

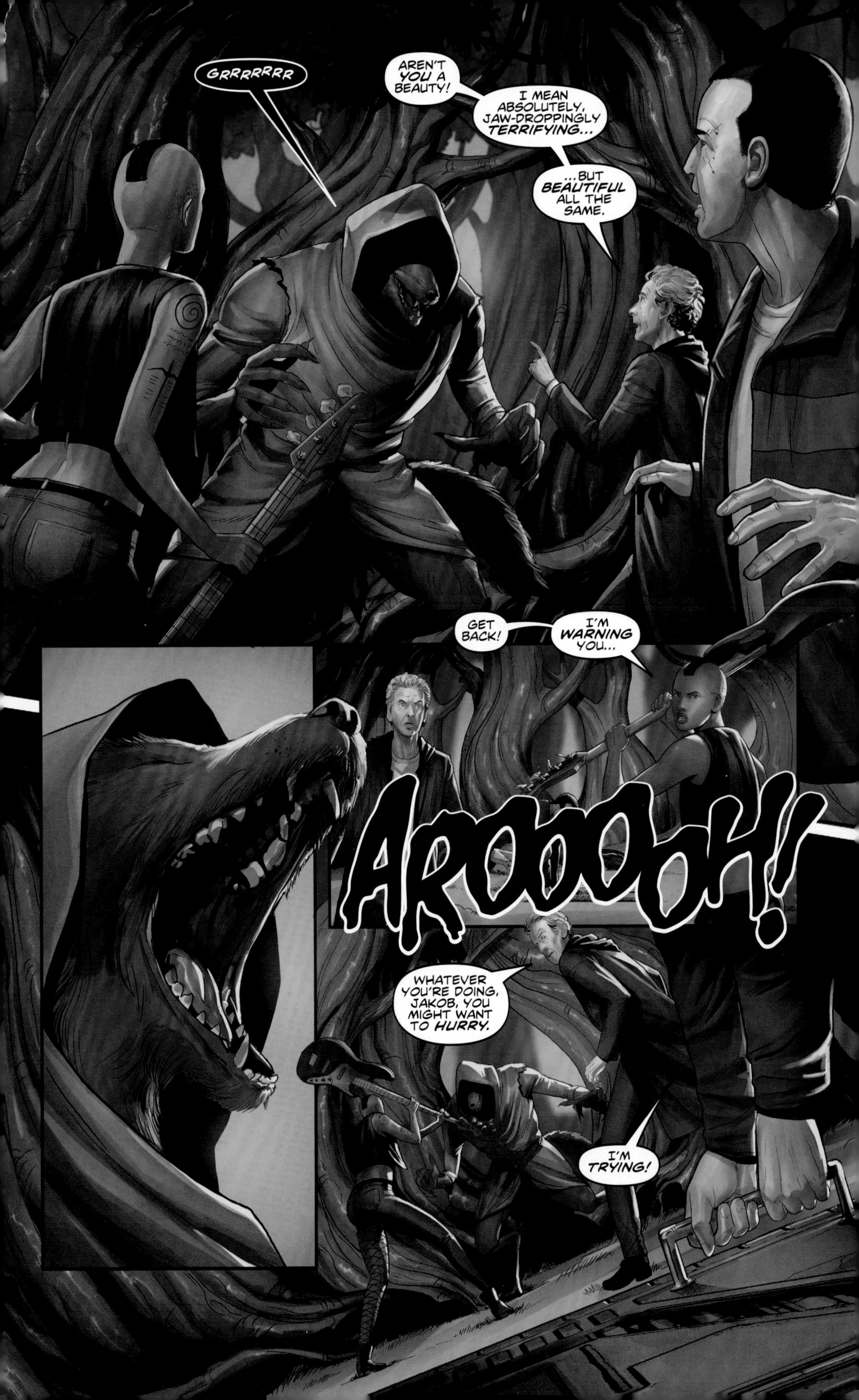
GRRRRRRR
AREN'T YOU A BEAUTY!
I MEAN ABSOLUTELY, JAW-DROPPINGLY TERRIFYING...
...BUT BEAUTIFUL ALL THE SAME.
GET BACK!
I'M WARNING YOU...
AROOOOH!
WHATEVER YOU'RE DOING, JAKOB, YOU MIGHT WANT TO HURRY.
I'M TRYING!

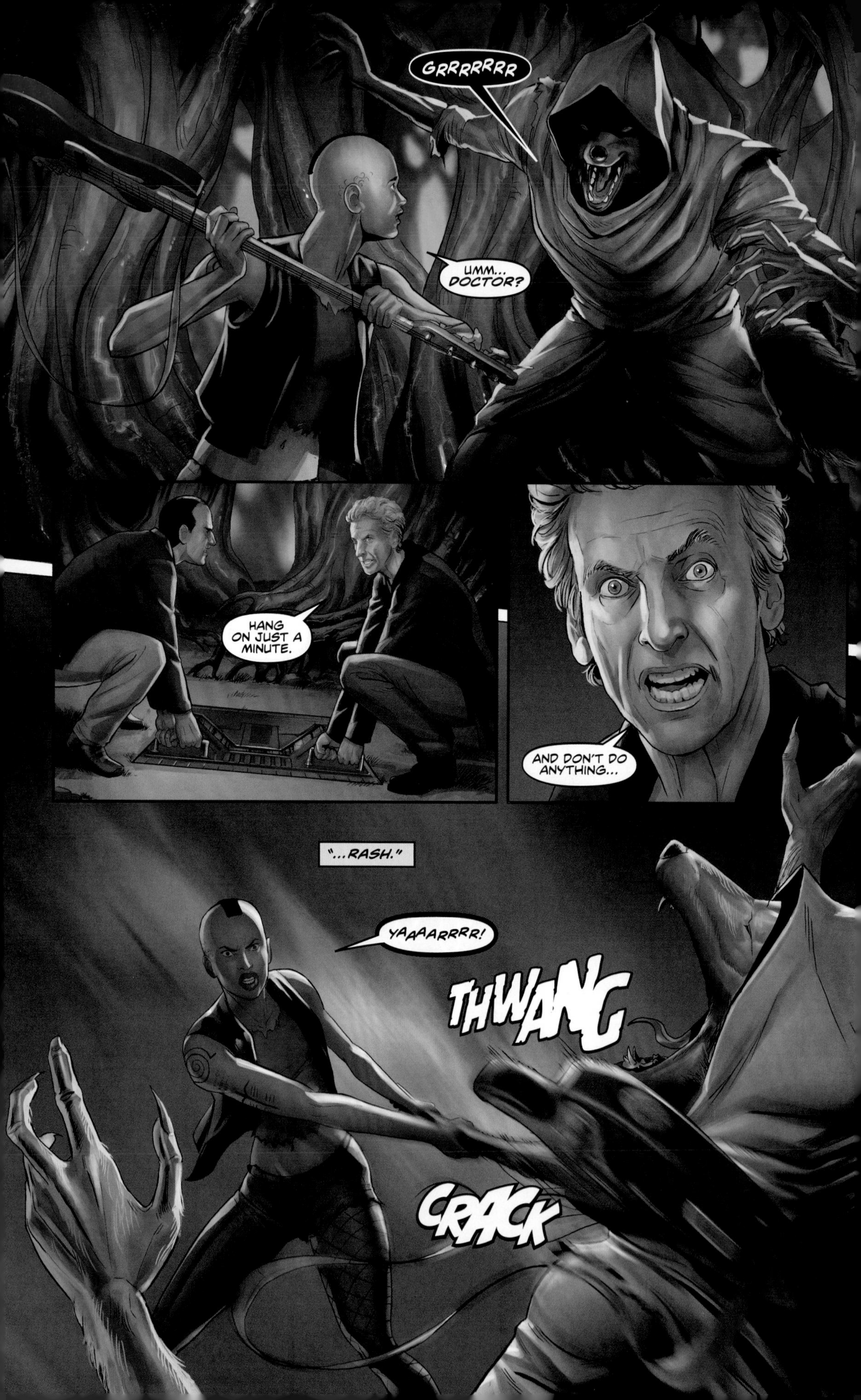
GRRRRRRR
UMM... DOCTOR?
HANG ON JUST A MINUTE.
AND DON'T DO ANYTHING...
"...RASH."
YAAAARRRR!
THWANG
CRACK

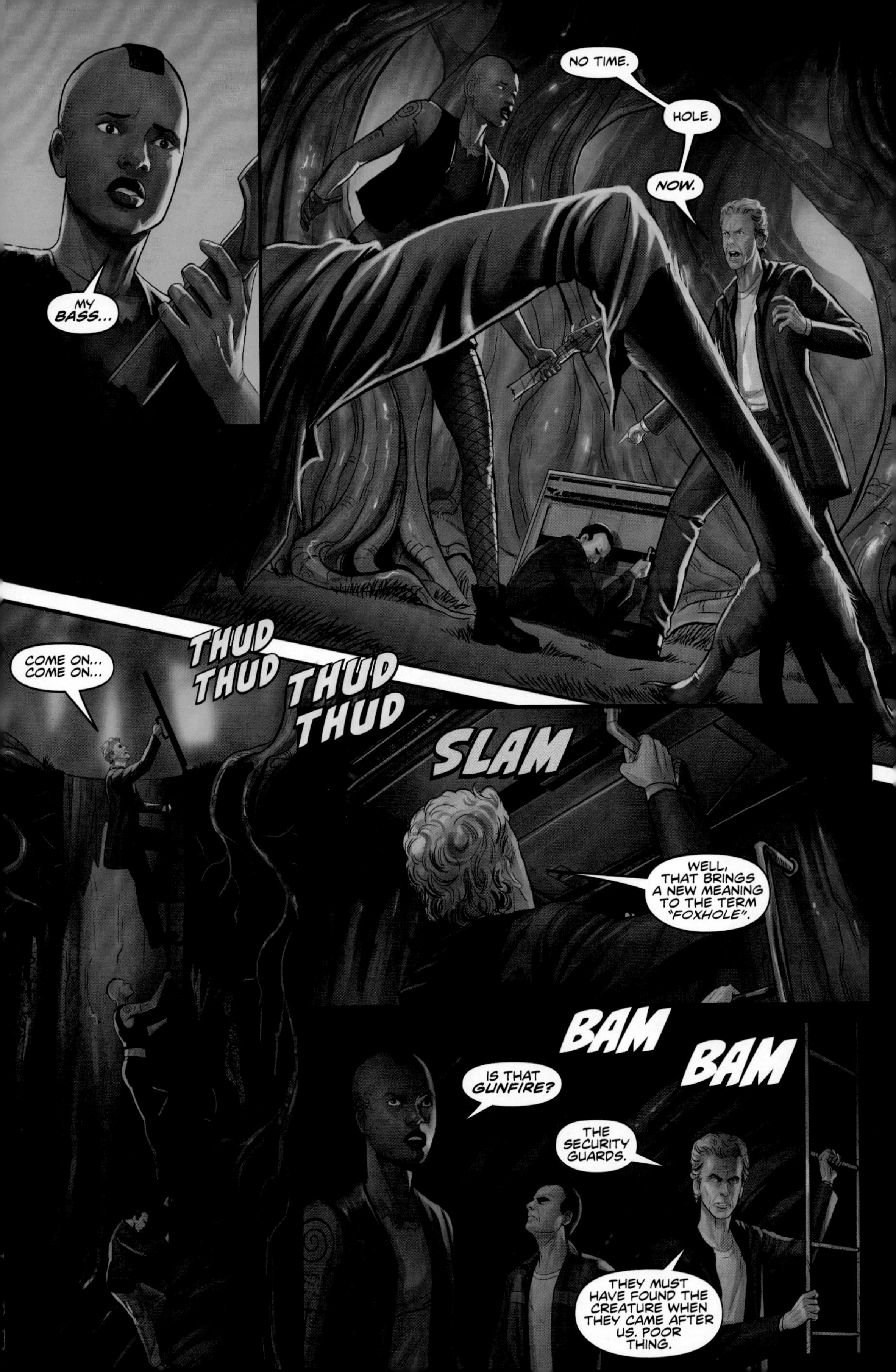
MY BASS...
NO TIME.
HOLE.
NOW.
COME ON... COME ON...
THUD THUD
THUD THUD
SLAM
WELL, THAT BRINGS A NEW MEANING TO THE TERM "FOXHOLE".
BAM
BAM
IS THAT GUNFIRE?
THE SECURITY GUARDS.
THEY MUST HAVE FOUND THE CREATURE WHEN THEY CAME AFTER US. POOR THING.

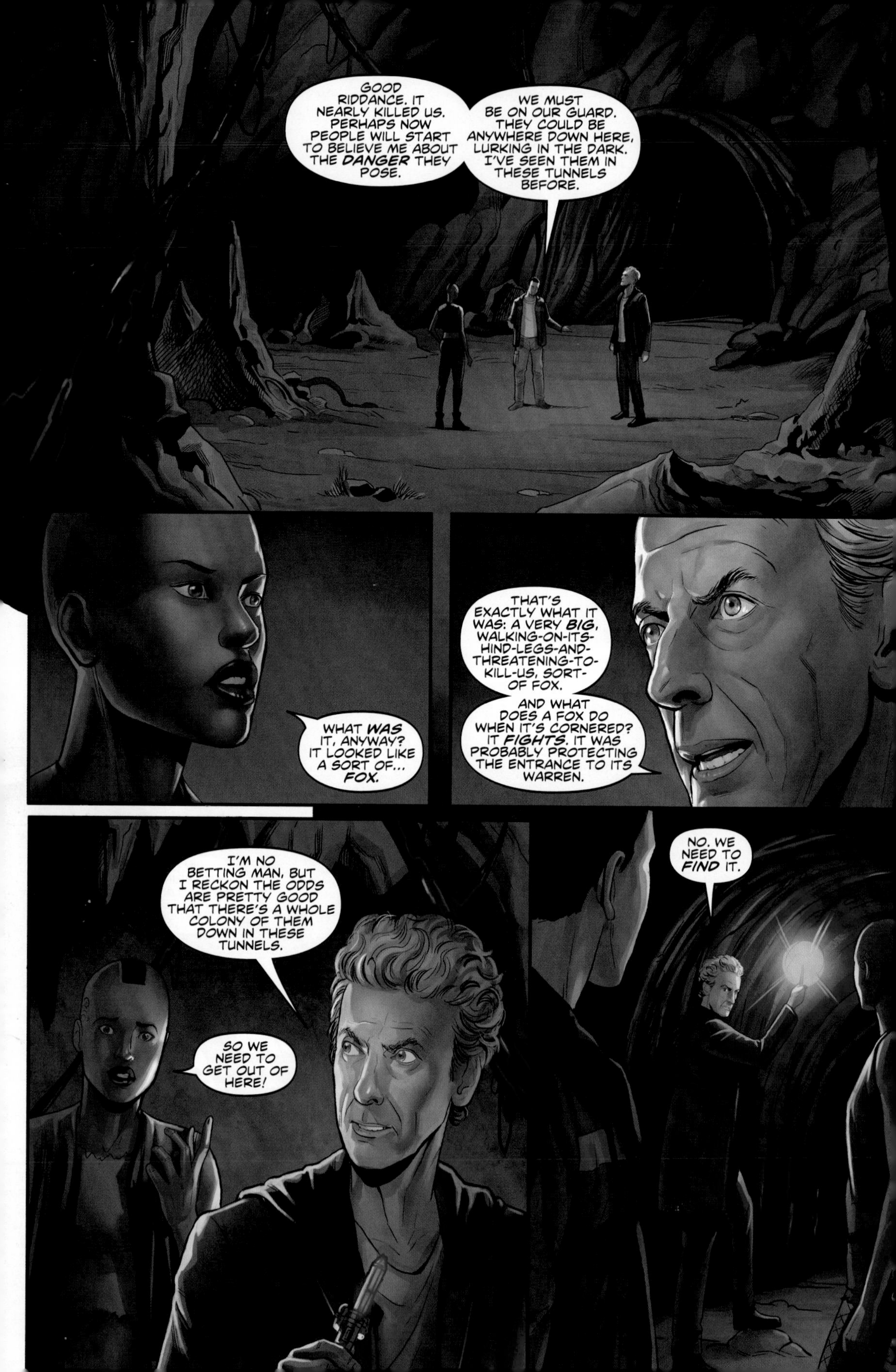

GOOD RIDDANCE. IT NEARLY KILLED US. PERHAPS NOW PEOPLE WILL START TO BELIEVE ME ABOUT THE *DANGER* THEY POSE.
WE MUST BE ON OUR GUARD. THEY COULD BE ANYWHERE DOWN HERE, LURKING IN THE DARK. I'VE SEEN THEM IN THESE TUNNELS BEFORE.
WHAT *WAS* IT, ANYWAY? IT LOOKED LIKE A SORT OF... *FOX.*
THAT'S EXACTLY WHAT IT WAS: A VERY *BIG*, WALKING-ON-ITS-HIND-LEGS-AND-THREATENING-TO-KILL-US, SORT-OF FOX.
AND WHAT DOES A FOX DO WHEN IT'S CORNERED? IT *FIGHTS*. IT WAS PROBABLY PROTECTING THE ENTRANCE TO ITS WARREN.
I'M NO BETTING MAN, BUT I RECKON THE ODDS ARE PRETTY GOOD THAT THERE'S A WHOLE COLONY OF THEM DOWN IN THESE TUNNELS.
SO WE NEED TO GET OUT OF HERE!
NO. WE NEED TO *FIND* IT.

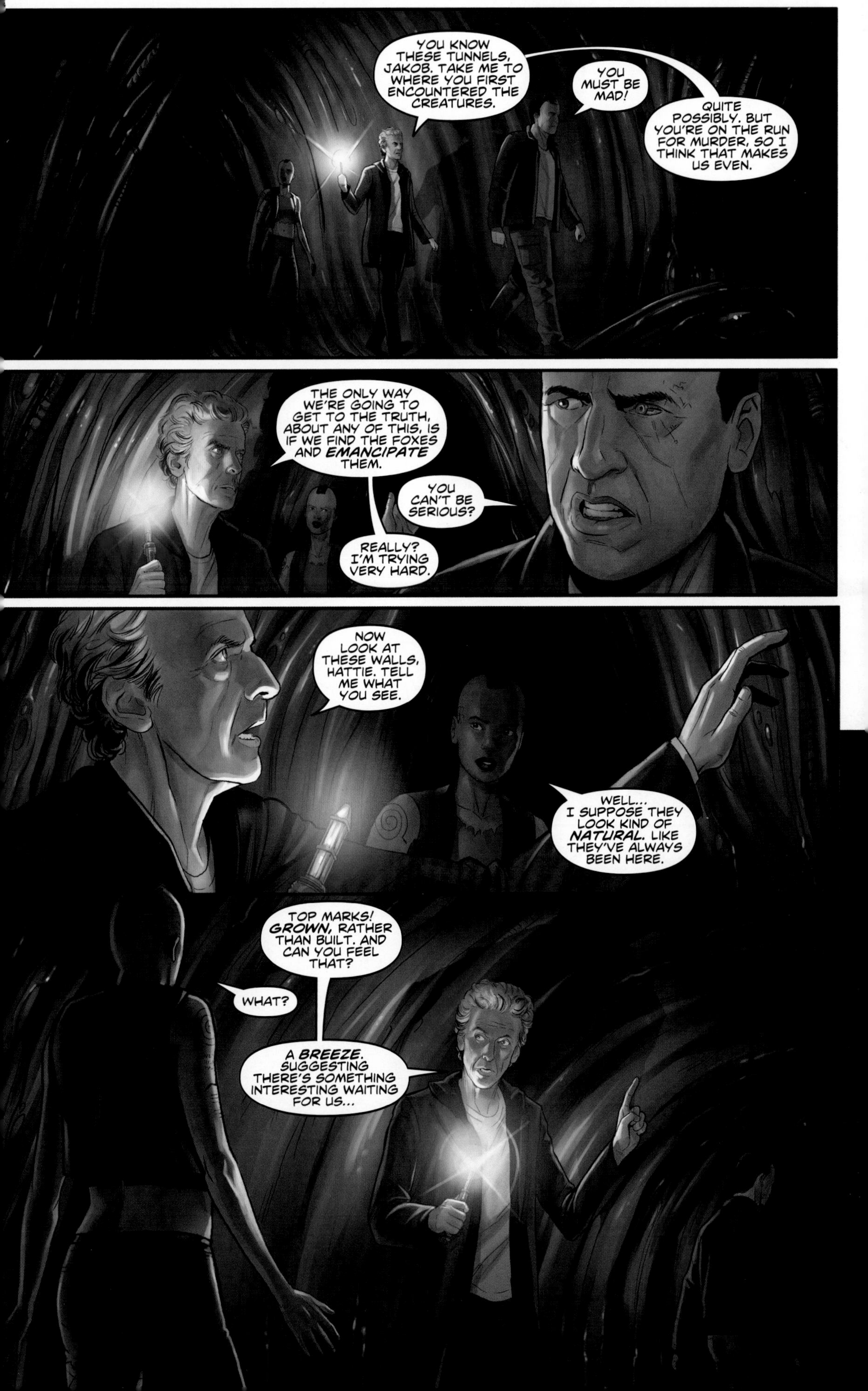
YOU KNOW THESE TUNNELS, JAKOB. TAKE ME TO WHERE YOU FIRST ENCOUNTERED THE CREATURES.
YOU MUST BE MAD!
QUITE POSSIBLY. BUT YOU'RE ON THE RUN FOR MURDER, SO I THINK THAT MAKES US EVEN.
THE ONLY WAY WE'RE GOING TO GET TO THE TRUTH, ABOUT ANY OF THIS, IS IF WE FIND THE FOXES AND EMANCIPATE THEM.
YOU CAN'T BE SERIOUS?
REALLY? I'M TRYING VERY HARD.
NOW LOOK AT THESE WALLS, HATTIE. TELL ME WHAT YOU SEE.
WELL... I SUPPOSE THEY LOOK KIND OF NATURAL. LIKE THEY'VE ALWAYS BEEN HERE.
TOP MARKS! GROWN, RATHER THAN BUILT. AND CAN YOU FEEL THAT?
WHAT?
A BREEZE. SUGGESTING THERE'S SOMETHING INTERESTING WAITING FOR US...

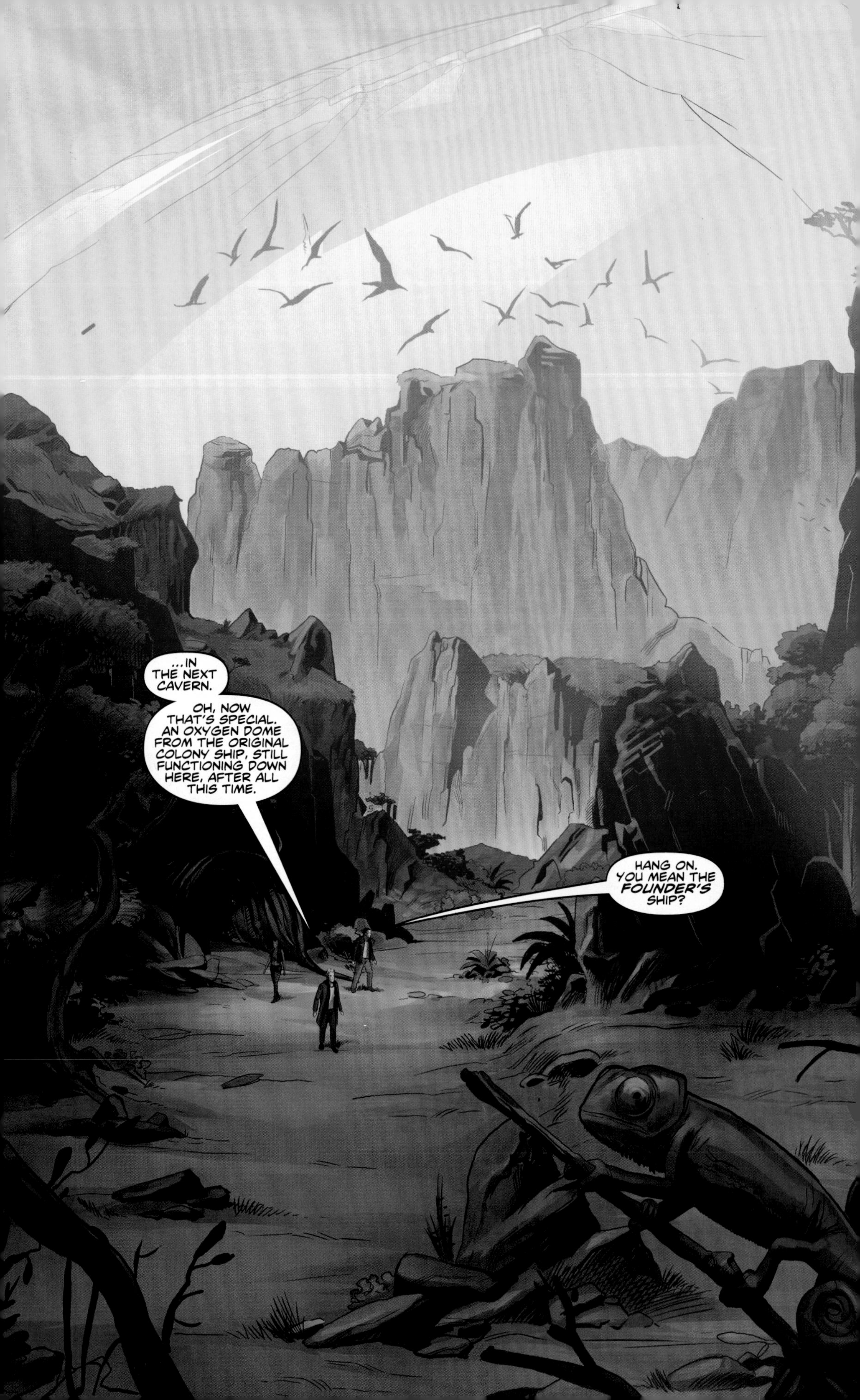
...IN THE NEXT CAVERN.
OH, NOW THAT'S SPECIAL. AN OXYGEN DOME FROM THE ORIGINAL COLONY SHIP, STILL FUNCTIONING DOWN HERE, AFTER ALL THIS TIME.
HANG ON. YOU MEAN THE *FOUNDER'S* SHIP?

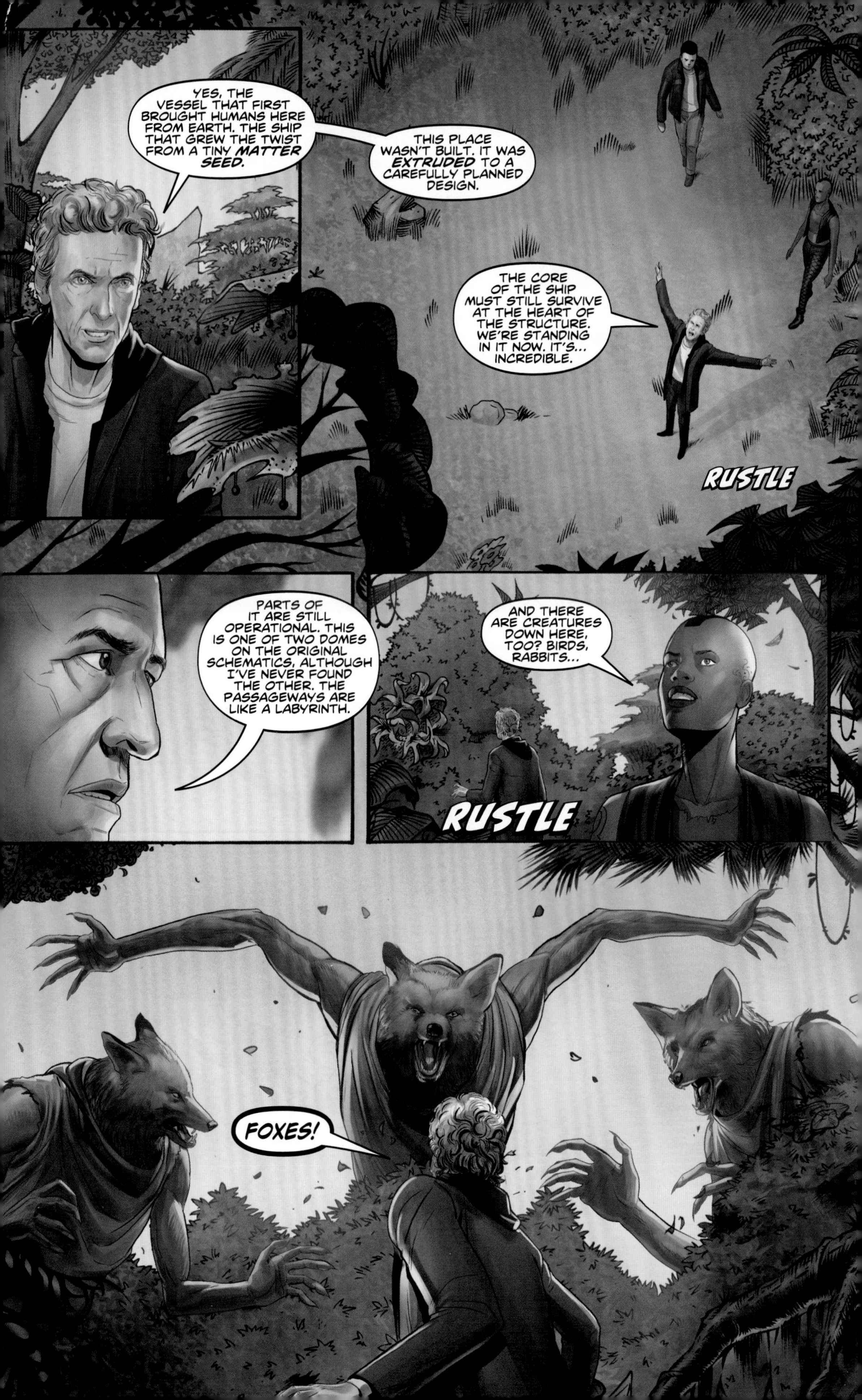
YES, THE VESSEL THAT FIRST BROUGHT HUMANS HERE FROM EARTH. THE SHIP THAT GREW THE TWIST FROM A TINY *MATTER SEED.*
THIS PLACE WASN'T BUILT. IT WAS *EXTRUDED* TO A CAREFULLY PLANNED DESIGN.
THE CORE OF THE SHIP MUST STILL SURVIVE AT THE HEART OF THE STRUCTURE. WE'RE STANDING IN IT NOW. IT'S... INCREDIBLE.
RUSTLE
PARTS OF IT ARE STILL OPERATIONAL. THIS IS ONE OF TWO DOMES ON THE ORIGINAL SCHEMATICS, ALTHOUGH I'VE NEVER FOUND THE OTHER. THE PASSAGEWAYS ARE LIKE A LABYRINTH.
AND THERE ARE CREATURES DOWN HERE, TOO? BIRDS, RABBITS...
RUSTLE
FOXES!

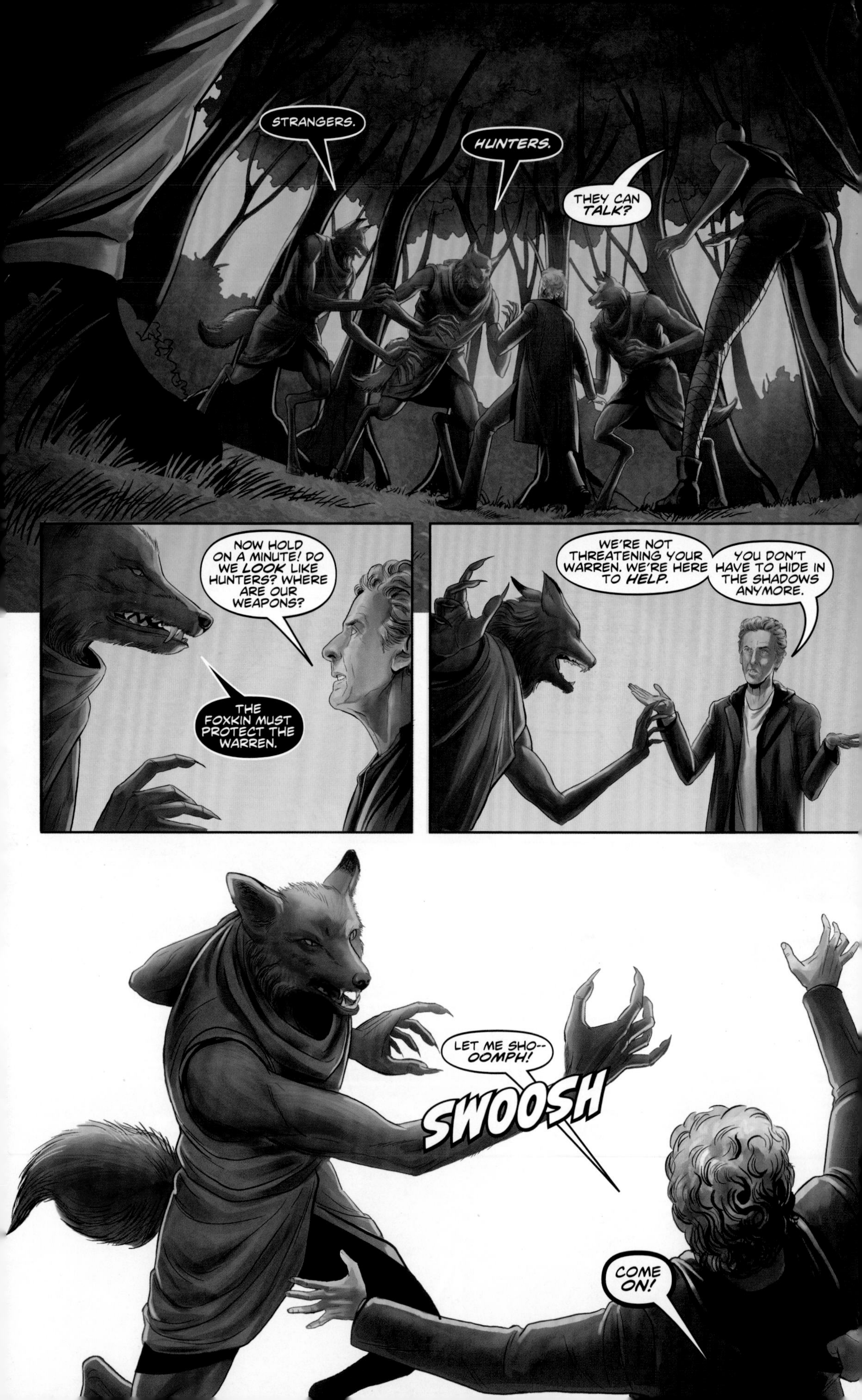
STRANGERS.
HUNTERS.
THEY CAN TALK?
NOW HOLD ON A MINUTE! DO WE LOOK LIKE HUNTERS? WHERE ARE OUR WEAPONS?
THE FOXKIN MUST PROTECT THE WARREN.
WE'RE NOT THREATENING YOUR WARREN. WE'RE HERE TO HELP.
YOU DON'T HAVE TO HIDE IN THE SHADOWS ANYMORE.
LET ME SHO-- OOMPH!
SWOOSH
COME ON!

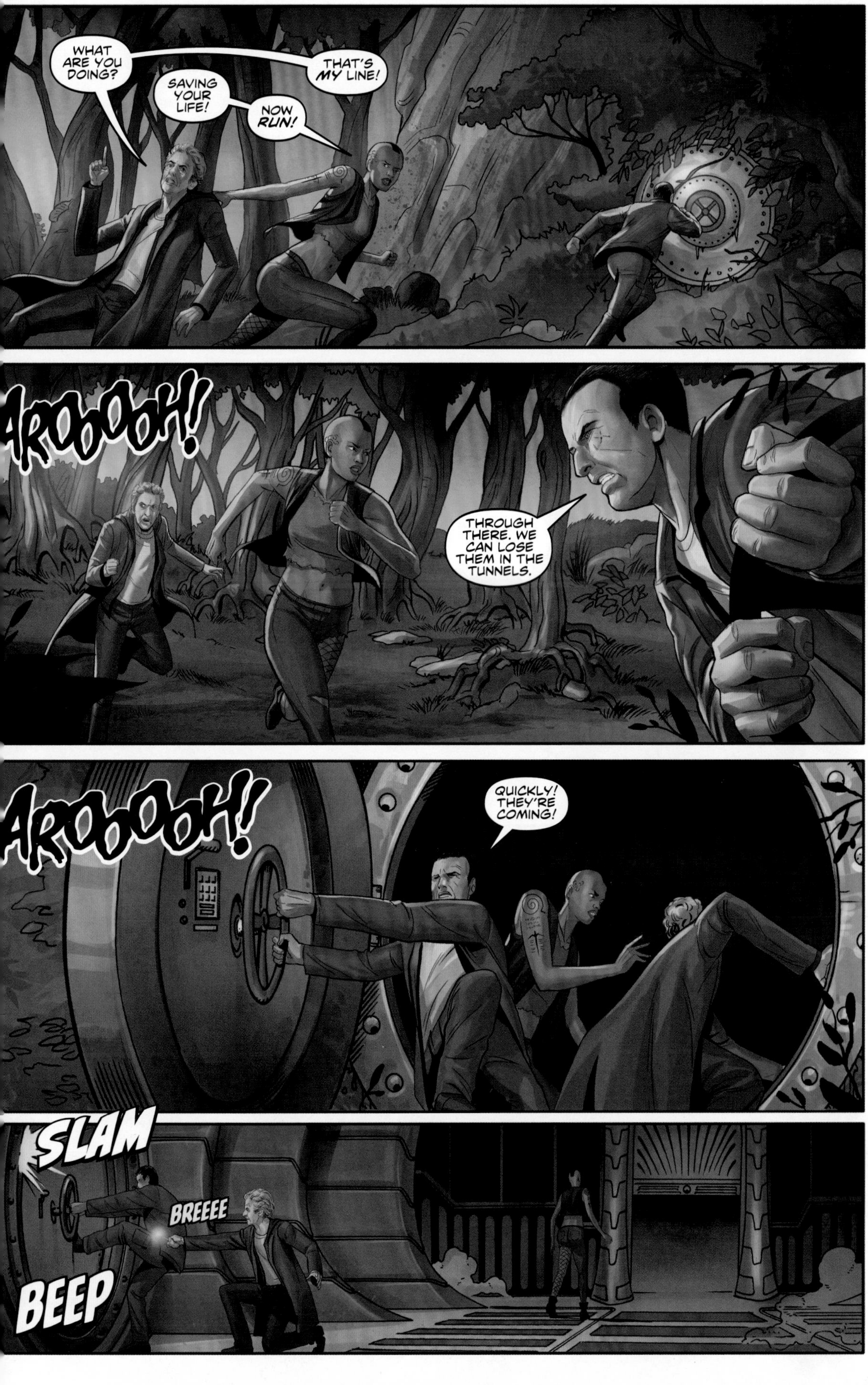
WHAT ARE YOU DOING?
SAVING YOUR LIFE!
THAT'S MY LINE!
NOW RUN!
AROOOOH!
THROUGH THERE. WE CAN LOSE THEM IN THE TUNNELS.
AROOOOH!
QUICKLY! THEY'RE COMING!
SLAM
BREEEE
BEEP

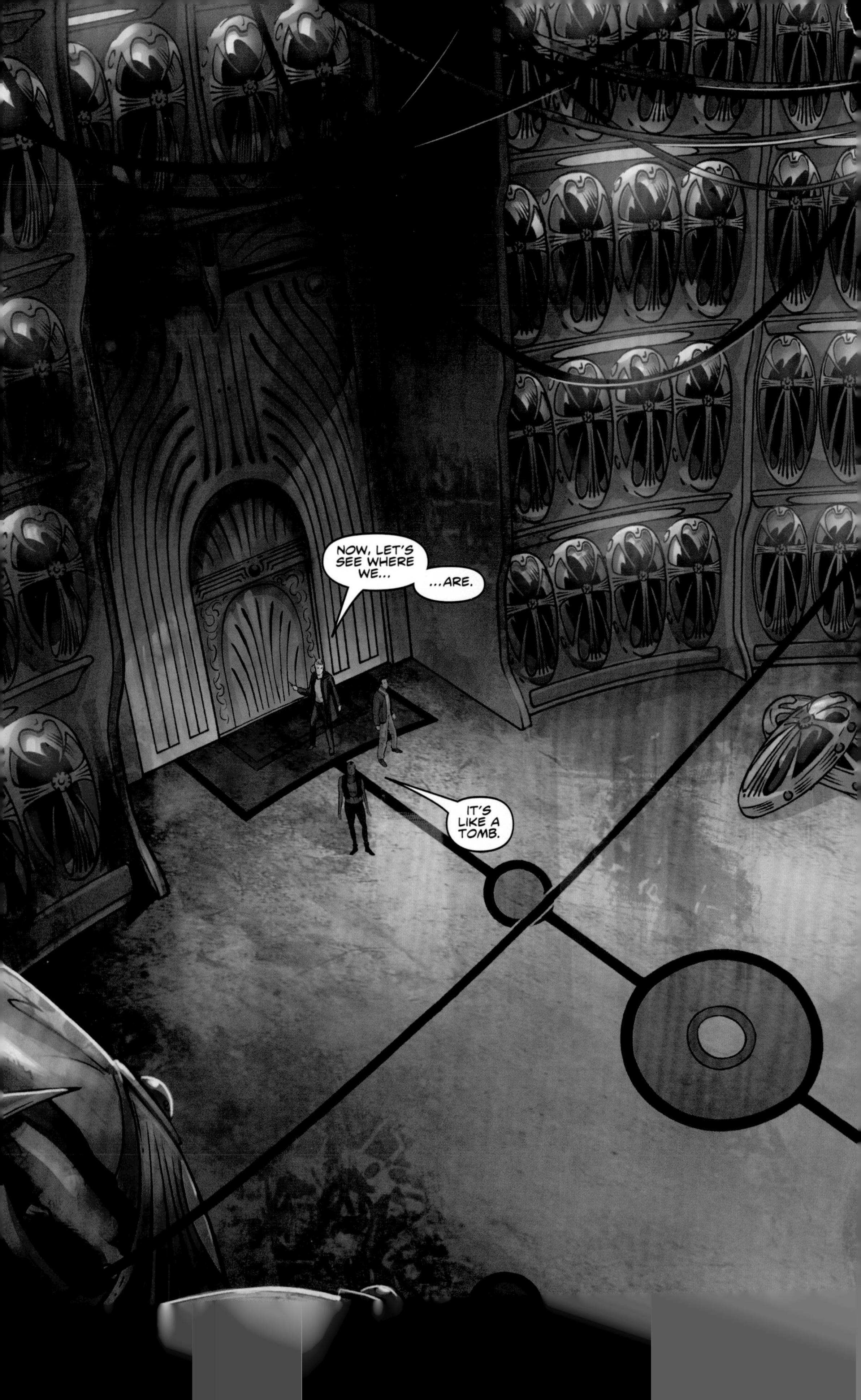
NOW, LET'S SEE WHERE WE...
...ARE.
IT'S LIKE A TOMB.

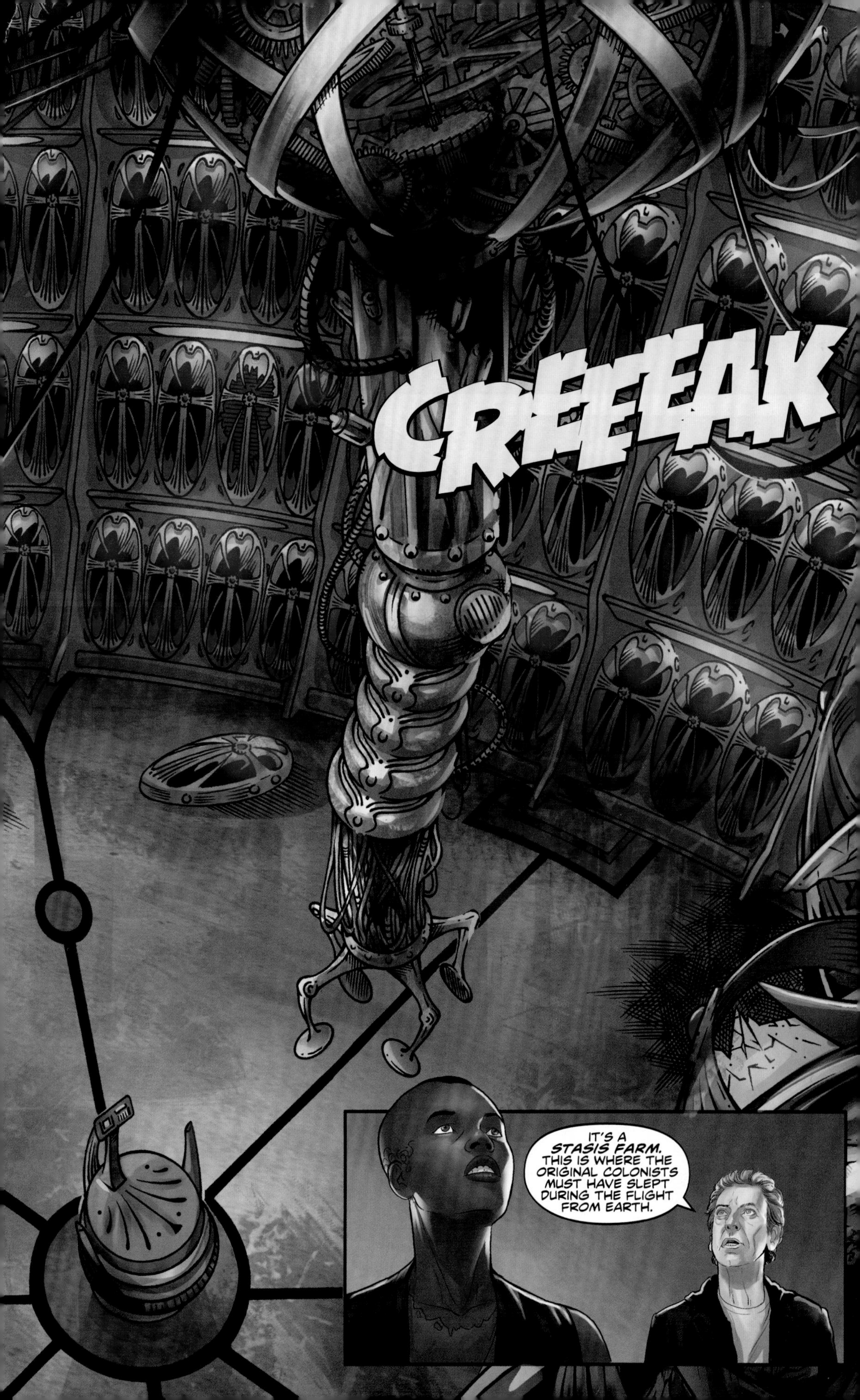
CREEEAK
IT'S A STASIS FARM. THIS IS WHERE THE ORIGINAL COLONISTS MUST HAVE SLEPT DURING THE FLIGHT FROM EARTH.

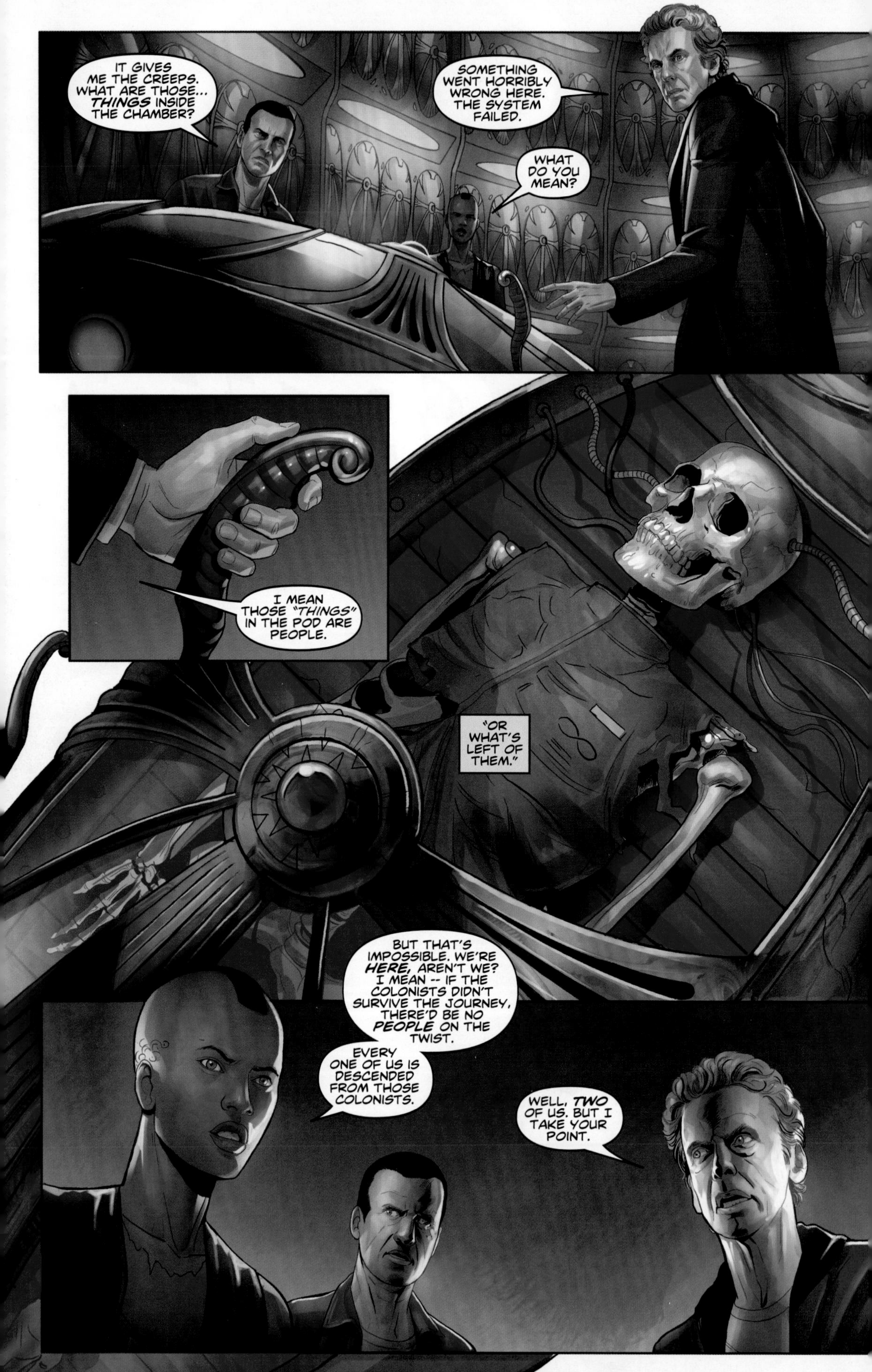
IT GIVES ME THE CREEPS. WHAT ARE THOSE... THINGS INSIDE THE CHAMBER?
SOMETHING WENT HORRIBLY WRONG HERE. THE SYSTEM FAILED.
WHAT DO YOU MEAN?
I MEAN THOSE "THINGS" IN THE POD ARE PEOPLE.
"OR WHAT'S LEFT OF THEM."
BUT THAT'S IMPOSSIBLE. WE'RE HERE, AREN'T WE? I MEAN -- IF THE COLONISTS DIDN'T SURVIVE THE JOURNEY, THERE'D BE NO PEOPLE ON THE TWIST.
EVERY ONE OF US IS DESCENDED FROM THOSE COLONISTS.
WELL, TWO OF US. BUT I TAKE YOUR POINT.

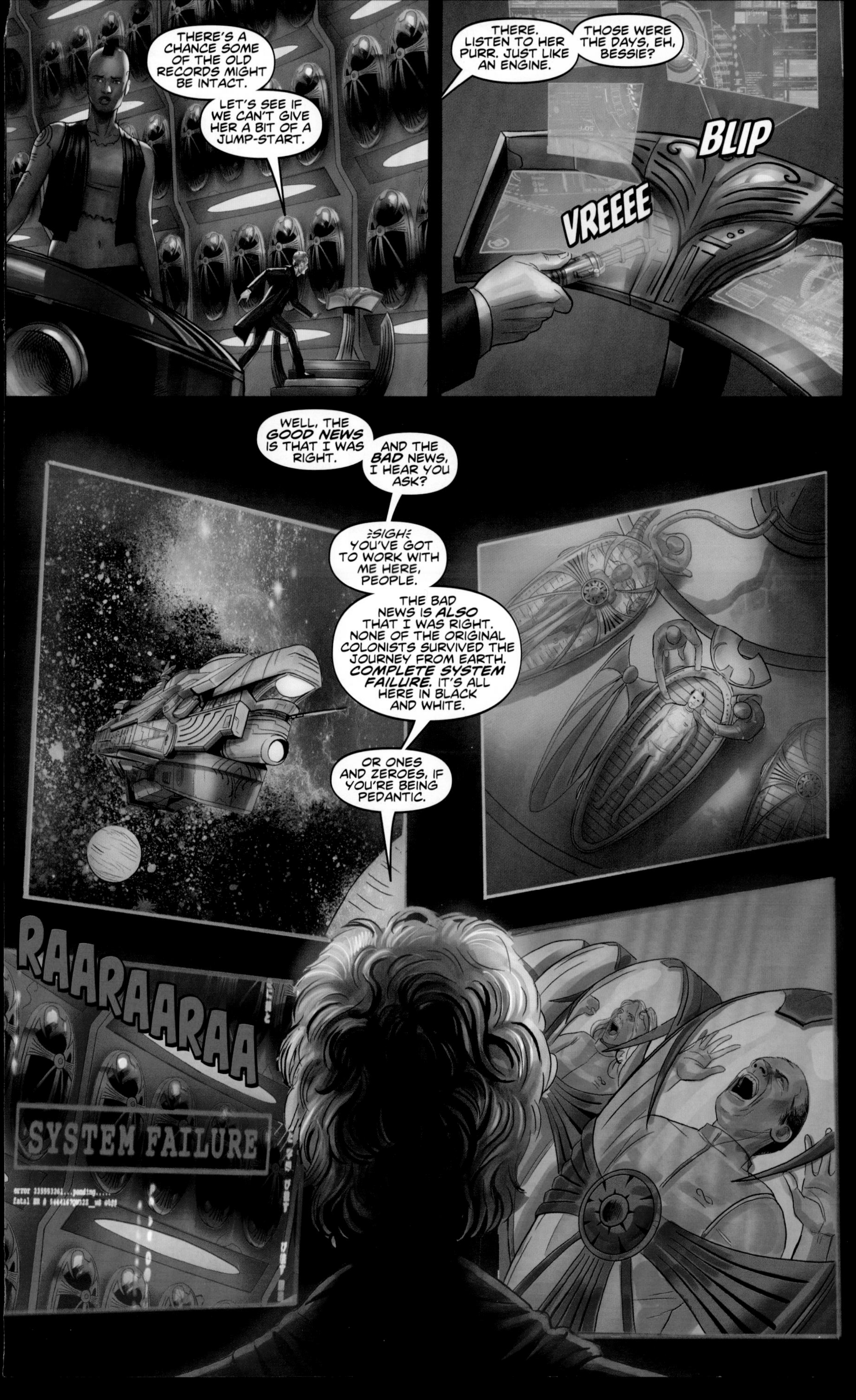
THERE'S A CHANCE SOME OF THE OLD RECORDS MIGHT BE INTACT.
LET'S SEE IF WE CAN'T GIVE HER A BIT OF A JUMP-START.
THERE. LISTEN TO HER PURR. JUST LIKE AN ENGINE.
THOSE WERE THE DAYS, EH, BESSIE?
BLIP
VREEEE
WELL, THE GOOD NEWS IS THAT I WAS RIGHT.
AND THE BAD NEWS, I HEAR YOU ASK?
SIGH YOU'VE GOT TO WORK WITH ME HERE, PEOPLE.
THE BAD NEWS IS ALSO THAT I WAS RIGHT. NONE OF THE ORIGINAL COLONISTS SURVIVED THE JOURNEY FROM EARTH. COMPLETE SYSTEM FAILURE. IT'S ALL HERE IN BLACK AND WHITE.
OR ONES AND ZEROES, IF YOU'RE BEING PEDANTIC.
RAARAARAA
SYSTEM FAILURE

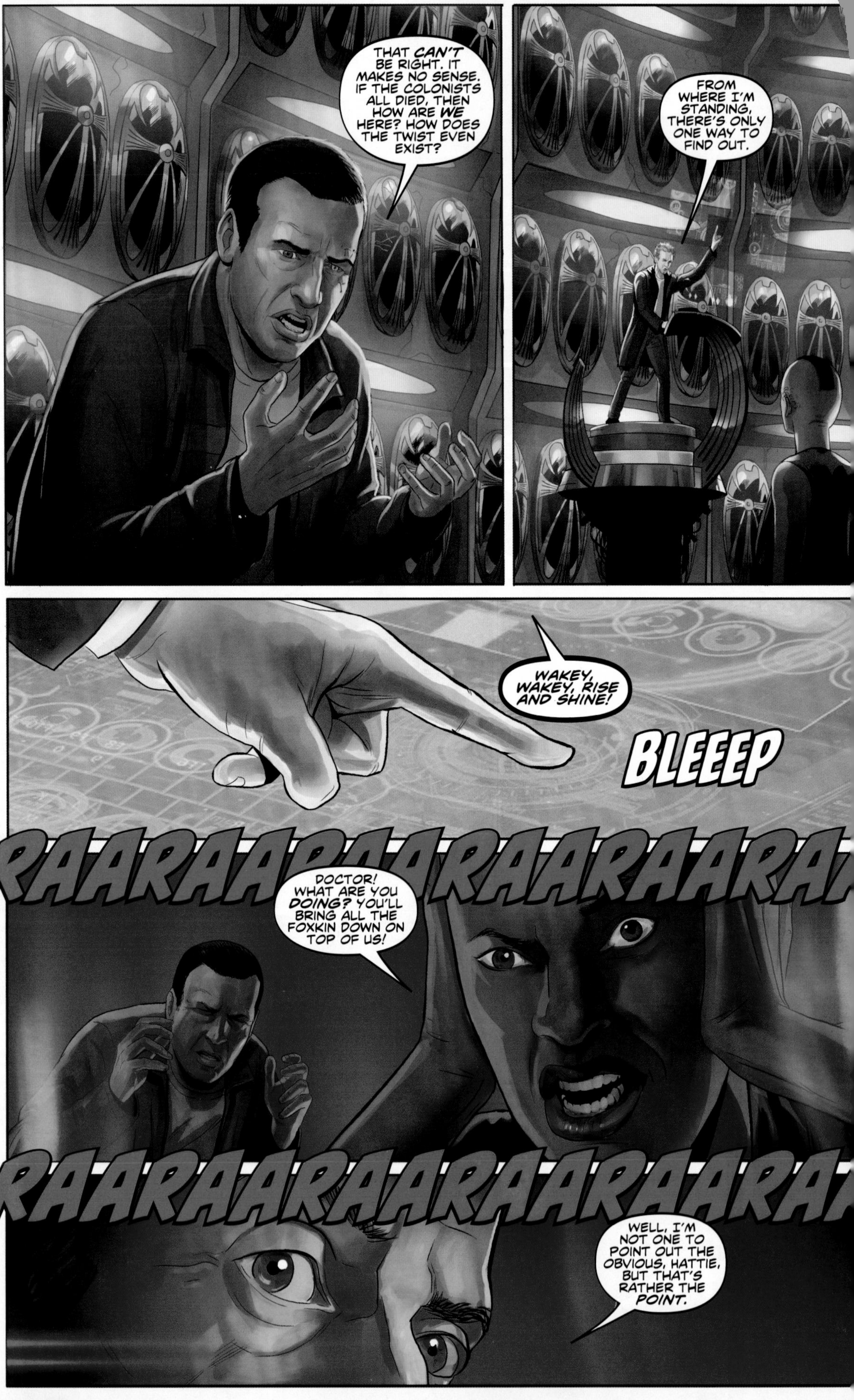
THAT CAN'T BE RIGHT. IT MAKES NO SENSE. IF THE COLONISTS ALL DIED, THEN HOW ARE WE HERE? HOW DOES THE TWIST EVEN EXIST?
FROM WHERE I'M STANDING, THERE'S ONLY ONE WAY TO FIND OUT.
WAKEY, WAKEY, RISE AND SHINE!
BLEEEP
RAARAARAARAARAARAARAARA
DOCTOR! WHAT ARE YOU DOING? YOU'LL BRING ALL THE FOXKIN DOWN ON TOP OF US!
RAARAARAARAARAARAARAARA
WELL, I'M NOT ONE TO POINT OUT THE OBVIOUS, HATTIE, BUT THAT'S RATHER THE POINT.

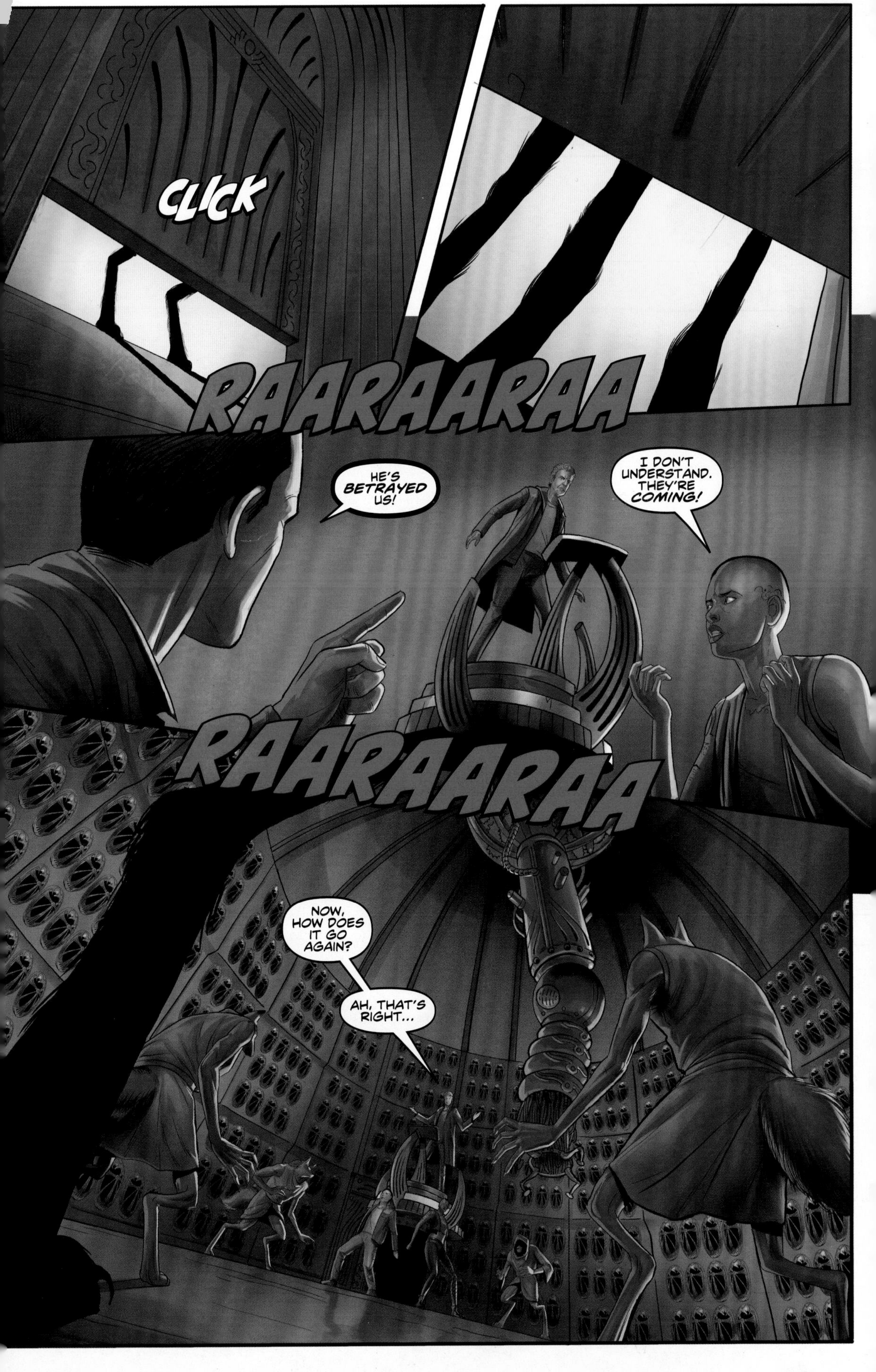
CLICK
RAARAARAA
HE'S BETRAYED US!
I DON'T UNDERSTAND. THEY'RE COMING!
RAARAARAA
NOW, HOW DOES IT GO AGAIN?
AH, THAT'S RIGHT...

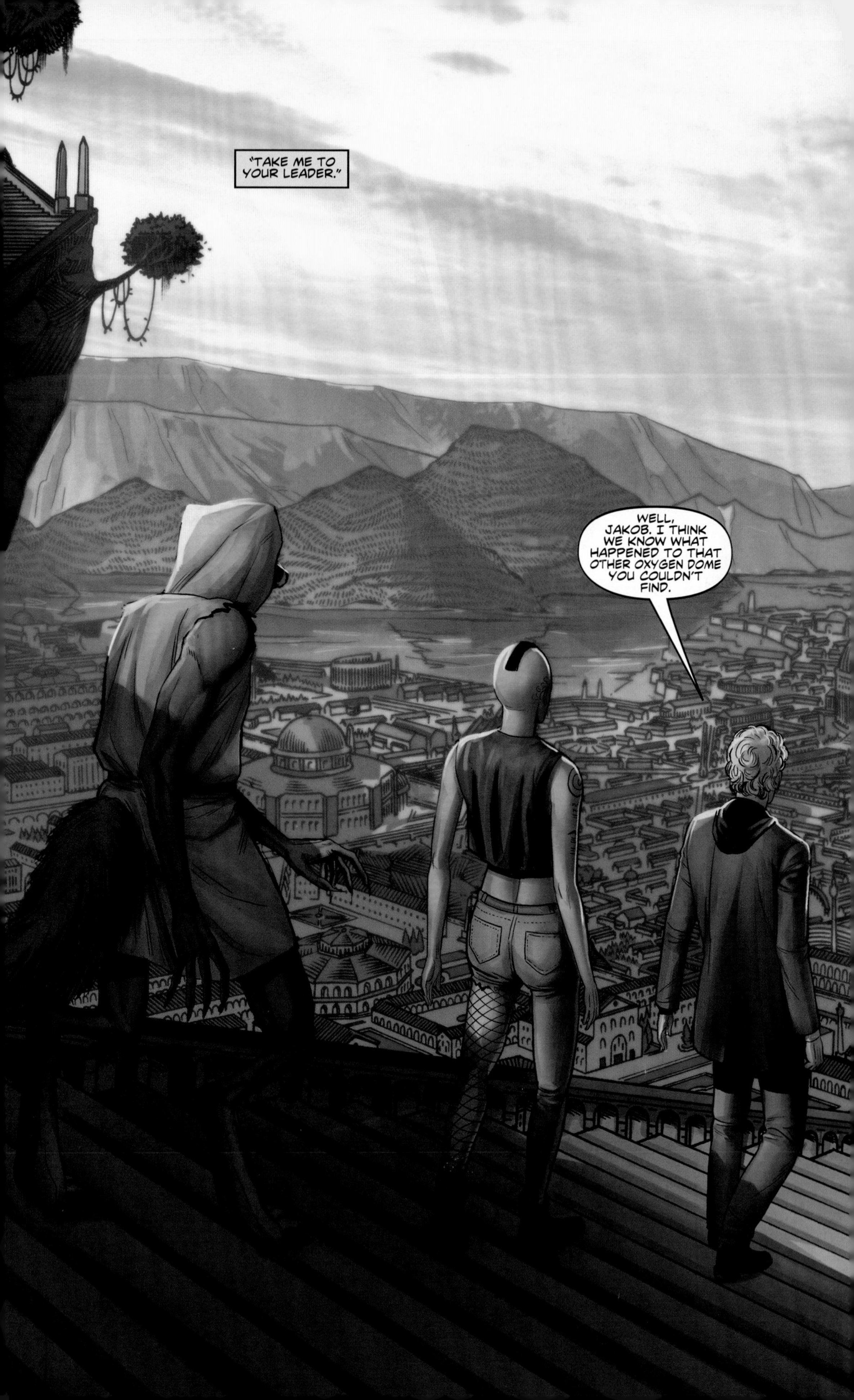
"TAKE ME TO YOUR LEADER."
WELL, JAKOB. I THINK WE KNOW WHAT HAPPENED TO THAT OTHER OXYGEN DOME YOU COULDN'T FIND.

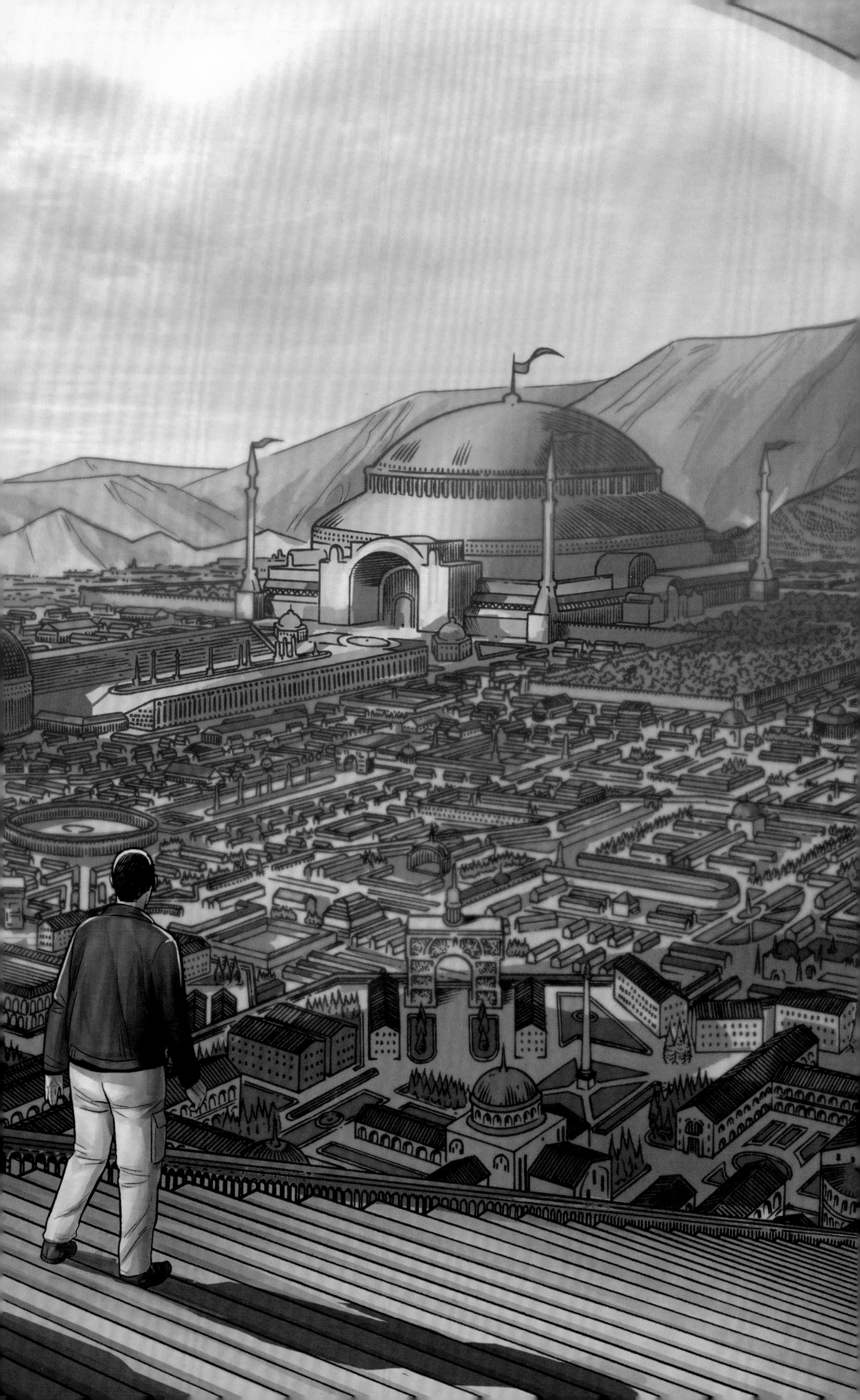

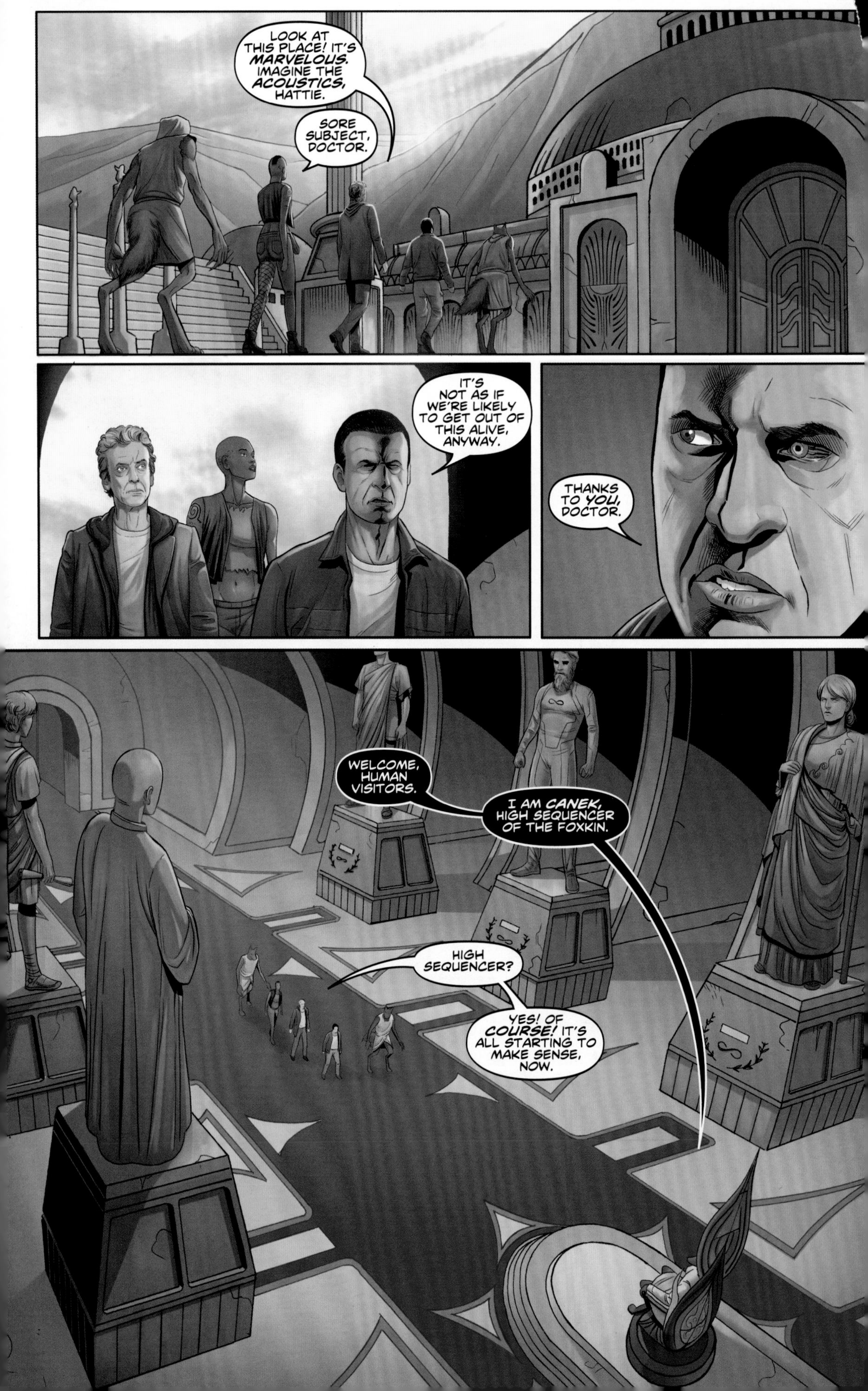
LOOK AT THIS PLACE! IT'S MARVELOUS. IMAGINE THE ACOUSTICS, HATTIE.
SORE SUBJECT, DOCTOR.
IT'S NOT AS IF WE'RE LIKELY TO GET OUT OF THIS ALIVE, ANYWAY.
THANKS TO YOU, DOCTOR.
WELCOME, HUMAN VISITORS.
I AM CANEK, HIGH SEQUENCER OF THE FOXKIN.
HIGH SEQUENCER?
YES! OF COURSE! IT'S ALL STARTING TO MAKE SENSE, NOW.

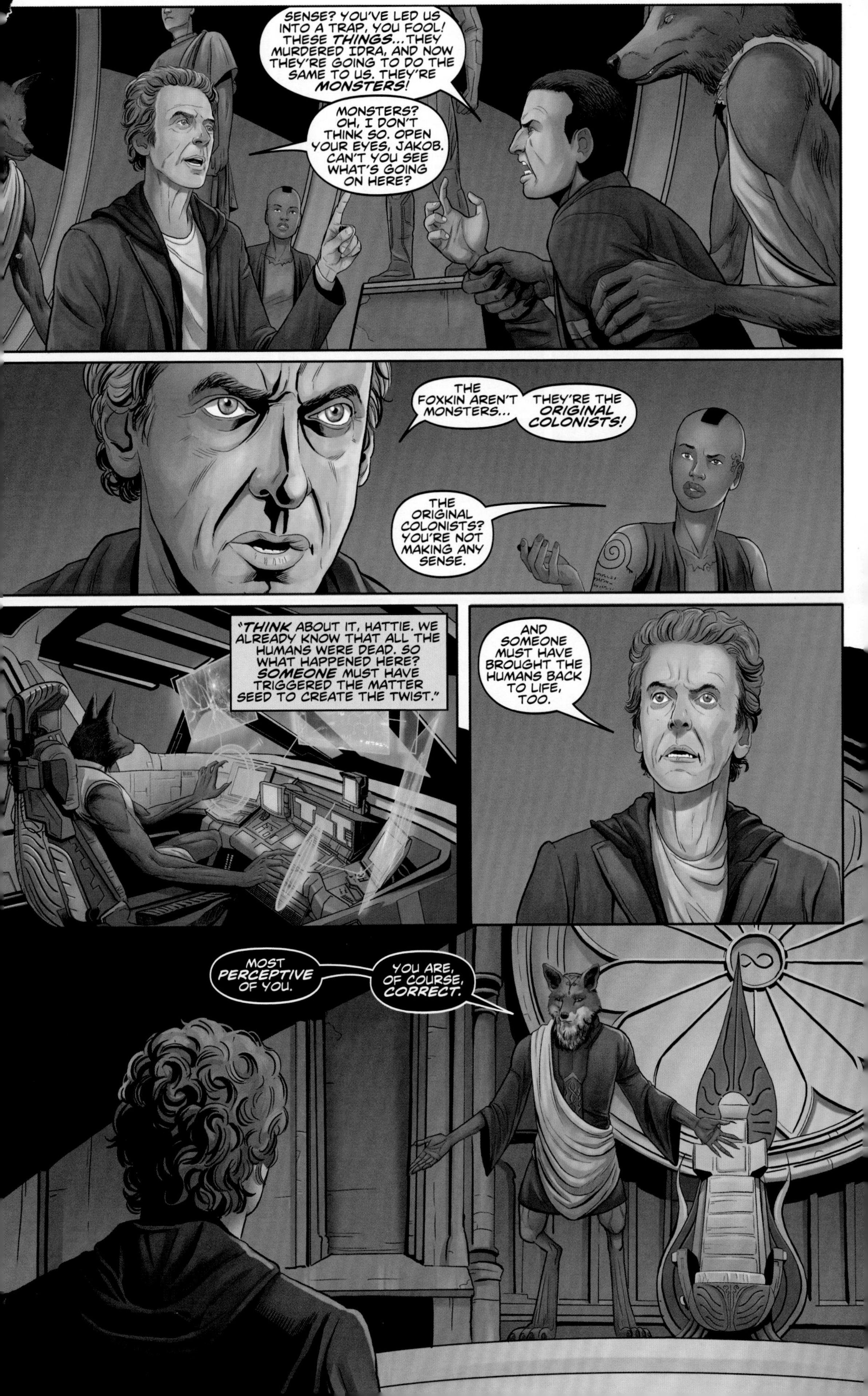
SENSE? YOU'VE LED US INTO A TRAP, YOU FOOL! THESE *THINGS*...THEY MURDERED IDRA, AND NOW THEY'RE GOING TO DO THE SAME TO US. THEY'RE ***MONSTERS***!
MONSTERS? OH, I DON'T THINK SO. OPEN YOUR EYES, JAKOB. CAN'T YOU SEE WHAT'S GOING ON HERE?
THE FOXKIN AREN'T MONSTERS...
THEY'RE THE ***ORIGINAL COLONISTS!***
THE ORIGINAL COLONISTS? YOU'RE NOT MAKING ANY SENSE.
"***THINK*** ABOUT IT, HATTIE. WE ALREADY KNOW THAT ALL THE HUMANS WERE DEAD. SO WHAT HAPPENED HERE? ***SOMEONE*** MUST HAVE TRIGGERED THE MATTER SEED TO CREATE THE TWIST."
AND SOMEONE MUST HAVE BROUGHT THE HUMANS BACK TO LIFE, TOO.
MOST ***PERCEPTIVE*** OF YOU.
YOU ARE, OF COURSE, ***CORRECT***.

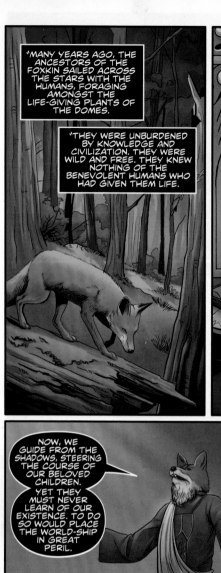

"MANY YEARS AGO, THE ANCESTORS OF THE FOXKIN SAILED ACROSS THE STARS WITH THE HUMANS, FORAGING AMONGST THE LIFE-GIVING PLANTS OF THE DOMES.

"THEY WERE UNBURDENED BY KNOWLEDGE AND CIVILIZATION. THEY WERE WILD AND FREE. THEY KNEW NOTHING OF THE BENEVOLENT HUMANS WHO HAD GIVEN THEM LIFE.

"BUT THEY EVOLVED, AND THEY GREW. AND AFTER A TIME, THEY DISCOVERED THERE HAD ONCE BEEN ANOTHER CIVILIZATION ON THE WORLD-SHIP, AN EXTINCT MASTER RACE, WHOSE TIMELESS SLEEP HAD BEEN DISTURBED.

"WE MADE IT OUR SACRED DUTY TO RETURN THEM TO LIFE. FOR GENERATIONS WE TOILED, STUDYING THE GREAT WORKS OF THE HUMANS, LEARNING. FINALLY, WE SUCCEEDED.

"WE CLONED THE HUMAN MASTERS FROM THEIR REMAINS, AND NURTURED THEM UNTIL THEY COULD ONCE AGAIN LIVE ALONE BENEATH THE STARS."

NOW, WE GUIDE FROM THE SHADOWS, STEERING THE COURSE OF OUR BELOVED CHILDREN. YET THEY MUST NEVER LEARN OF OUR EXISTENCE. TO DO SO WOULD PLACE THE WORLD-SHIP IN GREAT PERIL.

AND SO IT IS THAT THE THREE OF YOU MUST *CHOOSE*. YOU CANNOT BE ALLOWED TO RETURN TO THE SURFACE.

"SO I OFFER YOU A LIFE OF INCARCERATION, HERE, AMONGST THE FOXKIN, OR A SWIFT, PAINLESS DEATH.

"THE CHOICE IS *YOURS*."

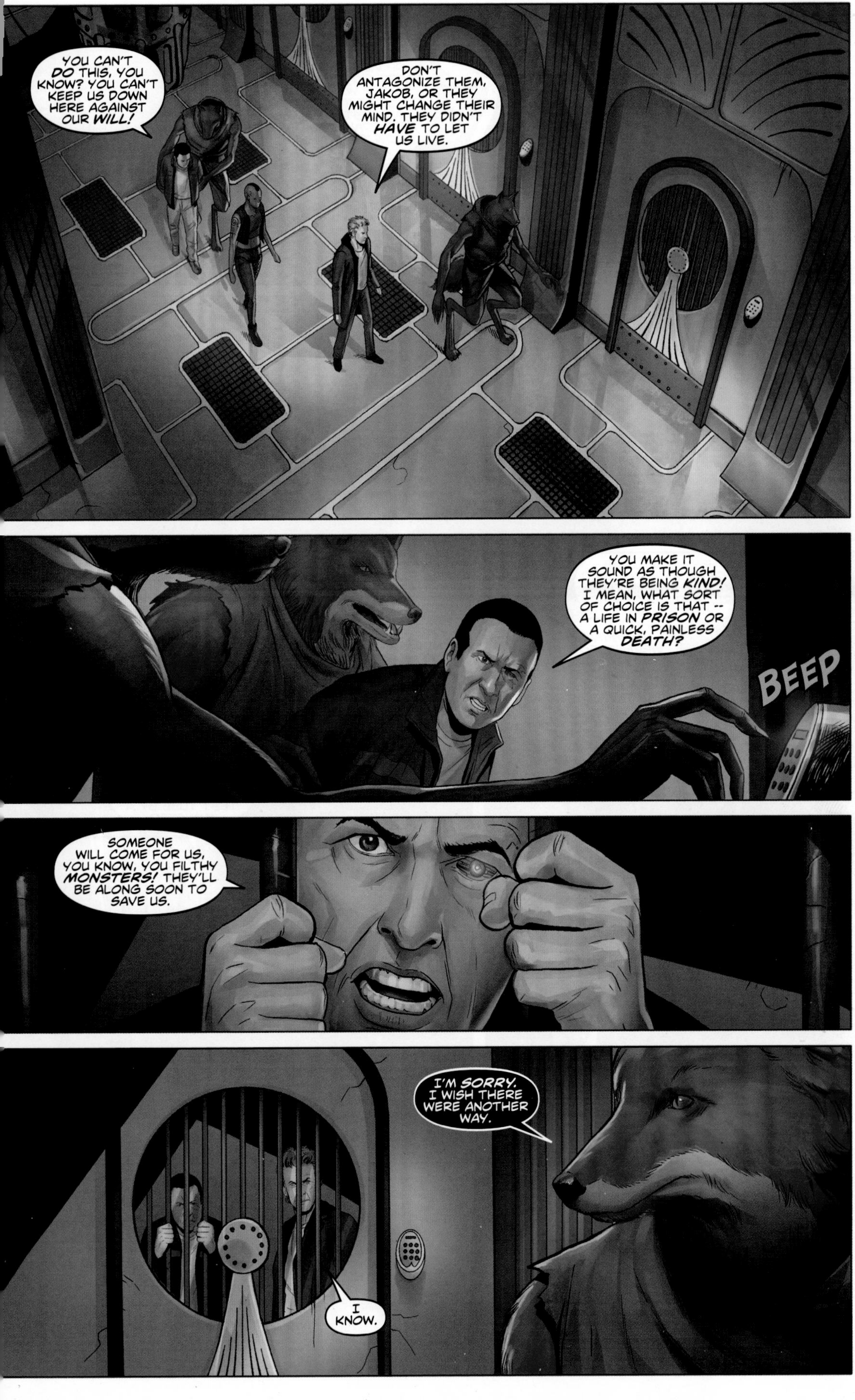

YOU CAN'T DO THIS, YOU KNOW? YOU CAN'T KEEP US DOWN HERE AGAINST OUR WILL!
DON'T ANTAGONIZE THEM, JAKOB, OR THEY MIGHT CHANGE THEIR MIND. THEY DIDN'T HAVE TO LET US LIVE.
YOU MAKE IT SOUND AS THOUGH THEY'RE BEING KIND! I MEAN, WHAT SORT OF CHOICE IS THAT -- A LIFE IN PRISON OR A QUICK, PAINLESS DEATH?
BEEP
SOMEONE WILL COME FOR US, YOU KNOW, YOU FILTHY MONSTERS! THEY'LL BE ALONG SOON TO SAVE US.
I'M SORRY. I WISH THERE WERE ANOTHER WAY.
I KNOW.

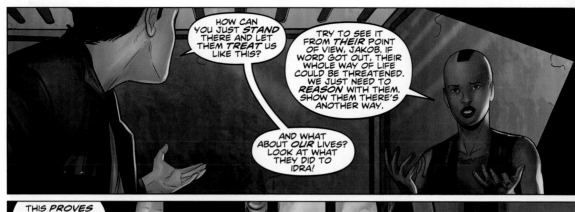

HOW CAN YOU JUST *STAND* THERE AND LET THEM *TREAT* US LIKE THIS?

TRY TO SEE IT FROM *THEIR* POINT OF VIEW, JAKOB. IF WORD GOT OUT, THEIR WHOLE WAY OF LIFE COULD BE THREATENED. WE JUST NEED TO *REASON* WITH THEM. SHOW THEM THERE'S ANOTHER WAY.

AND WHAT ABOUT *OUR* LIVES? LOOK AT WHAT THEY DID TO IDRA!

THIS *PROVES* I'M INNOCENT. THEY MUST HAVE KILLED HER TO PROTECT THEIR SECRET, JUST LIKE YOU SAID, DOCTOR.

HMMM.

BREEEE

THEY NEED TO BE *STOPPED.* DESTROYED LIKE THE VERMIN THEY ARE, SPREADING THEIR *DIRTY LIES.*

VERMIN? IF IT WEREN'T FOR THE FOXKIN, THERE'D BE NO HUMANS ON THE TWIST AT ALL! CAN'T YOU SEE? THEY'RE AN INTELLIGENT, CIVILIZED SPECIES. THEY DEMAND *RESPECT,* NOT HATRED.

YOU HUMANS COULD LEARN A LOT FROM THEM.

IF IT'S *TRUE,* IF THEY REALLY *DID* RECREATE ALL THE COLONISTS FROM THE REMAINS OF THEIR DNA, THEN WE OWE THEM *EVERYTHING.*

OH, IT'S TRUE. THOSE CREATURES BACK THERE MADE *ALL* OF YOU.

I *REFUSE* TO BELIEVE THAT. NOT *ME.* I WAS NOT BRED IN A TEST TUBE BY A MONSTER.

BUT YOU STILL MANAGED TO TURN *INTO* ONE, ALL BY YOURSELF. HOW *CLEVER* OF YOU.

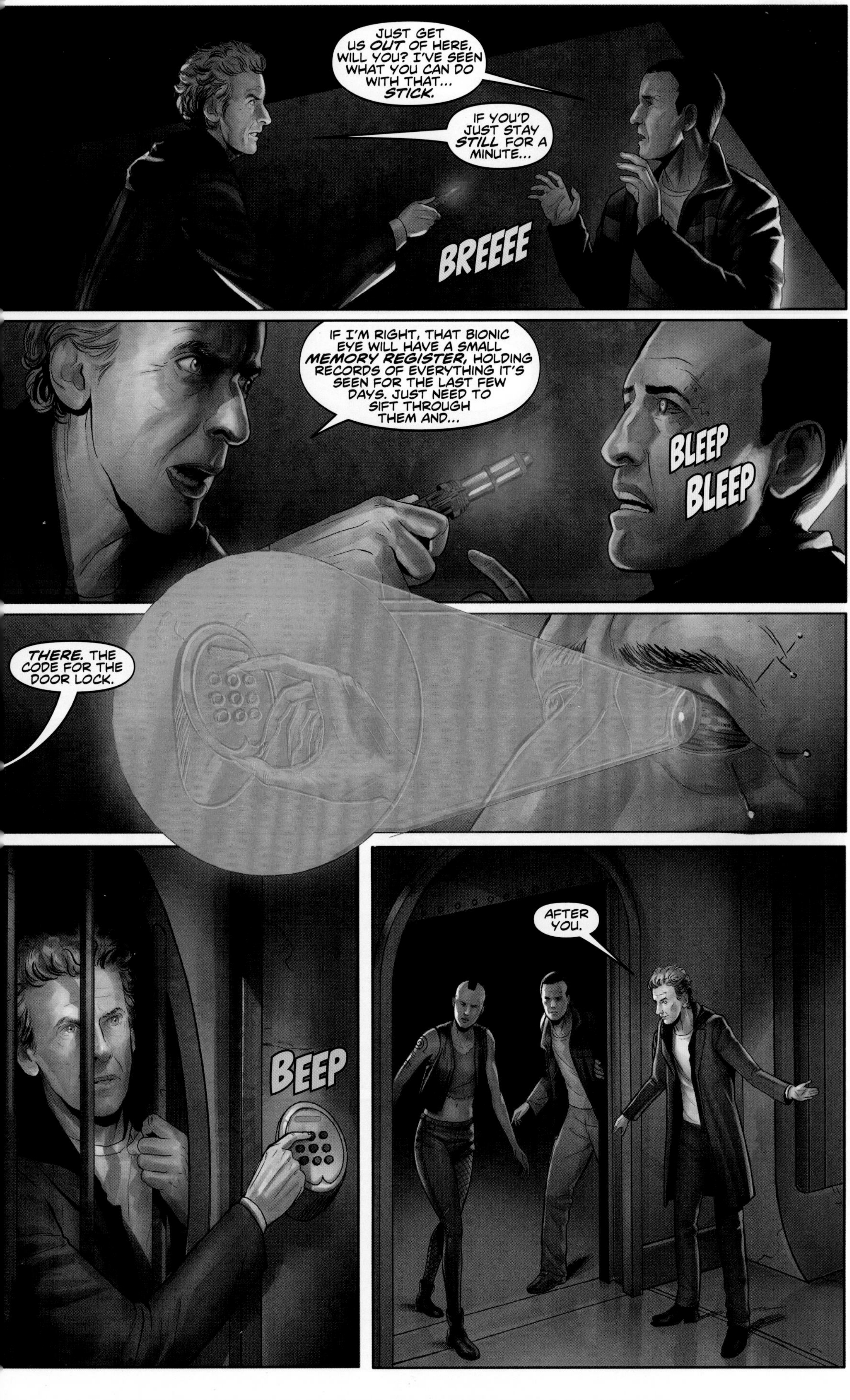
JUST GET US OUT OF HERE, WILL YOU? I'VE SEEN WHAT YOU CAN DO WITH THAT... STICK.
IF YOU'D JUST STAY STILL FOR A MINUTE...
BREEEE
IF I'M RIGHT, THAT BIONIC EYE WILL HAVE A SMALL MEMORY REGISTER, HOLDING RECORDS OF EVERYTHING IT'S SEEN FOR THE LAST FEW DAYS. JUST NEED TO SIFT THROUGH THEM AND...
BLEEP
BLEEP
THERE. THE CODE FOR THE DOOR LOCK.
BEEP
AFTER YOU.

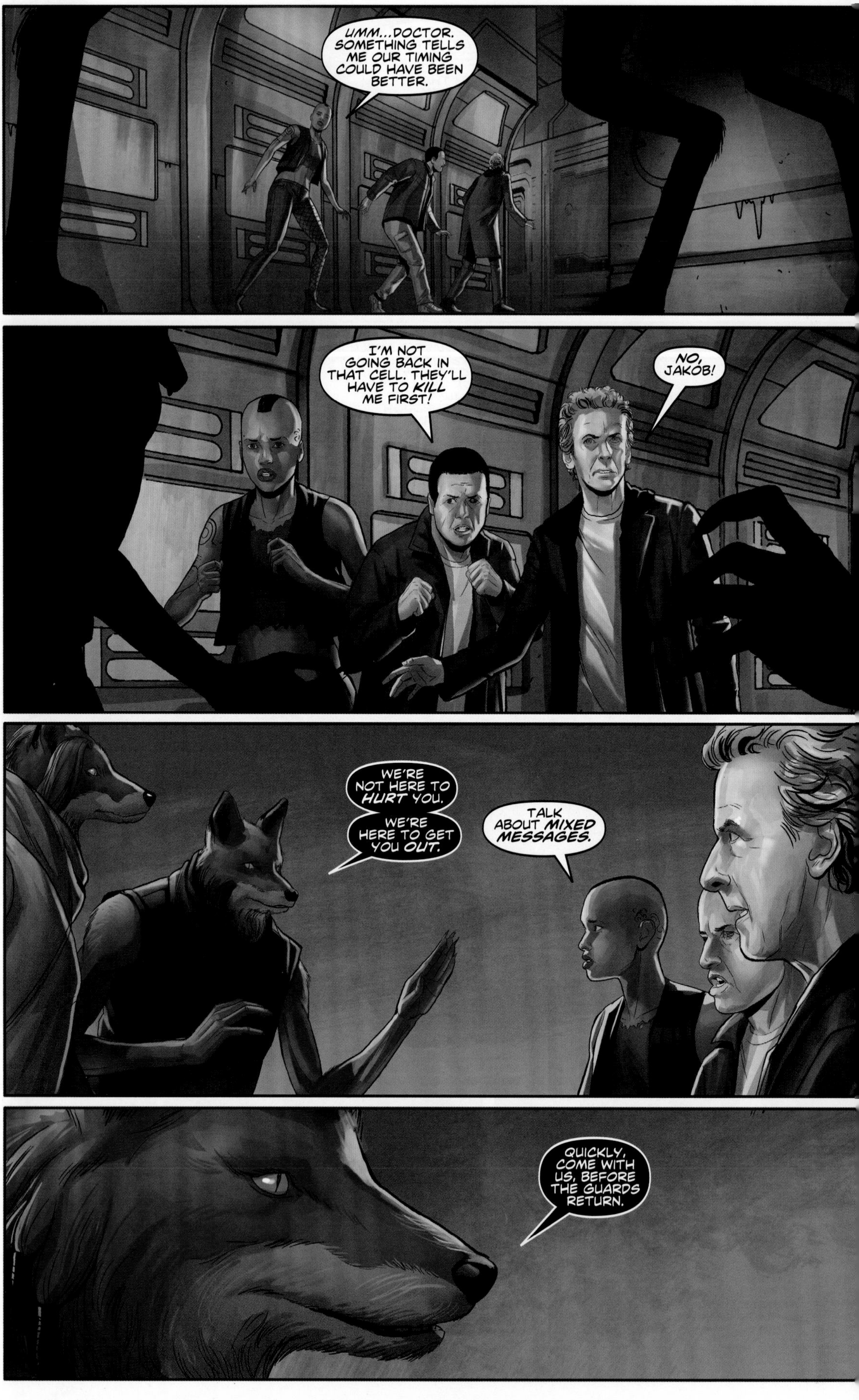
UMM...DOCTOR. SOMETHING TELLS ME OUR TIMING COULD HAVE BEEN BETTER.
I'M NOT GOING BACK IN THAT CELL. THEY'LL HAVE TO KILL ME FIRST!
NO, JAKOB!
WE'RE NOT HERE TO HURT YOU.
WE'RE HERE TO GET YOU OUT.
TALK ABOUT MIXED MESSAGES.
QUICKLY, COME WITH US, BEFORE THE GUARDS RETURN.

WE CAN'T *TRUST* THEM. IT'S A *TRAP.*

NO. WE'RE PART OF A MOVEMENT THAT BELIEVES THE FOXKIN SHOULD *REVEAL* THEMSELVES TO THE HUMANS. WE... DON'T *AGREE* WITH KEEPING YOU HERE. WE WANT TO GET OUR MESSAGE OUT, NO MATTER THE CONSEQUENCES.

WE WANT YOU TO DO THAT FOR US. TO TELL *EVERYONE* ON THE TWIST THAT WE'RE *HERE,* THAT OUR LEADERS ARE *WRONG* TO HIDE US AWAY, AND THAT WE'RE NOT GOING TO *HARM* ANYONE.

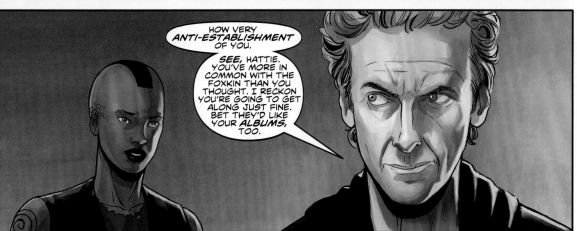

HOW VERY *ANTI-ESTABLISHMENT* OF YOU.

SEE, HATTIE. YOU'VE MORE IN COMMON WITH THE FOXKIN THAN YOU THOUGHT. I RECKON YOU'RE GOING TO GET ALONG JUST FINE. BET THEY'D LIKE YOUR *ALBUMS,* TOO.

COME. WE'LL GUIDE YOU SAFELY BACK TO THE SURFACE.

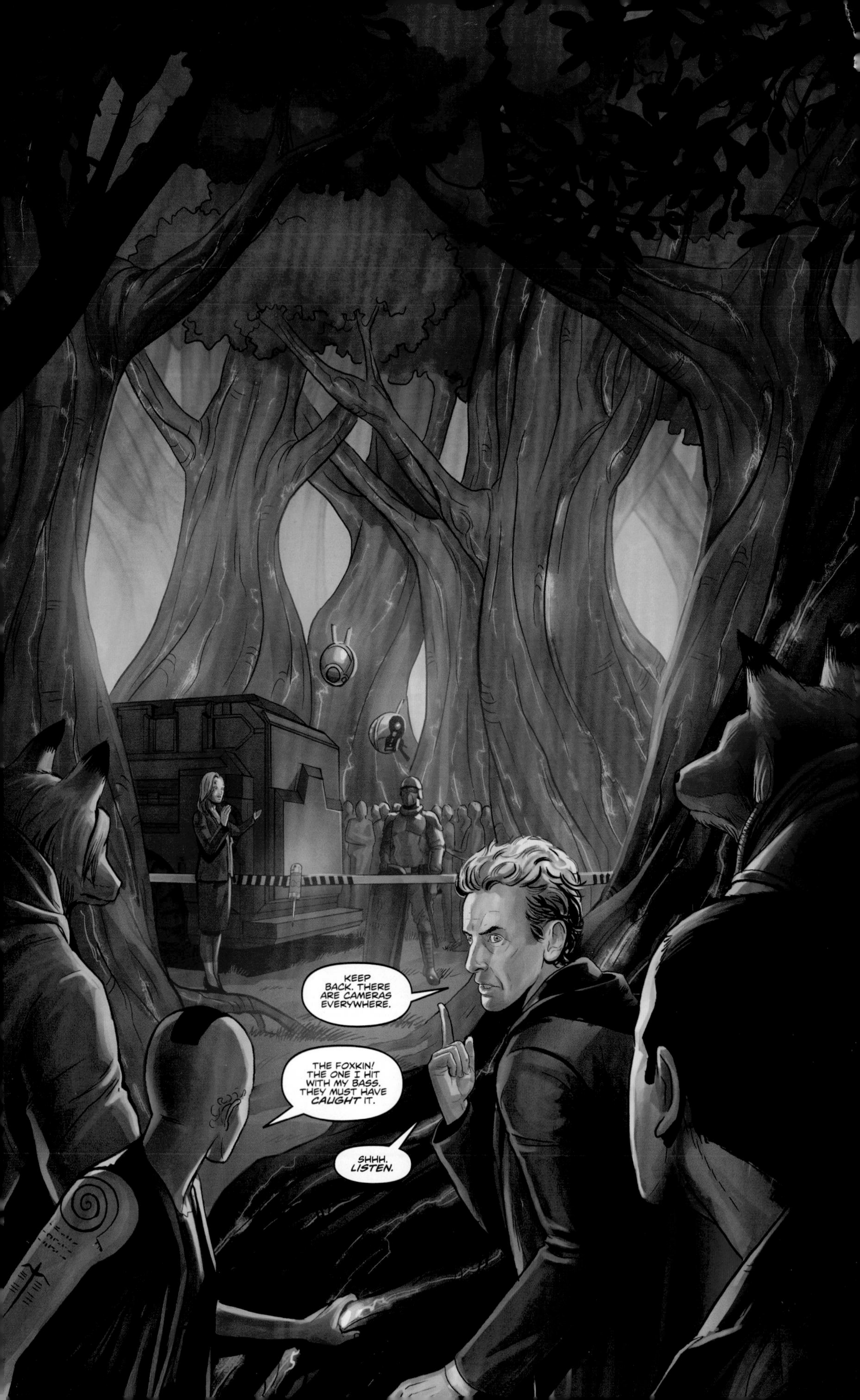
KEEP BACK. THERE ARE CAMERAS EVERYWHERE.
THE FOXKIN! THE ONE I HIT WITH MY BASS. THEY MUST HAVE *CAUGHT* IT.
SHHH. *LISTEN.*

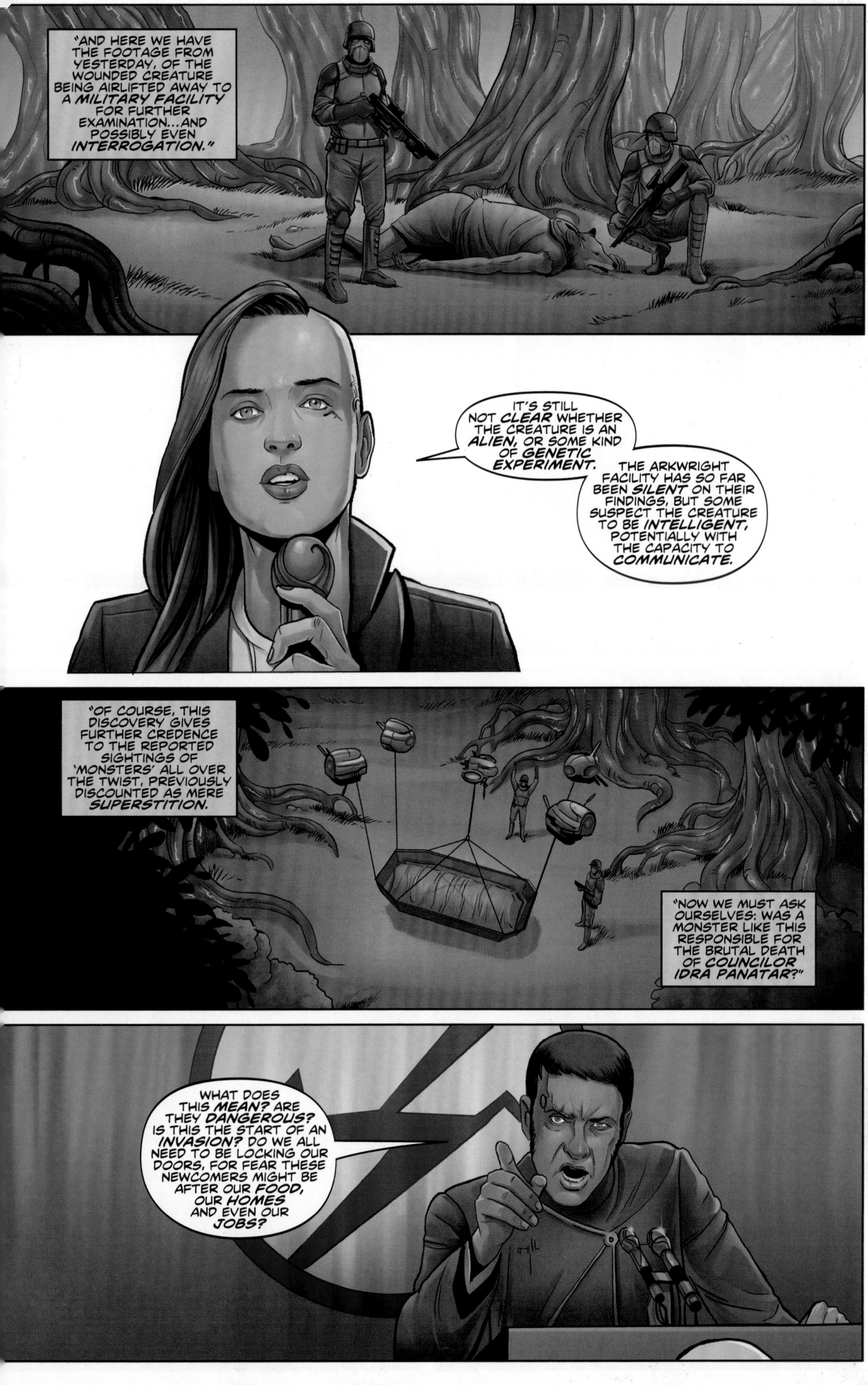
"AND HERE WE HAVE THE FOOTAGE FROM YESTERDAY, OF THE WOUNDED CREATURE BEING AIRLIFTED AWAY TO A MILITARY FACILITY FOR FURTHER EXAMINATION...AND POSSIBLY EVEN INTERROGATION."
IT'S STILL NOT CLEAR WHETHER THE CREATURE IS AN ALIEN, OR SOME KIND OF GENETIC EXPERIMENT.
THE ARKWRIGHT FACILITY HAS SO FAR BEEN SILENT ON THEIR FINDINGS, BUT SOME SUSPECT THE CREATURE TO BE INTELLIGENT, POTENTIALLY WITH THE CAPACITY TO COMMUNICATE.
"OF COURSE, THIS DISCOVERY GIVES FURTHER CREDENCE TO THE REPORTED SIGHTINGS OF 'MONSTERS' ALL OVER THE TWIST, PREVIOUSLY DISCOUNTED AS MERE SUPERSTITION.
"NOW WE MUST ASK OURSELVES: WAS A MONSTER LIKE THIS RESPONSIBLE FOR THE BRUTAL DEATH OF COUNCILOR IDRA PANATAR?"
WHAT DOES THIS MEAN? ARE THEY DANGEROUS? IS THIS THE START OF AN INVASION? DO WE ALL NEED TO BE LOCKING OUR DOORS, FOR FEAR THESE NEWCOMERS MIGHT BE AFTER OUR FOOD, OUR HOMES AND EVEN OUR JOBS?

WE'RE TOO LATE. THE FOX IS ALREADY OUT OF THE BAG. NO GOING BACK NOW.

GOING BACK WAS NEVER AN OPTION.

FINALLY! THIS IS THE CHANCE I'VE BEEN WAITING FOR. NOW SOMETHING CAN BE *DONE*. *NOW* PEOPLE WILL LISTEN.

I CAN SHOW EVERYONE WHAT A DANGER THEY ARE, WHAT THEY DID TO IDRA. I CAN LEAD THEM TO THE CREATURE'S NEST. *DESTROY* THEM.

THAT'S *ENOUGH*.

OH *NO*, DOCTOR. THIS IS JUST THE *START*.

NO, JAKOB. IT'S TIME YOU FACED UP TO WHAT YOU'VE DONE.

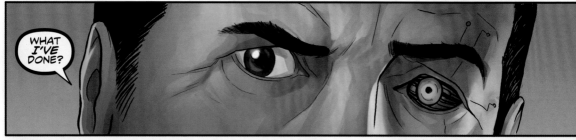

WHAT *I'VE* DONE?

IT'S TIME TO STOP THE *LIES*. YOU WERE *WRONG*, JAKOB. ABOUT THE FOXKIN, ABOUT IDRA...

YOU CROSSED A LINE YOU CAN NEVER COME BACK FROM.

DOCTOR?

IT WAS OBVIOUS FROM THE START. I JUST WANTED TO KNOW *WHY*. AND NOW I SEE IT. IDRA WAS GOING TO *TELL* EVERYONE, WASN'T SHE? SHE WAS GOING TO TELL THEM THE *TRUTH*.

WHAT...? I DON'T KNOW WHAT YOU'RE TALKING ABOUT...

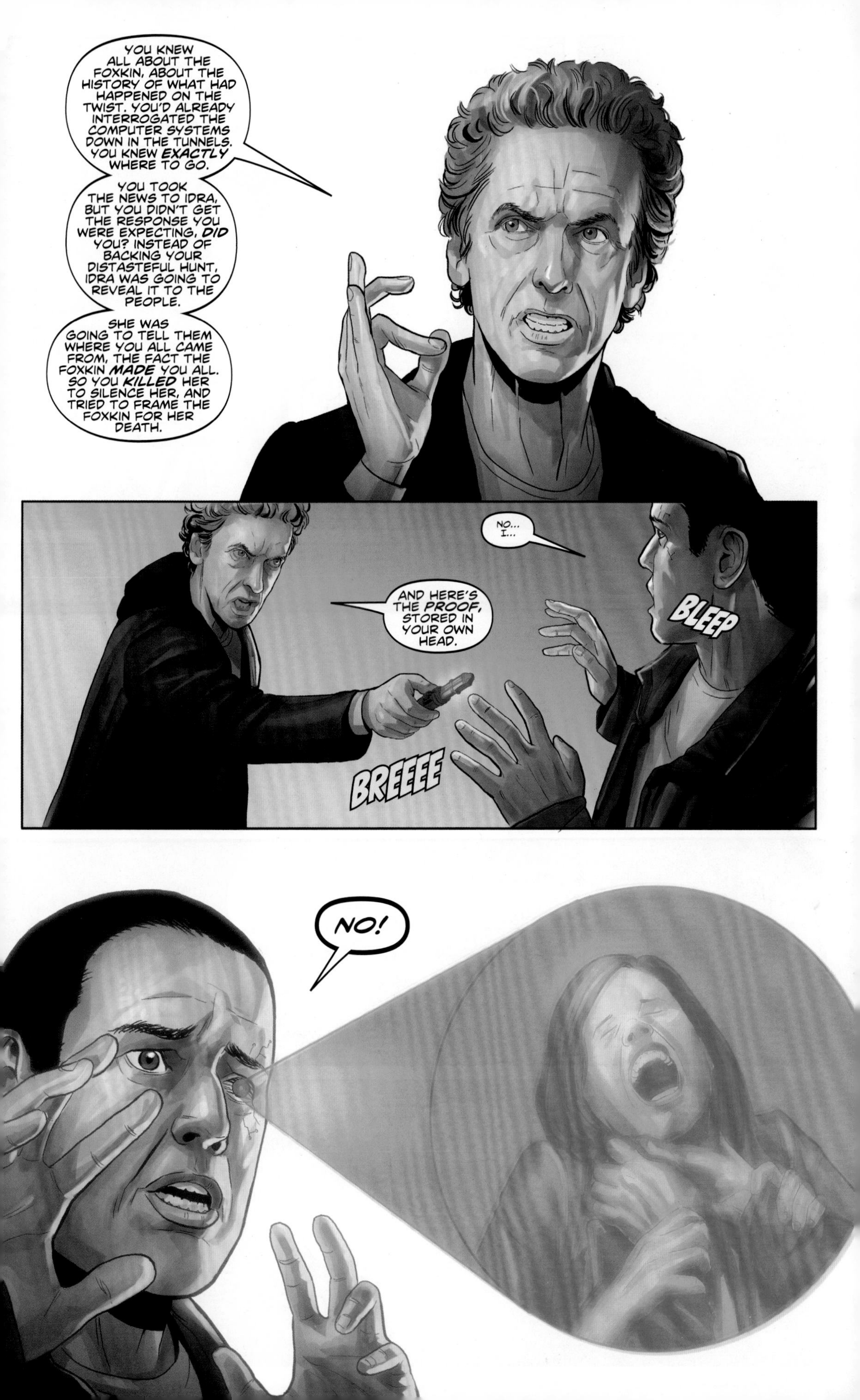
YOU KNEW ALL ABOUT THE FOXKIN, ABOUT THE HISTORY OF WHAT HAD HAPPENED ON THE TWIST. YOU'D ALREADY INTERROGATED THE COMPUTER SYSTEMS DOWN IN THE TUNNELS. YOU KNEW *EXACTLY* WHERE TO GO.
YOU TOOK THE NEWS TO IDRA, BUT YOU DIDN'T GET THE RESPONSE YOU WERE EXPECTING, *DID* YOU? INSTEAD OF BACKING YOUR DISTASTEFUL HUNT, IDRA WAS GOING TO REVEAL IT TO THE PEOPLE.
SHE WAS GOING TO TELL THEM WHERE YOU ALL CAME FROM, THE FACT THE FOXKIN *MADE* YOU ALL. SO YOU *KILLED* HER TO SILENCE HER, AND TRIED TO FRAME THE FOXKIN FOR HER DEATH.
NO... I...
AND HERE'S THE *PROOF*, STORED IN YOUR OWN HEAD.
BLEEP
BREEEE
NO!

IT WAS *HIM*? HE KILLED IDRA?

I DID IT FOR THE *GREATER GOOD*.

WHY CAN'T ANY OF YOU *SEE* THAT?

WE'RE LIVING ON TOP OF A NEST OF MONSTERS. THEY CONTROL OUR VERY *DNA*. THEY *HAVE* TO BE STOPPED!

THIS WAY, *EVERYONE* COULD SEE WHAT SORT OF MONSTERS THEY REALLY ARE.

HATTIE!

GRRRRRRR

GRRRR.

LET HIM *GO*, THERE'S BEEN *ENOUGH* BLOODSHED. DON'T GIVE HIM THE SATISFACTION OF LAYING ANOTHER DEATH AT YOUR DOOR.

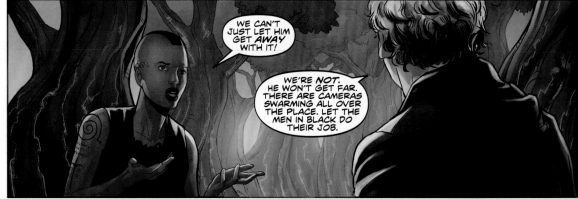

WE CAN'T JUST LET HIM GET *AWAY* WITH IT!

WE'RE *NOT*. HE WON'T GET FAR. THERE ARE CAMERAS SWARMING ALL OVER THE PLACE. LET THE MEN IN BLACK DO THEIR JOB.

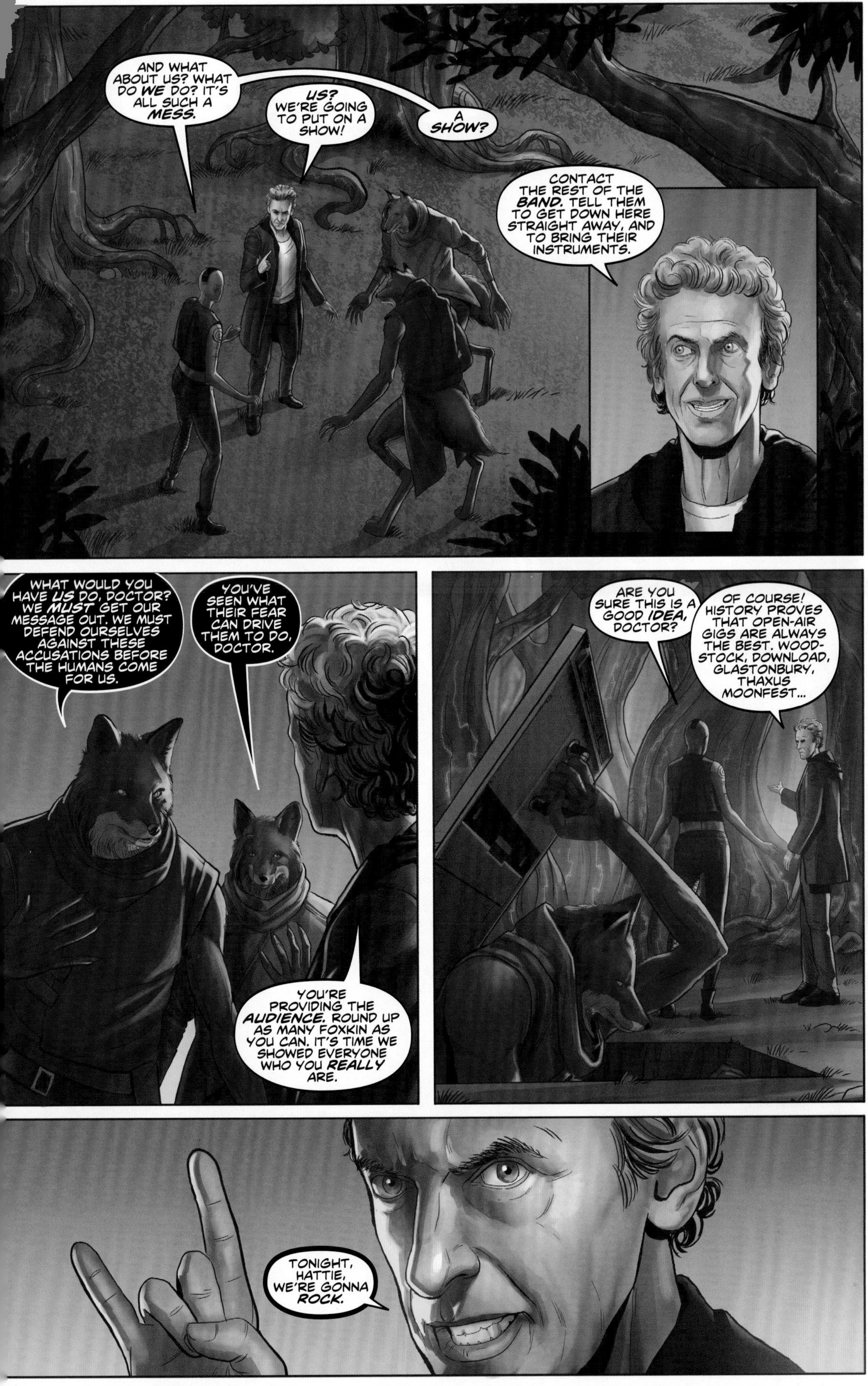
AND WHAT ABOUT US? WHAT DO WE DO? IT'S ALL SUCH A MESS.
US? WE'RE GOING TO PUT ON A SHOW!
A SHOW?
CONTACT THE REST OF THE BAND. TELL THEM TO GET DOWN HERE STRAIGHT AWAY, AND TO BRING THEIR INSTRUMENTS.
WHAT WOULD YOU HAVE US DO, DOCTOR? WE MUST GET OUR MESSAGE OUT. WE MUST DEFEND OURSELVES AGAINST THESE ACCUSATIONS BEFORE THE HUMANS COME FOR US.
YOU'VE SEEN WHAT THEIR FEAR CAN DRIVE THEM TO DO, DOCTOR.
YOU'RE PROVIDING THE AUDIENCE. ROUND UP AS MANY FOXKIN AS YOU CAN. IT'S TIME WE SHOWED EVERYONE WHO YOU REALLY ARE.
ARE YOU SURE THIS IS A GOOD IDEA, DOCTOR?
OF COURSE! HISTORY PROVES THAT OPEN-AIR GIGS ARE ALWAYS THE BEST. WOODSTOCK, DOWNLOAD, GLASTONBURY, THAXUS MOONFEST...
TONIGHT, HATTIE, WE'RE GONNA ROCK.

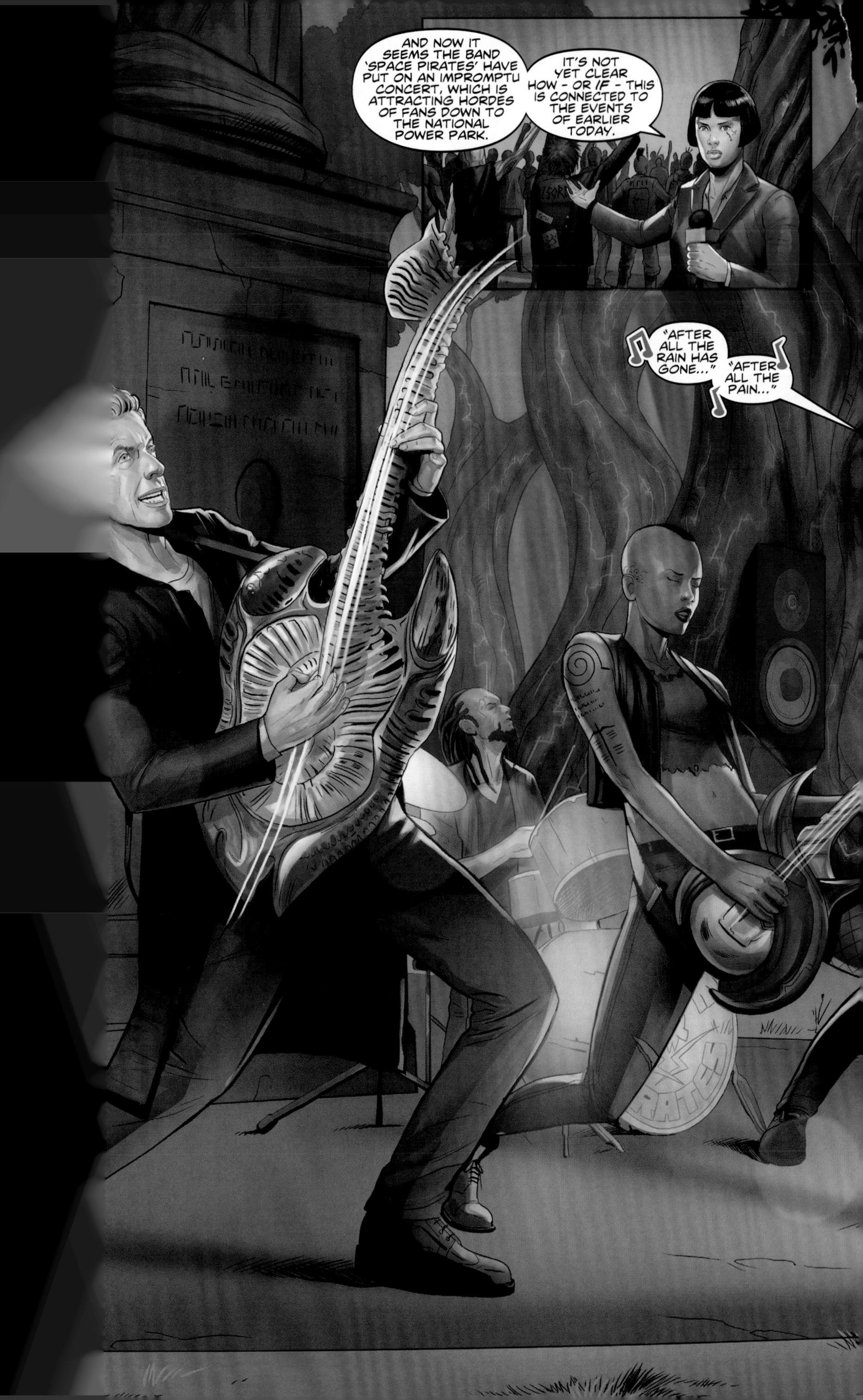
AND NOW IT SEEMS THE BAND 'SPACE PIRATES' HAVE PUT ON AN IMPROMPTU CONCERT, WHICH IS ATTRACTING HORDES OF FANS DOWN TO THE NATIONAL POWER PARK.
IT'S NOT YET CLEAR HOW - OR *IF* - THIS IS CONNECTED TO THE EVENTS OF EARLIER TODAY.
"AFTER ALL THE RAIN HAS GONE..."
"AFTER ALL THE PAIN..."

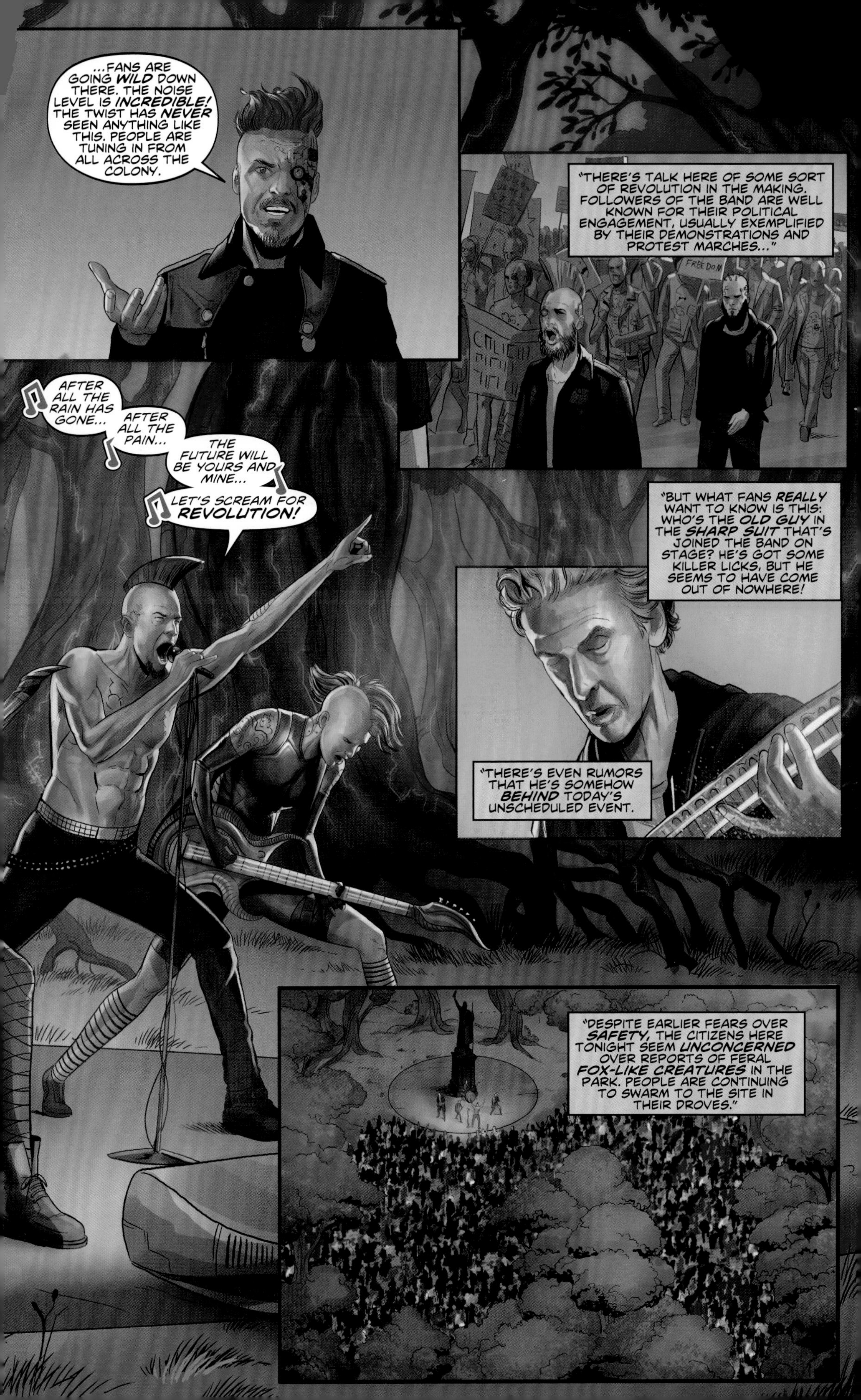
...FANS ARE GOING WILD DOWN THERE. THE NOISE LEVEL IS INCREDIBLE! THE TWIST HAS NEVER SEEN ANYTHING LIKE THIS. PEOPLE ARE TUNING IN FROM ALL ACROSS THE COLONY.
"THERE'S TALK HERE OF SOME SORT OF REVOLUTION IN THE MAKING. FOLLOWERS OF THE BAND ARE WELL KNOWN FOR THEIR POLITICAL ENGAGEMENT, USUALLY EXEMPLIFIED BY THEIR DEMONSTRATIONS AND PROTEST MARCHES..."
FREEDOM
AFTER ALL THE RAIN HAS GONE...
AFTER ALL THE PAIN...
THE FUTURE WILL BE YOURS AND MINE...
LET'S SCREAM FOR REVOLUTION!
"BUT WHAT FANS REALLY WANT TO KNOW IS THIS: WHO'S THE OLD GUY IN THE SHARP SUIT THAT'S JOINED THE BAND ON STAGE? HE'S GOT SOME KILLER LICKS, BUT HE SEEMS TO HAVE COME OUT OF NOWHERE!
"THERE'S EVEN RUMORS THAT HE'S SOMEHOW BEHIND TODAY'S UNSCHEDULED EVENT.
"DESPITE EARLIER FEARS OVER SAFETY, THE CITIZENS HERE TONIGHT SEEM UNCONCERNED OVER REPORTS OF FERAL FOX-LIKE CREATURES IN THE PARK. PEOPLE ARE CONTINUING TO SWARM TO THE SITE IN THEIR DROVES."

EVENING,
WOOD-SHOCK!

SEE WHAT
I DID THERE?
POWER TREES...?
ANYBODY?

NOW I'VE
GOT YOUR *ATTENTION*,
THERE'S SOMETHING YOU
ALL NEED TO HEAR.

THE
HISTORY YOU'VE
BEEN TAUGHT -- THE
STORIES YOU LEARNED
IN SCHOOL ABOUT THE
ORIGINS OF THE TWIST,
ABOUT THE FOUNDING
OF YOUR COLONY --
THEY'RE *NOT
TRUE*.

THAT WAS
HOW IT WAS
MEANT TO HAPPEN.
BUT IT *DIDN'T*. IT
ALL WENT WRONG.
LUCKY FOR YOU,
THERE WERE
OTHERS ON HAND
TO HELP.

YOU SEE,
THERE'S ANOTHER
RACE OF PEOPLE
LIVING IN YOUR
MIDST -- *PEOPLE* WHO
SAVED YOU ALL, WHO
ESTABLISHED THIS
COLONY WHEN THE
ORIGINAL MISSION
FAILED.

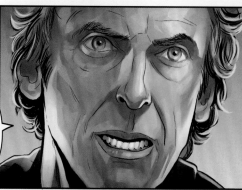

THESE PEOPLE
ENSURED *YOUR*
SURVIVAL. YOUR
SECURITY FORCES
FOUND ONE OF THEM
EARLIER TODAY -- A
FOXKIN -- AND NOW
YOU NEED TO BE
READY, BECAUSE
IT'S TIME THEY
STOPPED
HIDING.

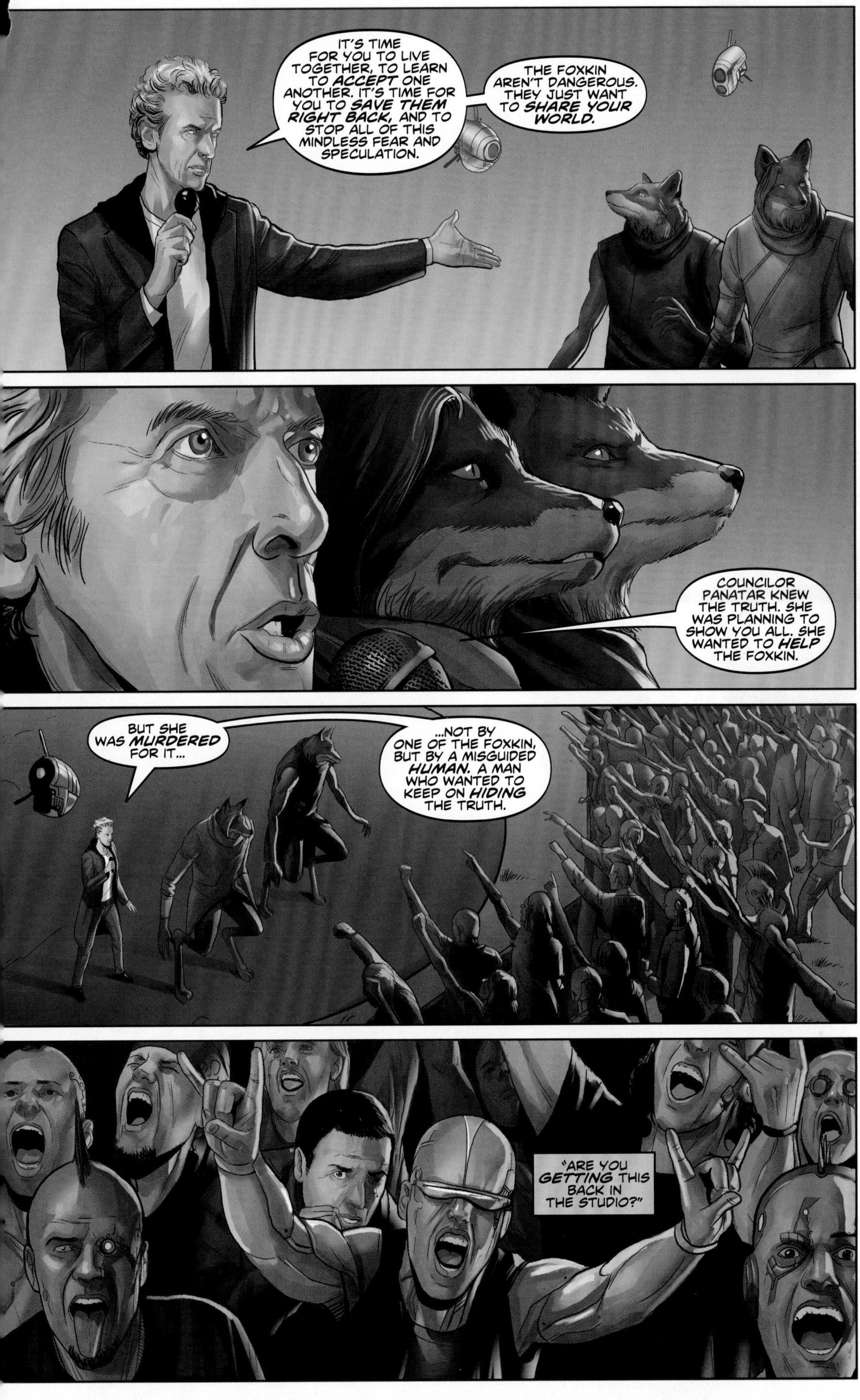
IT'S TIME FOR YOU TO LIVE TOGETHER, TO LEARN TO ACCEPT ONE ANOTHER. IT'S TIME FOR YOU TO SAVE THEM RIGHT BACK, AND TO STOP ALL OF THIS MINDLESS FEAR AND SPECULATION.
THE FOXKIN AREN'T DANGEROUS. THEY JUST WANT TO SHARE YOUR WORLD.
COUNCILOR PANATAR KNEW THE TRUTH. SHE WAS PLANNING TO SHOW YOU ALL. SHE WANTED TO HELP THE FOXKIN.
BUT SHE WAS MURDERED FOR IT...
...NOT BY ONE OF THE FOXKIN, BUT BY A MISGUIDED HUMAN. A MAN WHO WANTED TO KEEP ON HIDING THE TRUTH.
"ARE YOU GETTING THIS BACK IN THE STUDIO?"

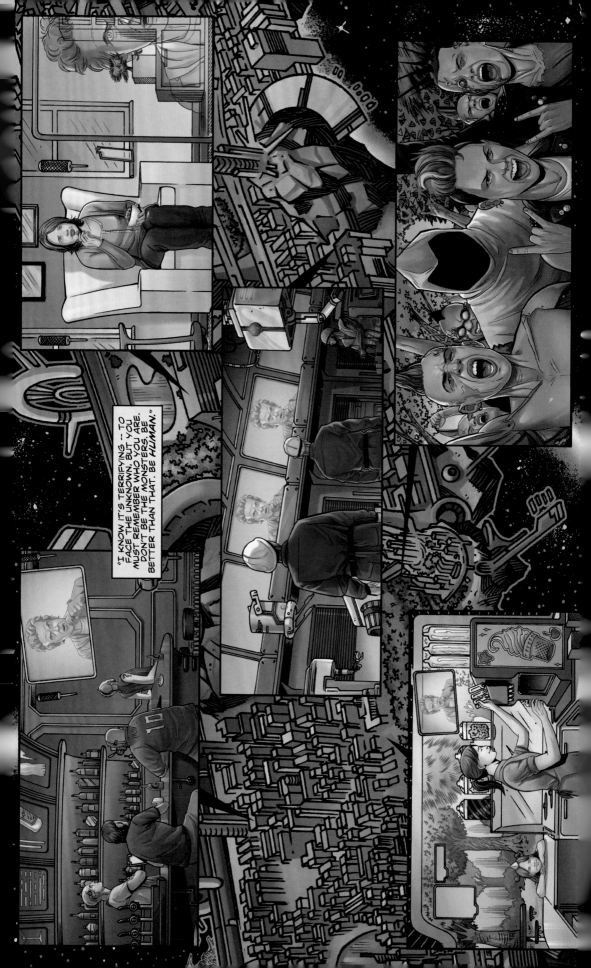

"I KNOW IT'S TERRIFYING -- TO FACE THE UNKNOWN, BUT YOU MUST REMEMBER WHO YOU ARE. DON'T BE THE MONSTERS. BE BETTER THAN THAT. BE *HUMAN*."

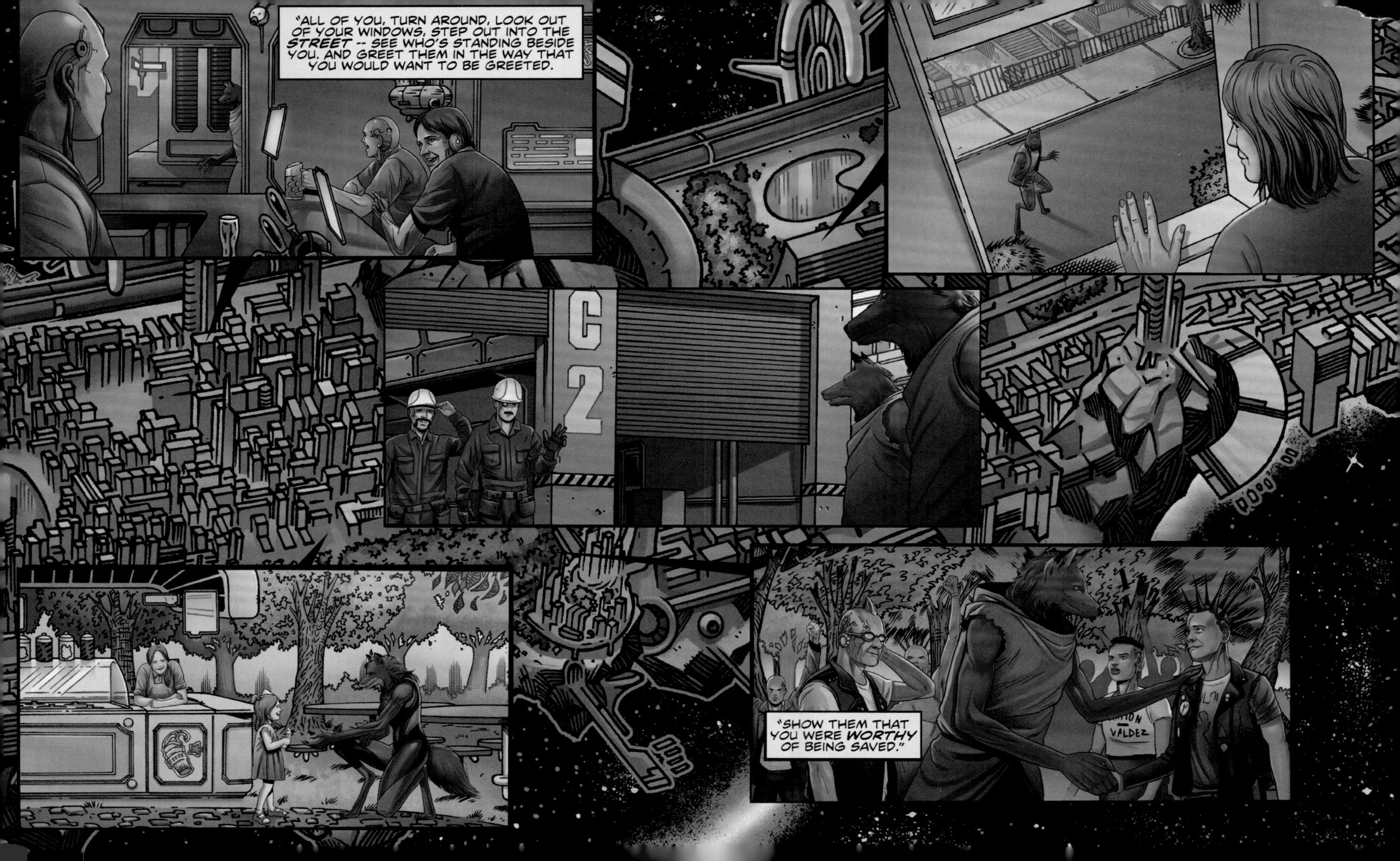
"ALL OF YOU, TURN AROUND, LOOK OUT OF YOUR WINDOWS, STEP OUT INTO THE STREET -- SEE WHO'S STANDING BESIDE YOU. AND GREET THEM IN THE WAY THAT YOU WOULD WANT TO BE GREETED.
C2
"SHOW THEM THAT YOU WERE WORTHY OF BEING SAVED."

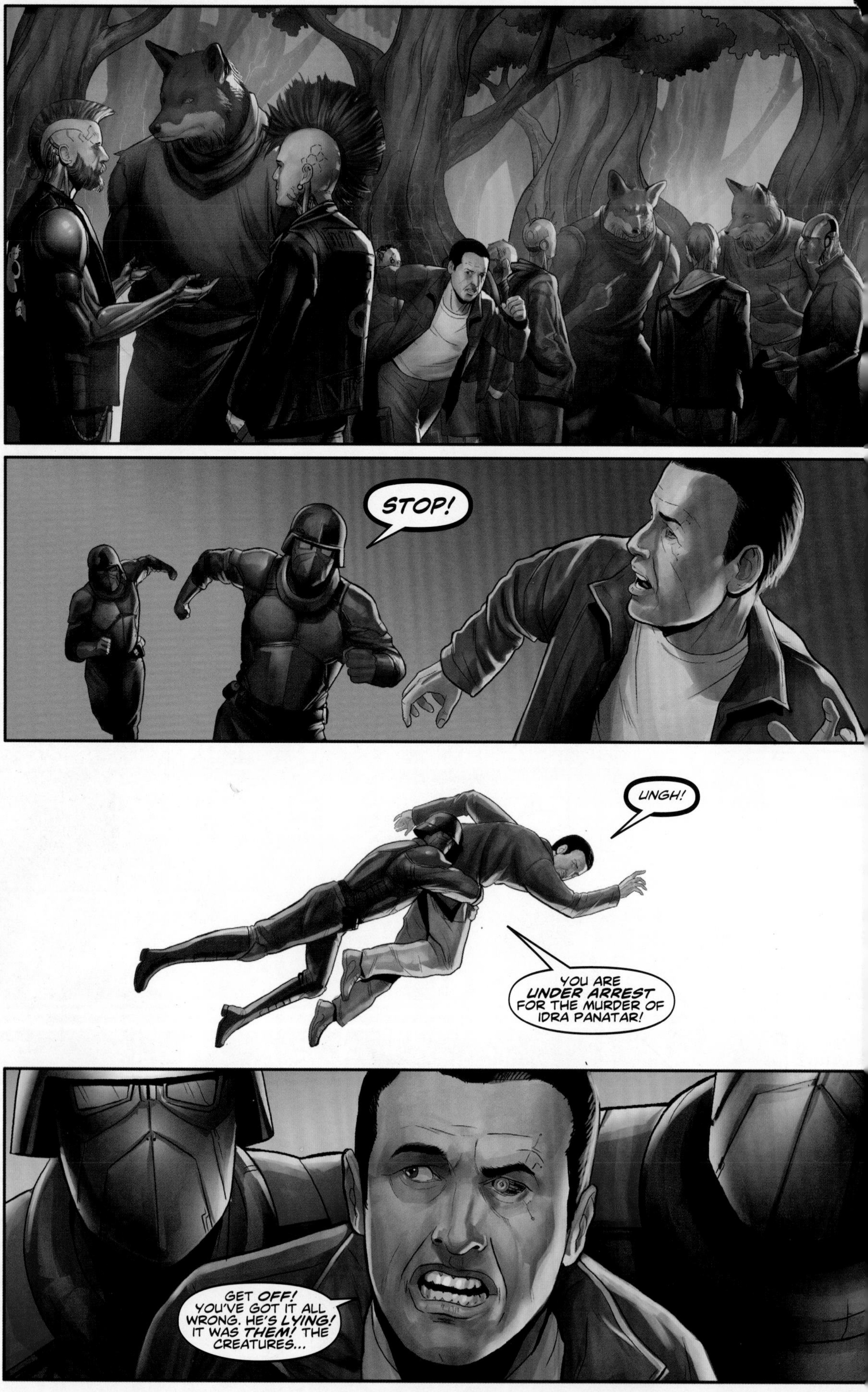
STOP!
UNGH!
YOU ARE UNDER ARREST FOR THE MURDER OF IDRA PANATAR!
GET OFF! YOU'VE GOT IT ALL WRONG. HE'S LYING! IT WAS THEM! THE CREATURES...

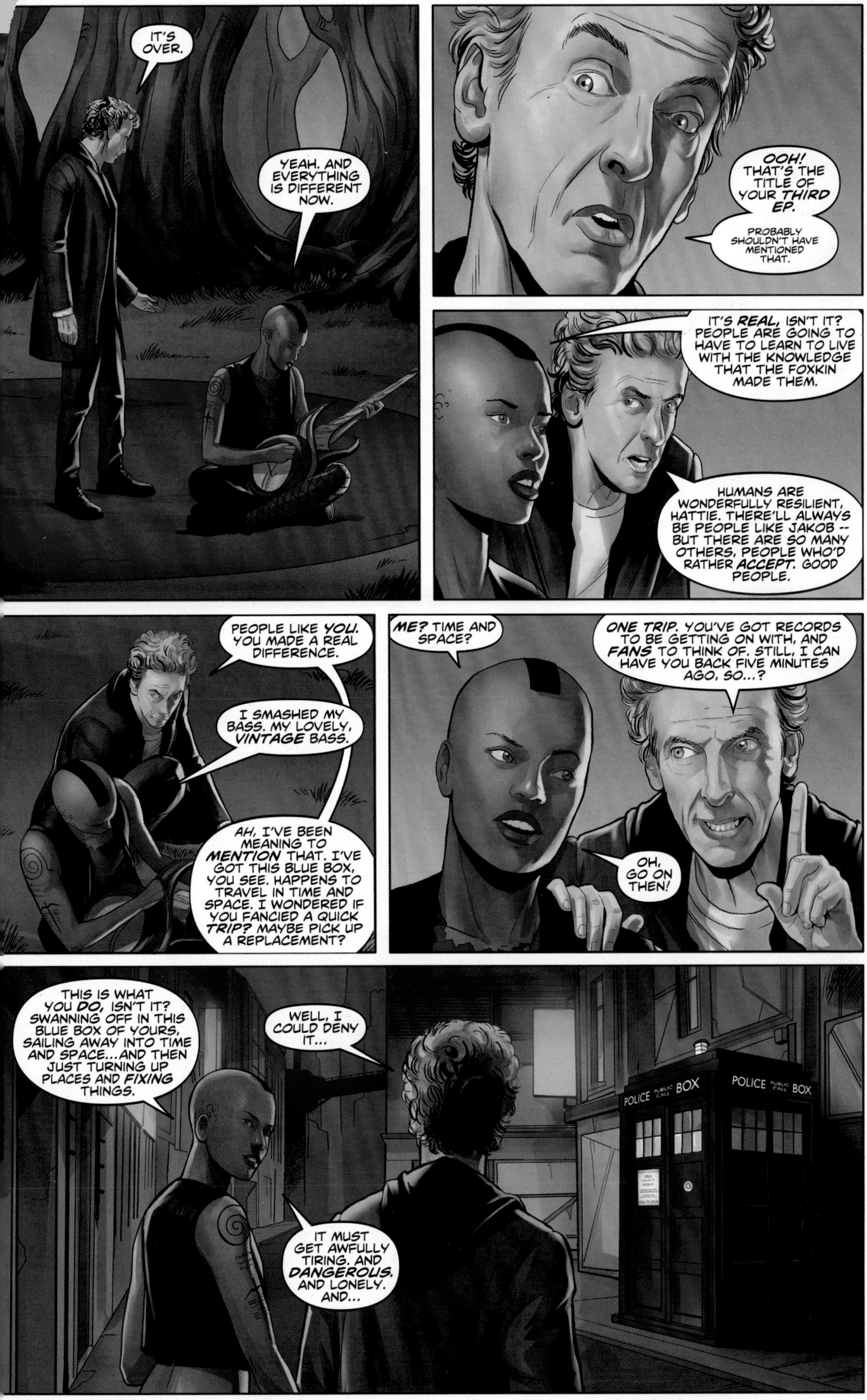
IT'S OVER.
YEAH. AND EVERYTHING IS DIFFERENT NOW.
OOH! THAT'S THE TITLE OF YOUR THIRD EP.
PROBABLY SHOULDN'T HAVE MENTIONED THAT.
IT'S REAL, ISN'T IT? PEOPLE ARE GOING TO HAVE TO LEARN TO LIVE WITH THE KNOWLEDGE THAT THE FOXKIN MADE THEM.
HUMANS ARE WONDERFULLY RESILIENT, HATTIE. THERE'LL ALWAYS BE PEOPLE LIKE JAKOB -- BUT THERE ARE SO MANY OTHERS, PEOPLE WHO'D RATHER ACCEPT. GOOD PEOPLE.
PEOPLE LIKE YOU. YOU MADE A REAL DIFFERENCE.
I SMASHED MY BASS. MY LOVELY, VINTAGE BASS.
AH, I'VE BEEN MEANING TO MENTION THAT. I'VE GOT THIS BLUE BOX, YOU SEE. HAPPENS TO TRAVEL IN TIME AND SPACE. I WONDERED IF YOU FANCIED A QUICK TRIP? MAYBE PICK UP A REPLACEMENT?
ME? TIME AND SPACE?
ONE TRIP. YOU'VE GOT RECORDS TO BE GETTING ON WITH, AND FANS TO THINK OF. STILL, I CAN HAVE YOU BACK FIVE MINUTES AGO, SO...?
OH, GO ON THEN!
THIS IS WHAT YOU DO, ISN'T IT? SWANNING OFF IN THIS BLUE BOX OF YOURS, SAILING AWAY INTO TIME AND SPACE...AND THEN JUST TURNING UP PLACES AND FIXING THINGS.
WELL, I COULD DENY IT...
POLICE PUBLIC CALL BOX
POLICE PUBLIC CALL BOX
IT MUST GET AWFULLY TIRING. AND DANGEROUS. AND LONELY. AND...

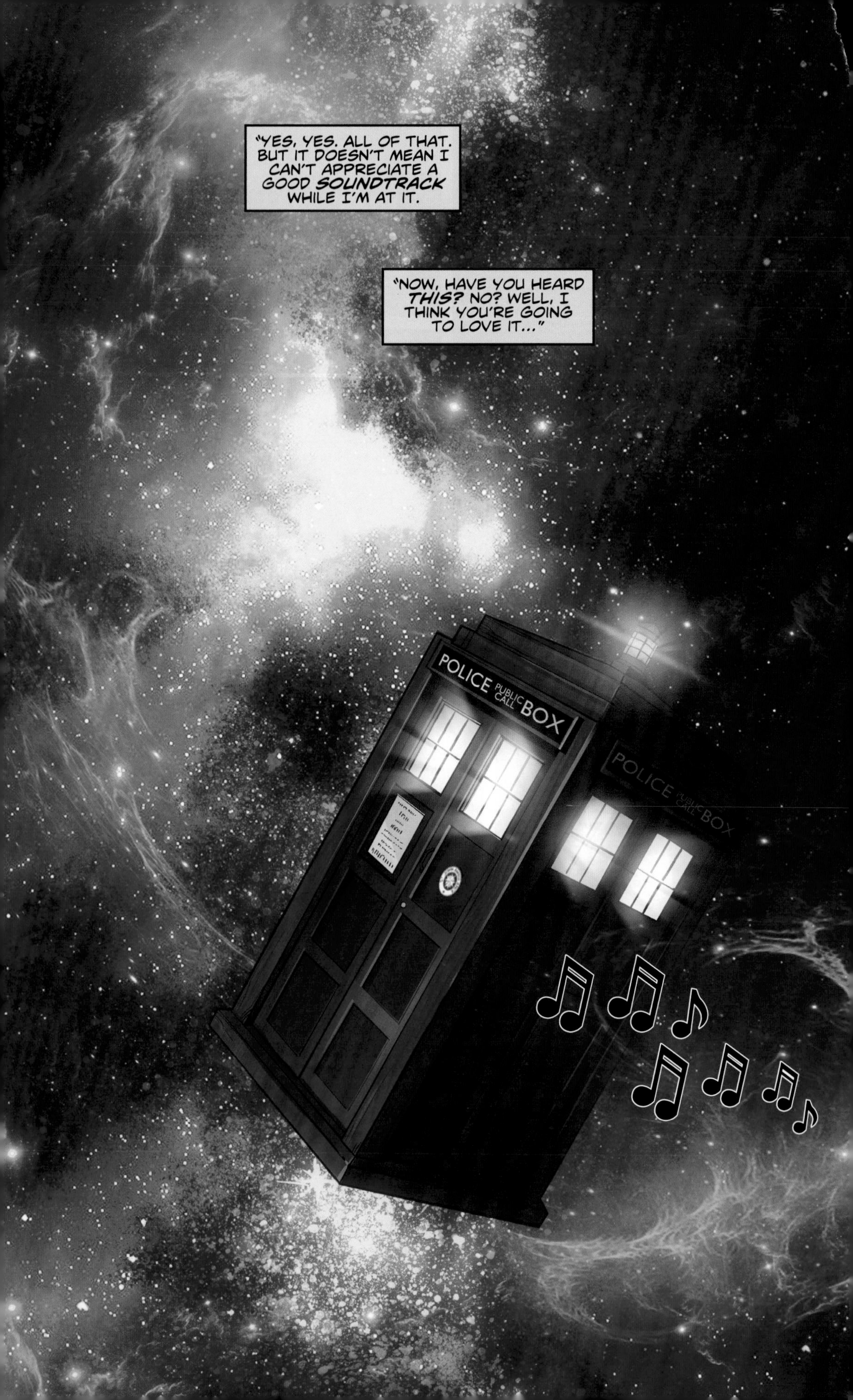
"YES, YES. ALL OF THAT. BUT IT DOESN'T MEAN I CAN'T APPRECIATE A GOOD SOUNDTRACK WHILE I'M AT IT.
"NOW, HAVE YOU HEARD THIS? NO? WELL, I THINK YOU'RE GOING TO LOVE IT..."
POLICE PUBLIC CALL BOX
POLICE PUBLIC CALL BOX

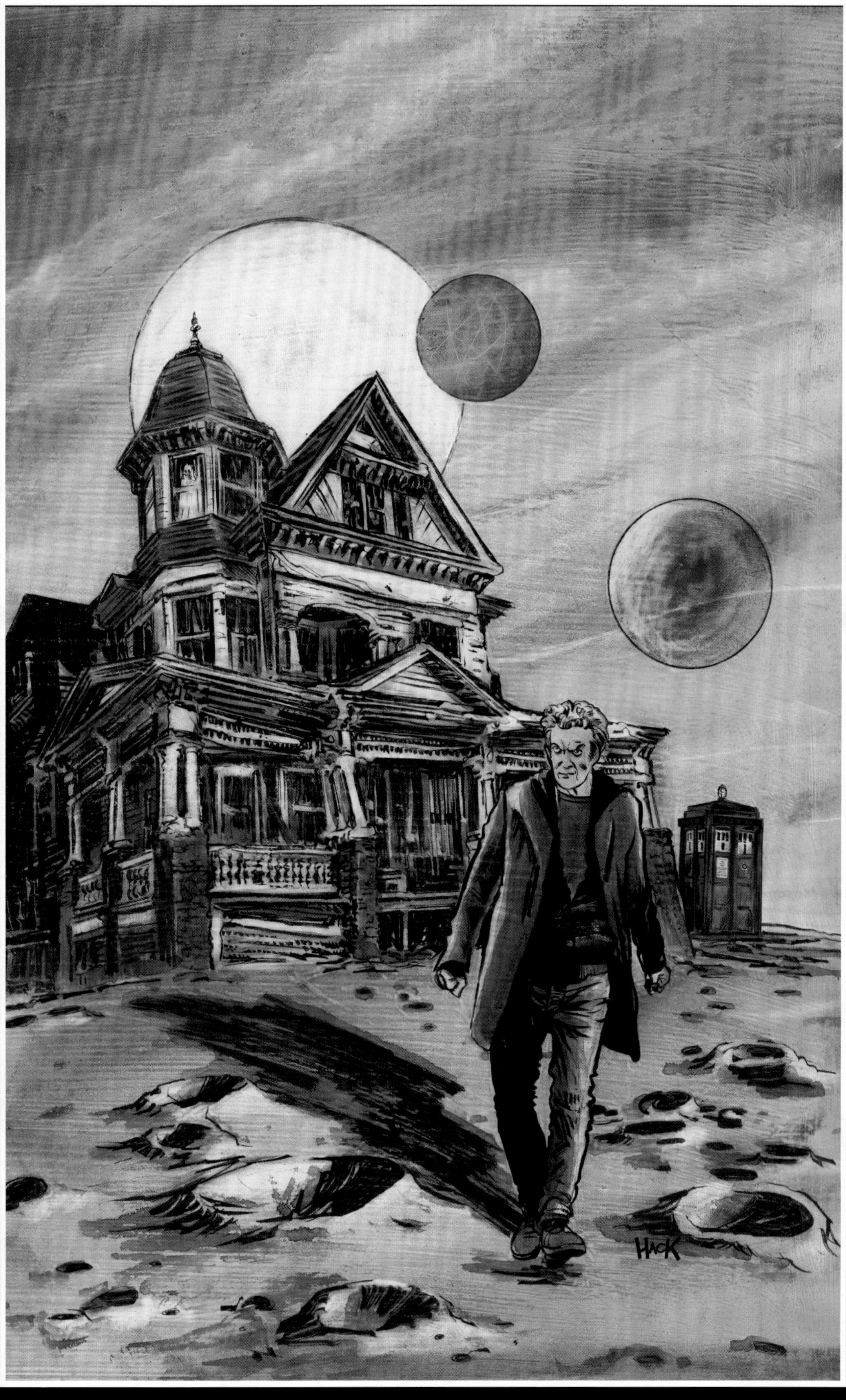
HACK

THE TWIST: ISSUE #6

Cover: ROBERT HACK

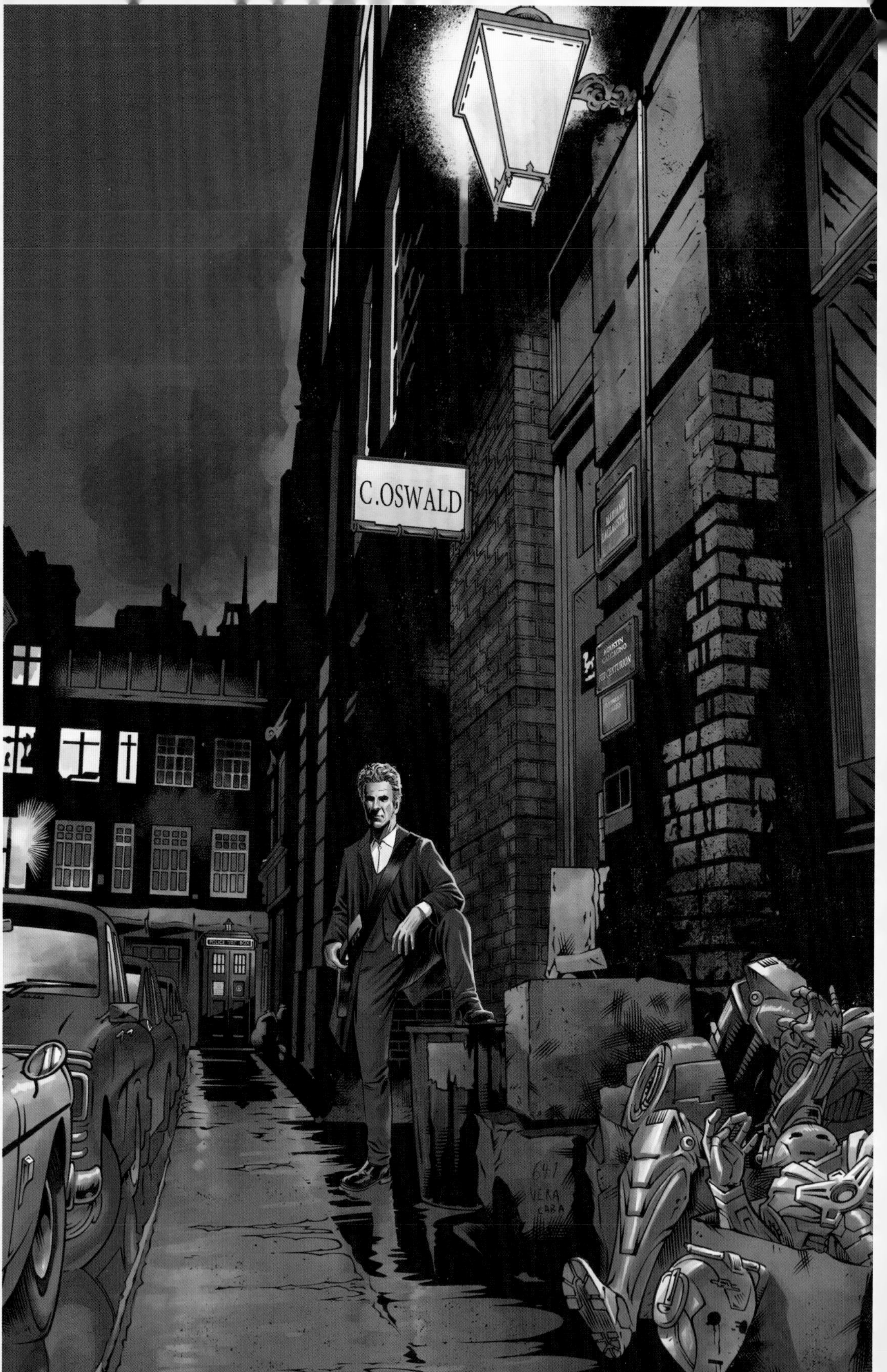
C.OSWALD
AGUSTIN CALCAGNO
FER CENTURION
647 VERA CABA

Cover: MARIA

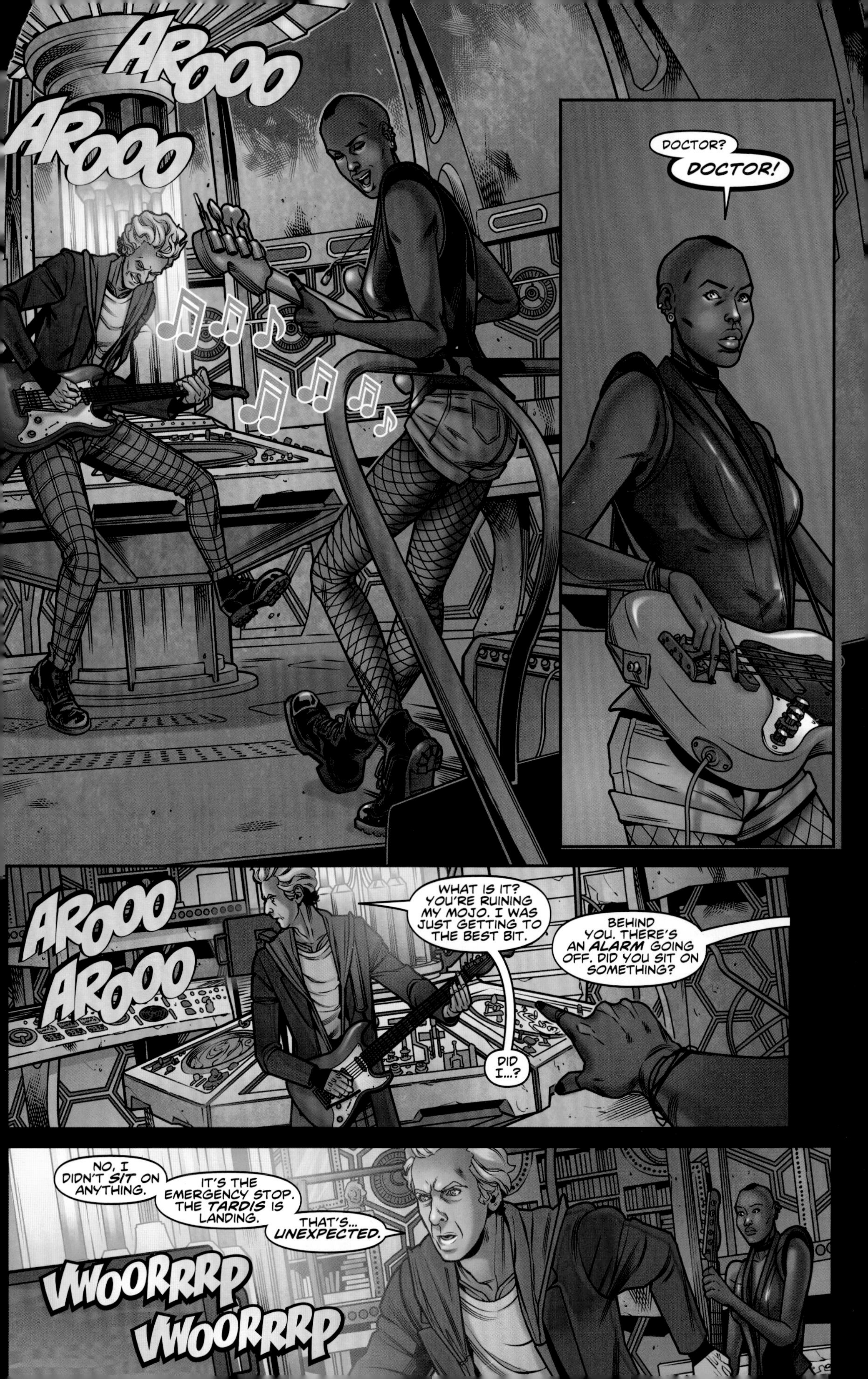
AROOO
AROOO
DOCTOR? DOCTOR!
AROOO
AROOO
WHAT IS IT? YOU'RE RUINING MY MOJO. I WAS JUST GETTING TO THE BEST BIT.
BEHIND YOU. THERE'S AN ALARM GOING OFF. DID YOU SIT ON SOMETHING?
DID I...?
NO, I DIDN'T SIT ON ANYTHING.
IT'S THE EMERGENCY STOP. THE TARDIS IS LANDING.
THAT'S... UNEXPECTED.
VWOORRRP
VWOORRRP

UNEXPECTED **GOOD**, OR UNEXPECTED **BAD**?

OH, EVERYONE LIKES **SURPRISES**, HATTIE!

DEPENDS ON THE SURPRISE.

WELL, EVEN THE **TARDIS** DOESN'T SEEM TO KNOW **EXACTLY** WHAT'S GOING ON. SHE'S PICKED UP SOME ALARMING READINGS. I THINK SHE WANTS US TO CHECK IT OUT.

READINGS?

SOMETHING'S LEAKING **DANGEROUS** AMOUNTS OF TEMPORAL RADIATION. AND TEMPORAL RADIATION SHOULDN'T EVEN **EXIST** ON EARTH IN THE 21ST CENTURY.

I TAKE IT THAT'S THE END OF OUR JAMMING SESSION, THEN?

THERE'LL BE PLENTY OF TIME FOR THAT LATER. DON'T YOU WANT TO KNOW WHERE WE **ARE**? THERE COULD BE **ANYTHING** OUTSIDE THAT DOOR.

A WORLD CARVED FROM MOON-SIZED GLACIERS. A FLOTILLA OF **SARKOVIAN NIGHTSHIPS.** A FLOATING PALACE OF **GOLD.** A...

POLICE TELEPHONE

FREE
FOR USE OF
PUBLIC

ADVICE & ASSISTANCE
OBTAINABLE IMMEDIATELY
OFFICERS & CARS
RESPOND TO ALL CALLS

PULL TO OPEN

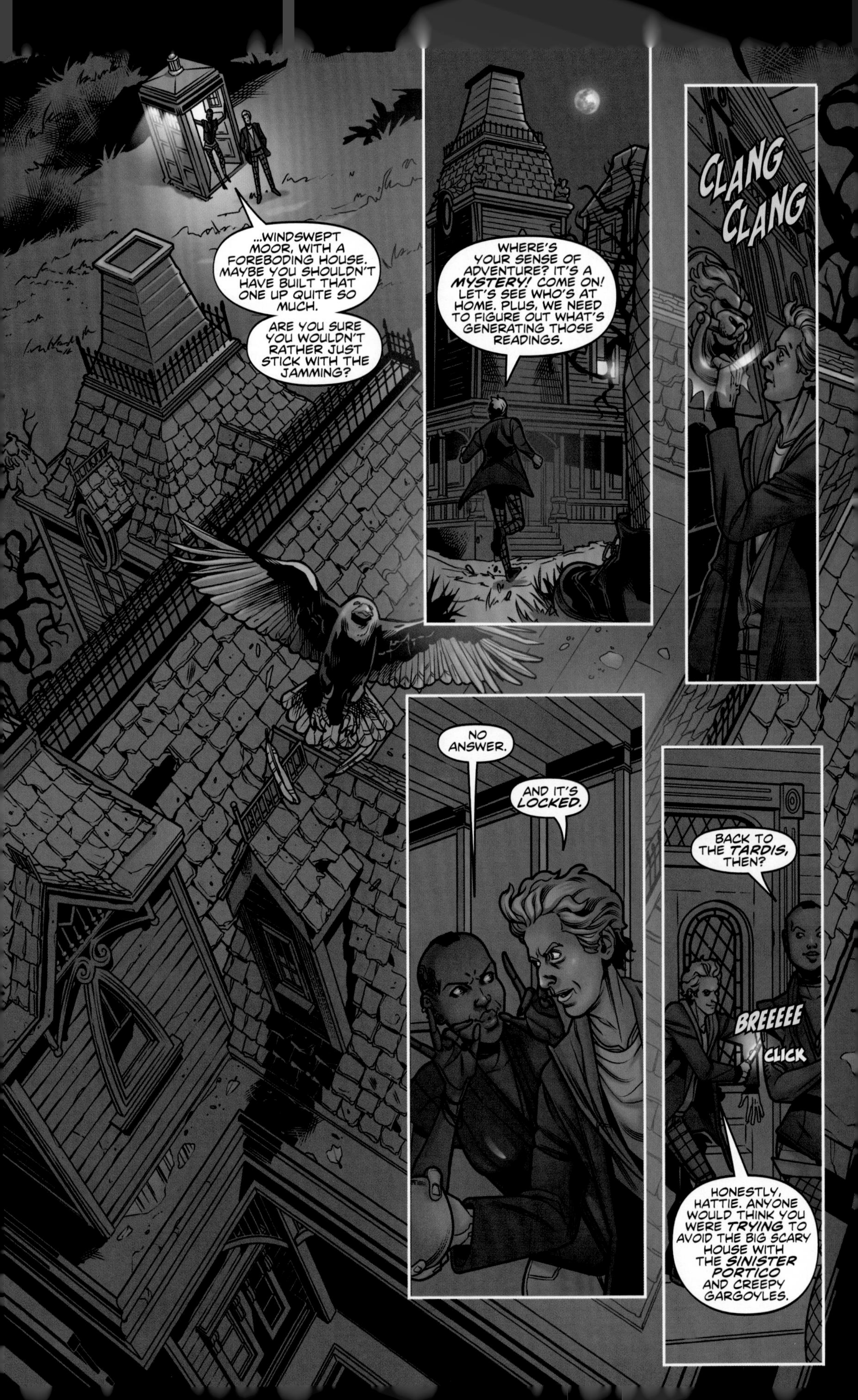
...WINDSWEPT MOOR, WITH A FOREBODING HOUSE. MAYBE YOU SHOULDN'T HAVE BUILT THAT ONE UP QUITE SO MUCH.
ARE YOU SURE YOU WOULDN'T RATHER JUST STICK WITH THE JAMMING?
WHERE'S YOUR SENSE OF ADVENTURE? IT'S A MYSTERY! COME ON! LET'S SEE WHO'S AT HOME. PLUS, WE NEED TO FIGURE OUT WHAT'S GENERATING THOSE READINGS.
CLANG CLANG
NO ANSWER.
AND IT'S LOCKED.
BACK TO THE TARDIS, THEN?
BREEEEE
CLICK
HONESTLY, HATTIE. ANYONE WOULD THINK YOU WERE TRYING TO AVOID THE BIG SCARY HOUSE WITH THE SINISTER PORTICO AND CREEPY GARGOYLES.

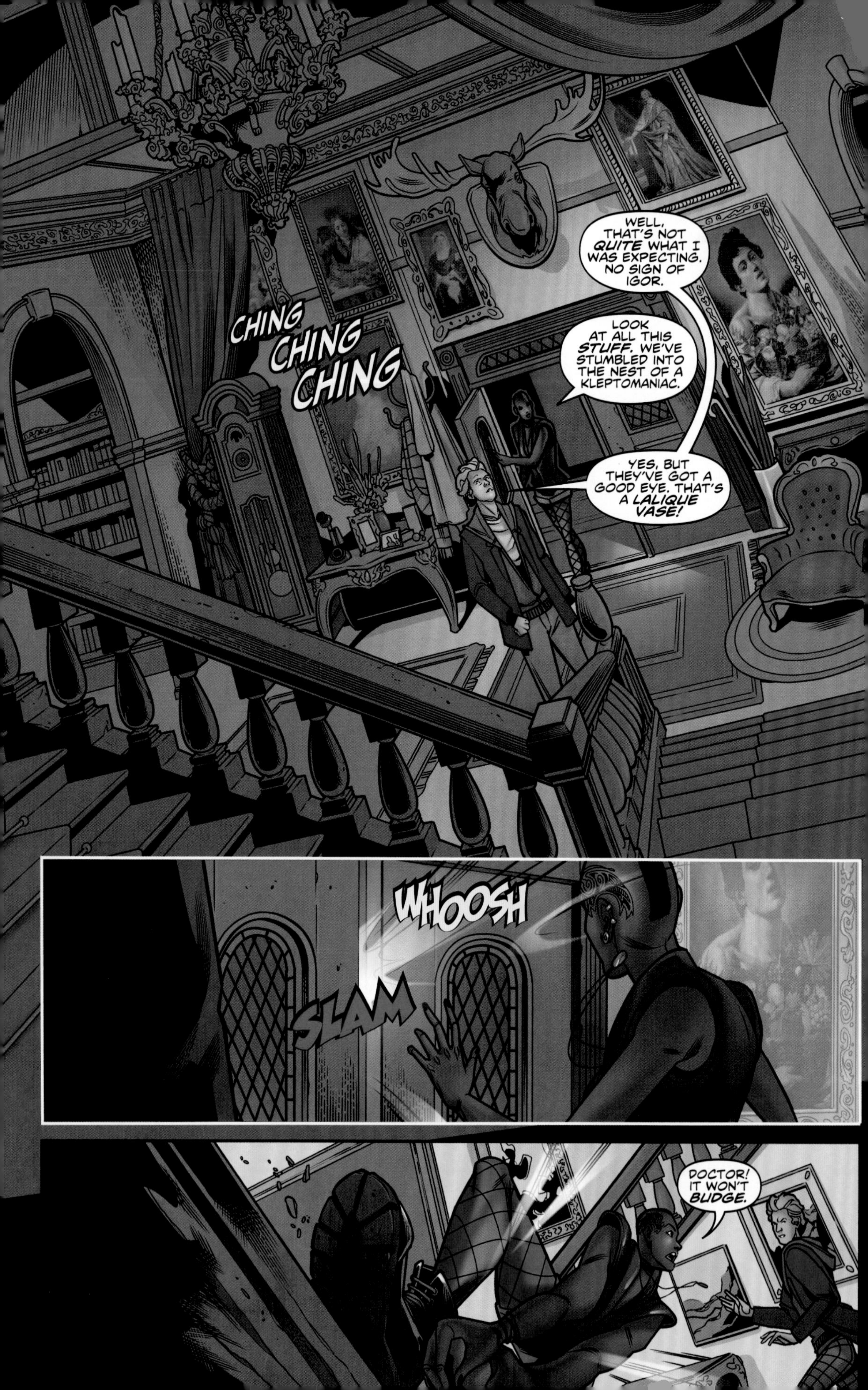

WELL, THAT'S NOT QUITE WHAT I WAS EXPECTING. NO SIGN OF IGOR.
CHING CHING CHING
LOOK AT ALL THIS STUFF. WE'VE STUMBLED INTO THE NEST OF A KLEPTOMANIAC.
YES, BUT THEY'VE GOT A GOOD EYE. THAT'S A LALIQUE VASE!
WHOOSH
SLAM
DOCTOR! IT WON'T BUDGE.

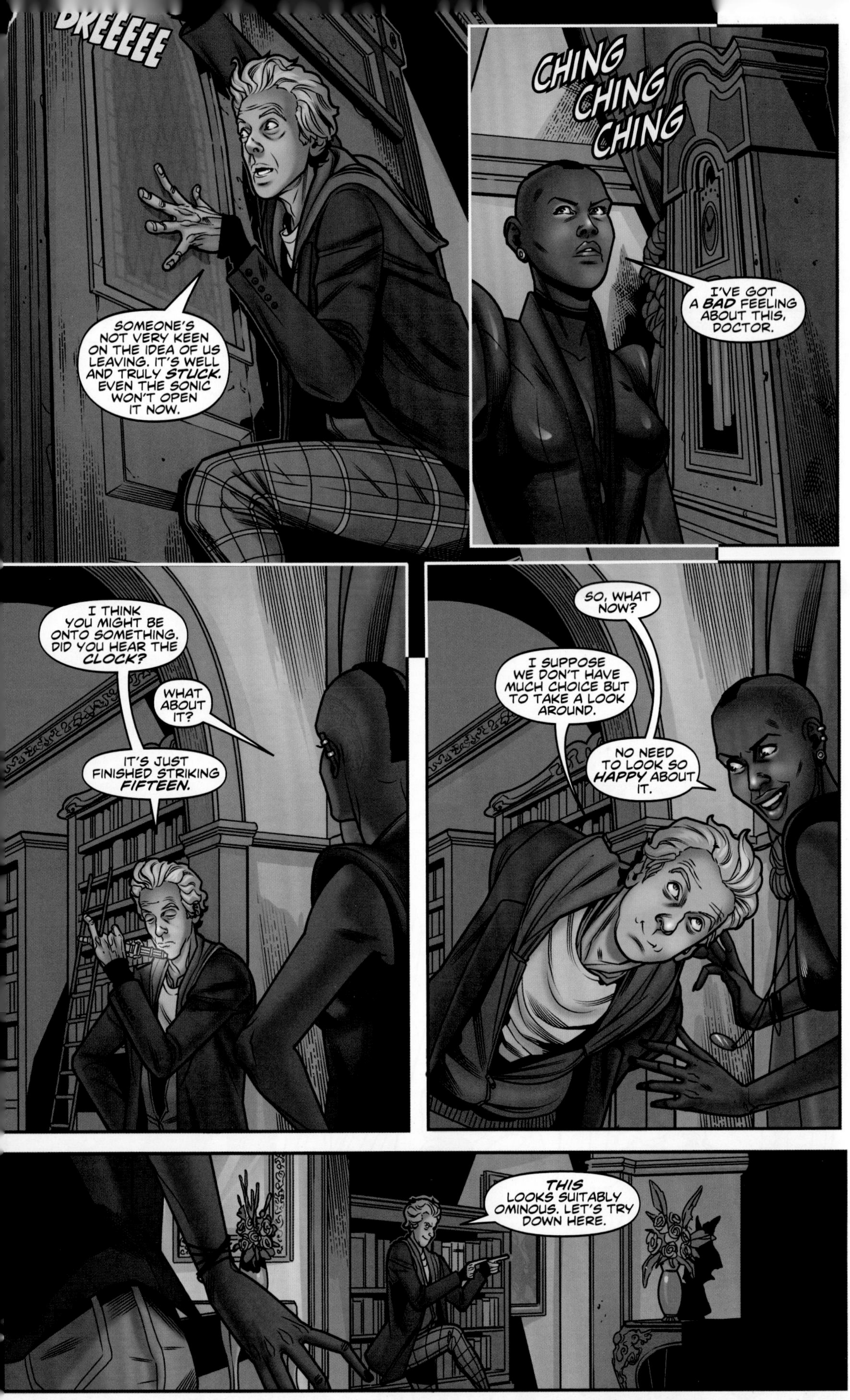
BREEEEE
SOMEONE'S NOT VERY KEEN ON THE IDEA OF US LEAVING. IT'S WELL AND TRULY STUCK. EVEN THE SONIC WON'T OPEN IT NOW.
CHING CHING CHING
I'VE GOT A BAD FEELING ABOUT THIS, DOCTOR.
I THINK YOU MIGHT BE ONTO SOMETHING. DID YOU HEAR THE CLOCK?
WHAT ABOUT IT?
IT'S JUST FINISHED STRIKING FIFTEEN.
SO, WHAT NOW?
I SUPPOSE WE DON'T HAVE MUCH CHOICE BUT TO TAKE A LOOK AROUND.
NO NEED TO LOOK SO HAPPY ABOUT IT.
THIS LOOKS SUITABLY OMINOUS. LET'S TRY DOWN HERE.

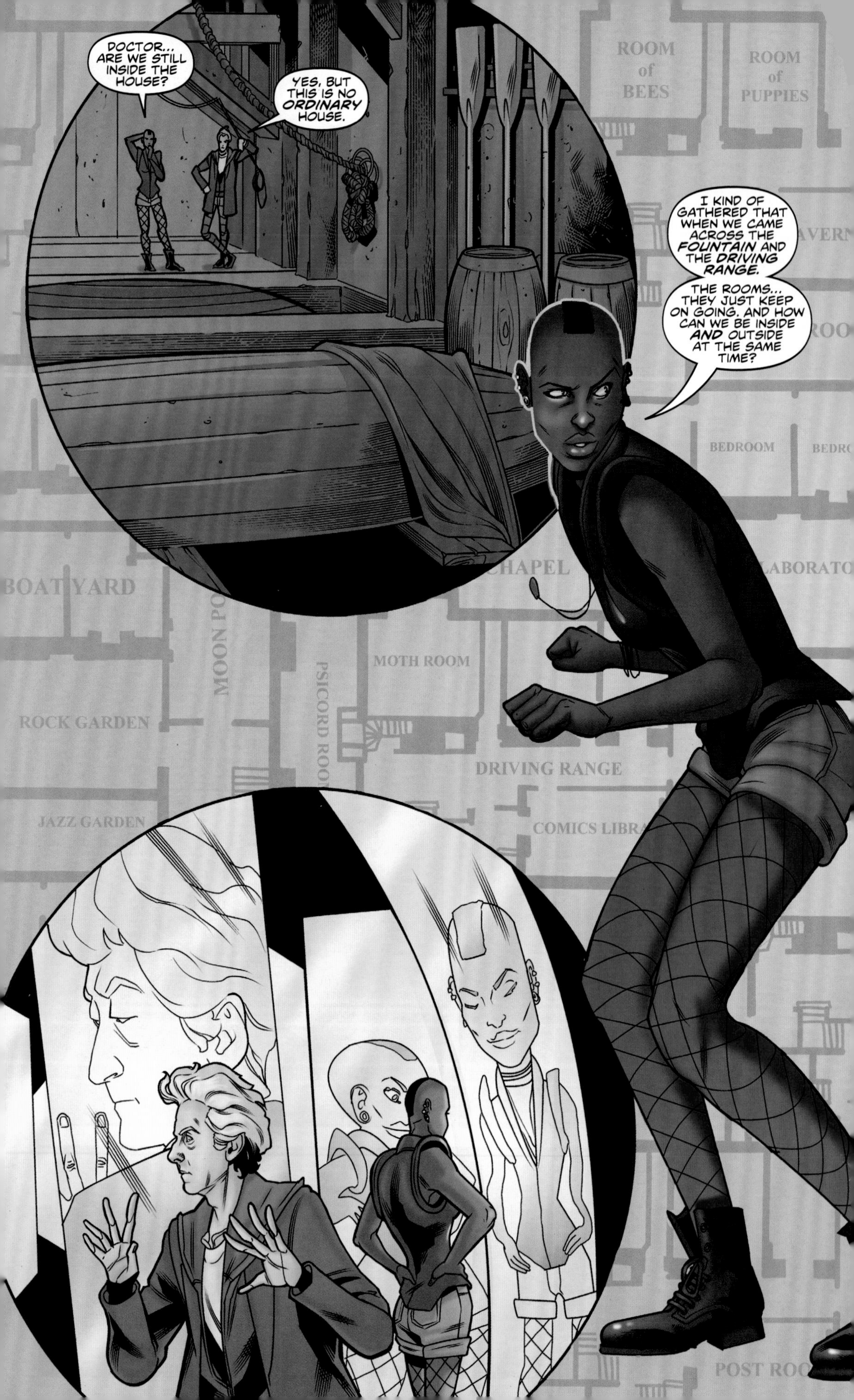
DOCTOR... ARE WE STILL INSIDE THE HOUSE?
YES, BUT THIS IS NO *ORDINARY* HOUSE.
I KIND OF GATHERED THAT WHEN WE CAME ACROSS THE *FOUNTAIN* AND THE *DRIVING RANGE.*
THE ROOMS... THEY JUST KEEP ON GOING. AND HOW CAN WE BE INSIDE *AND* OUTSIDE AT THE SAME TIME?
ROOM of BEES
ROOM of PUPPIES
BEDROOM
CHAPEL
BOAT YARD
MOTH ROOM
ROCK GARDEN
DRIVING RANGE
JAZZ GARDEN

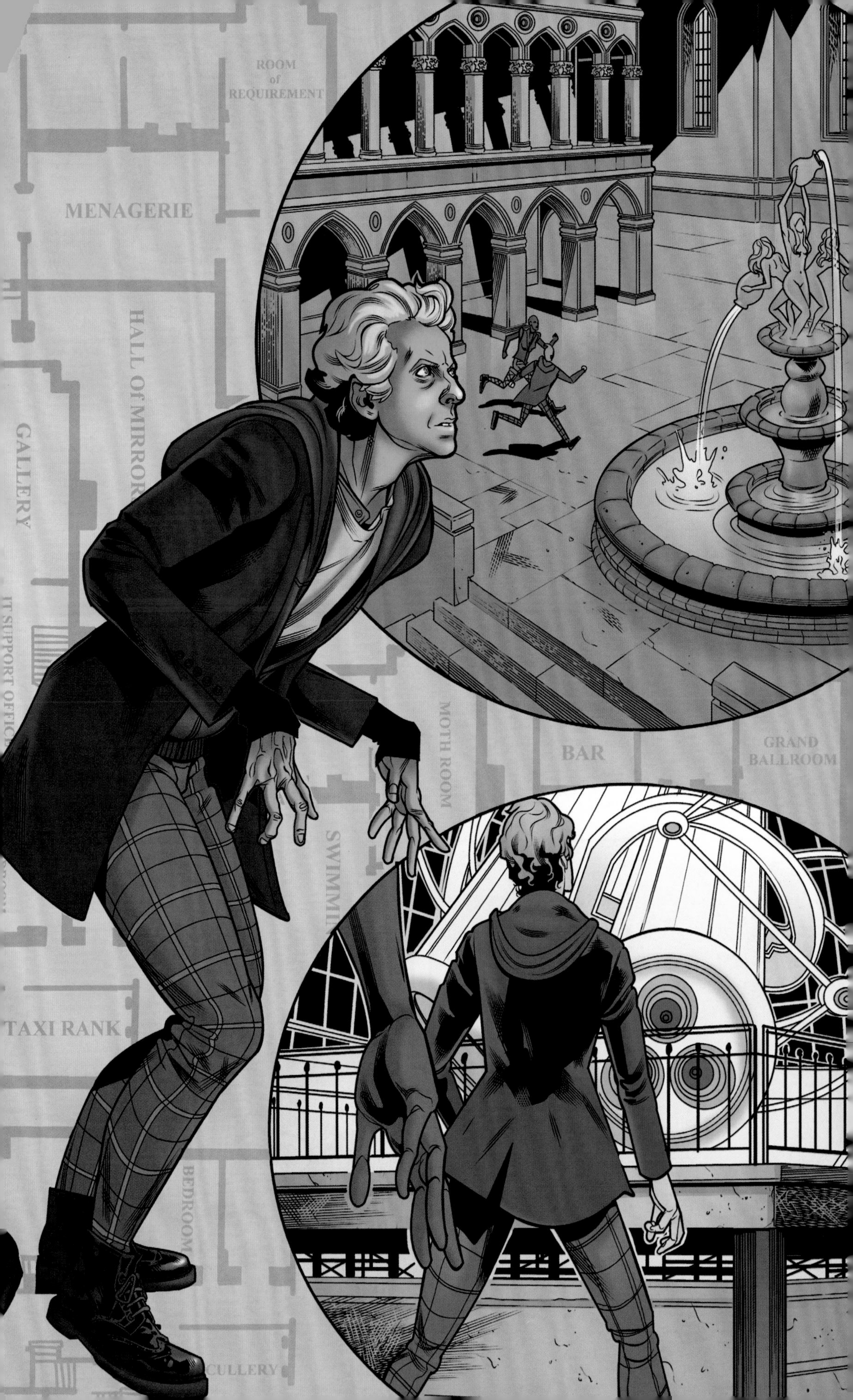
ROOM of REQUIREMENT
MENAGERIE
GALLERY
MOTH ROOM
BAR
GRAND BALLROOM
TAXI RANK
BEDROOM

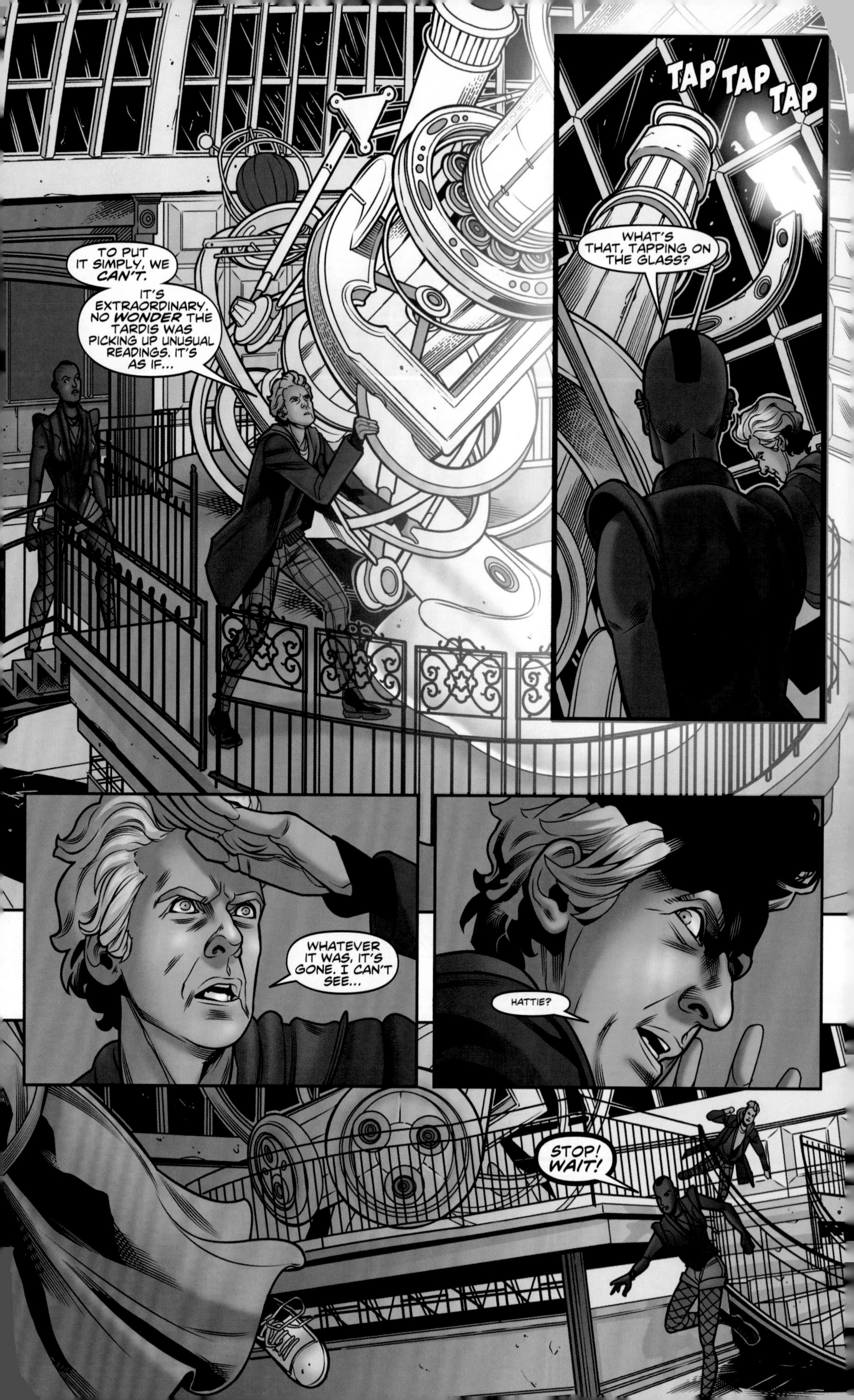

TO PUT IT SIMPLY, WE CAN'T.
IT'S EXTRAORDINARY. NO WONDER THE TARDIS WAS PICKING UP UNUSUAL READINGS. IT'S AS IF...
TAP TAP TAP
WHAT'S THAT, TAPPING ON THE GLASS?
WHATEVER IT WAS, IT'S GONE. I CAN'T SEE...
HATTIE?
STOP! WAIT!

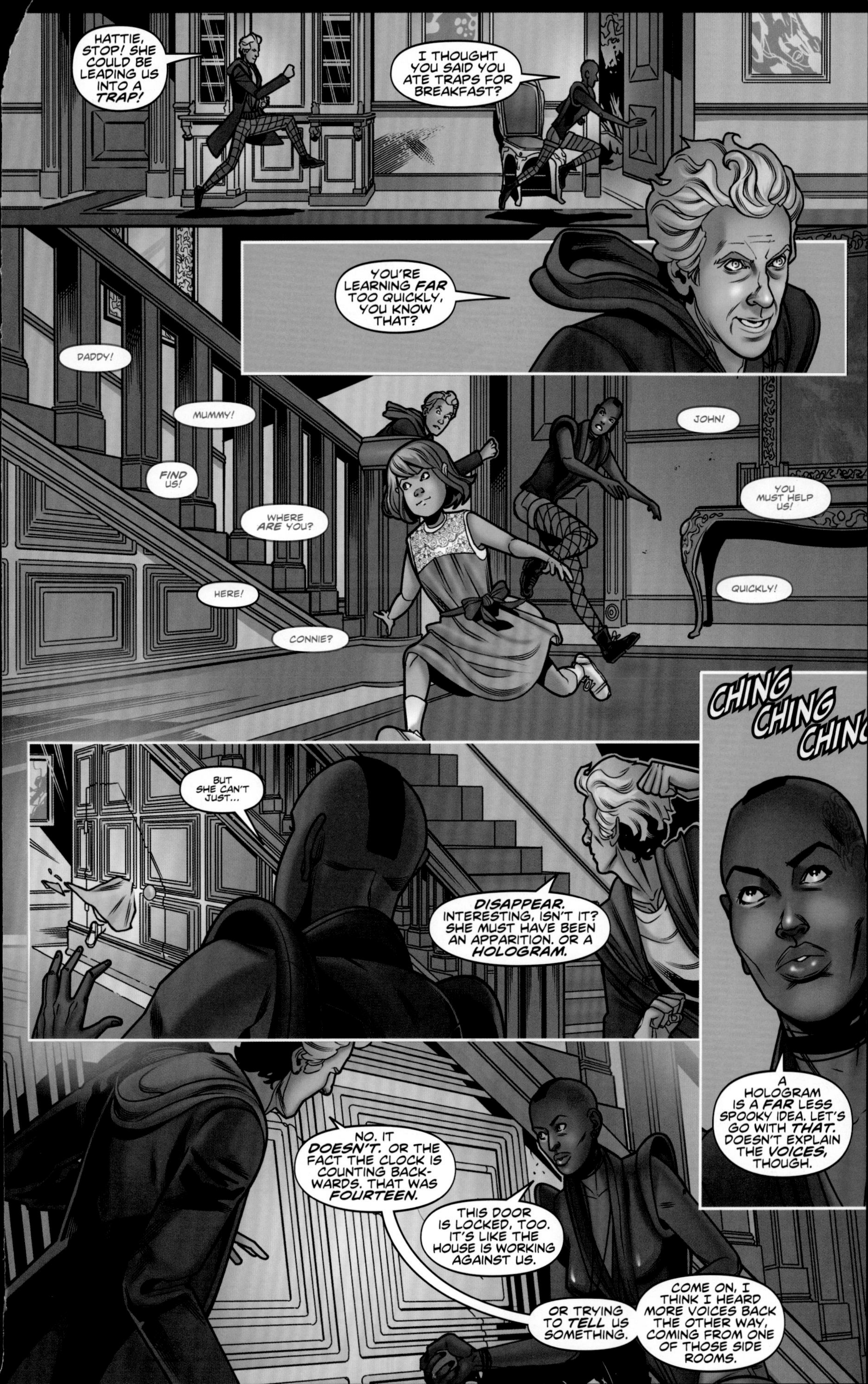
HATTIE, STOP! SHE COULD BE LEADING US INTO A TRAP!
I THOUGHT YOU SAID YOU ATE TRAPS FOR BREAKFAST?
YOU'RE LEARNING FAR TOO QUICKLY, YOU KNOW THAT?
DADDY!
MUMMY!
FIND US!
WHERE ARE YOU?
HERE!
CONNIE?
JOHN!
YOU MUST HELP US!
QUICKLY!
BUT SHE CAN'T JUST...
DISAPPEAR. INTERESTING, ISN'T IT? SHE MUST HAVE BEEN AN APPARITION. OR A HOLOGRAM.
CHING CHING CHING
A HOLOGRAM IS A FAR LESS SPOOKY IDEA. LET'S GO WITH THAT. DOESN'T EXPLAIN THE VOICES, THOUGH.
NO. IT DOESN'T. OR THE FACT THE CLOCK IS COUNTING BACK-WARDS. THAT WAS FOURTEEN.
THIS DOOR IS LOCKED, TOO. IT'S LIKE THE HOUSE IS WORKING AGAINST US.
OR TRYING TO TELL US SOMETHING.
COME ON, I THINK I HEARD MORE VOICES BACK THE OTHER WAY, COMING FROM ONE OF THOSE SIDE ROOMS.

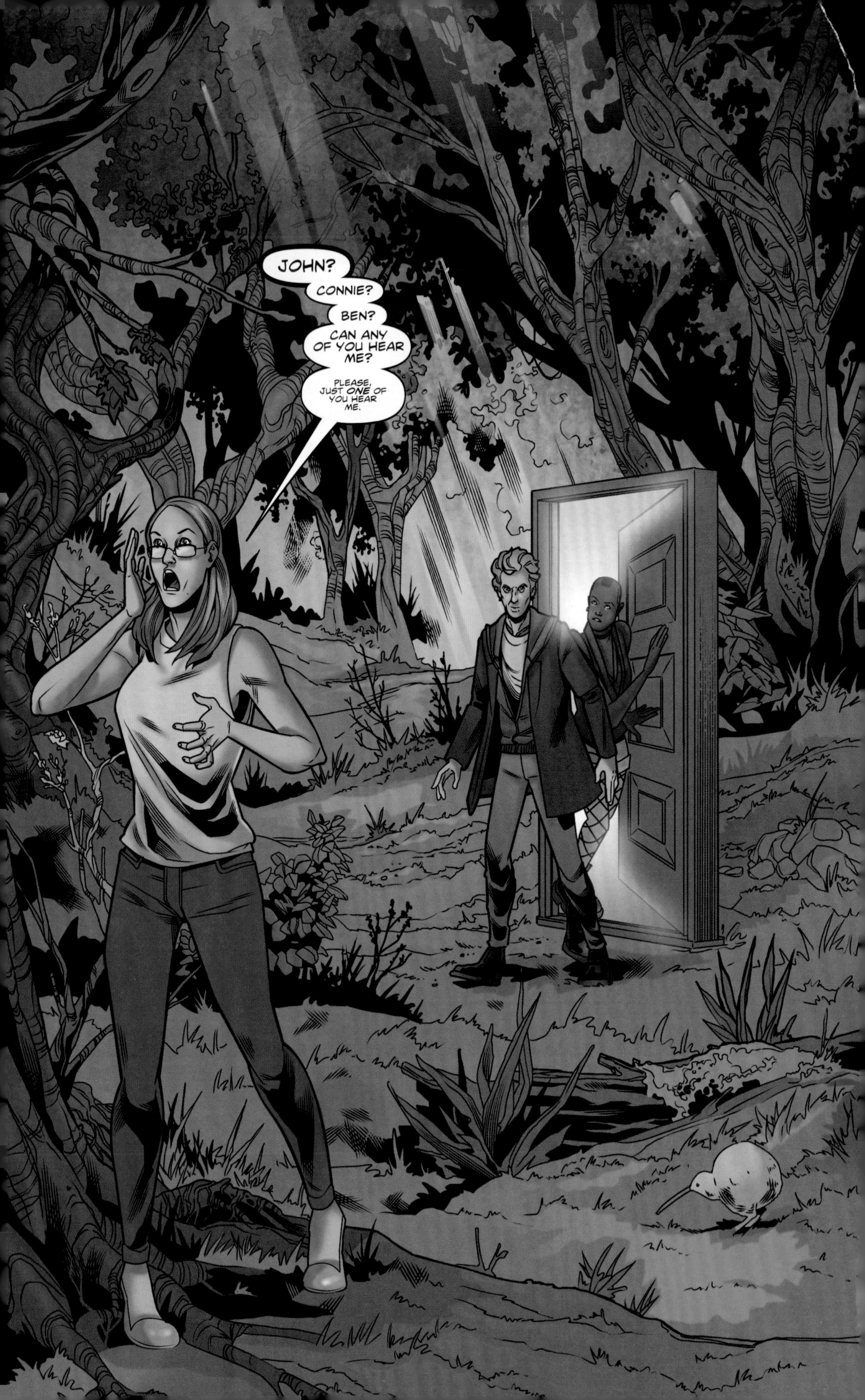
JOHN?
CONNIE?
BEN?
CAN ANY OF YOU HEAR ME?
PLEASE, JUST *ONE* OF YOU HEAR ME.

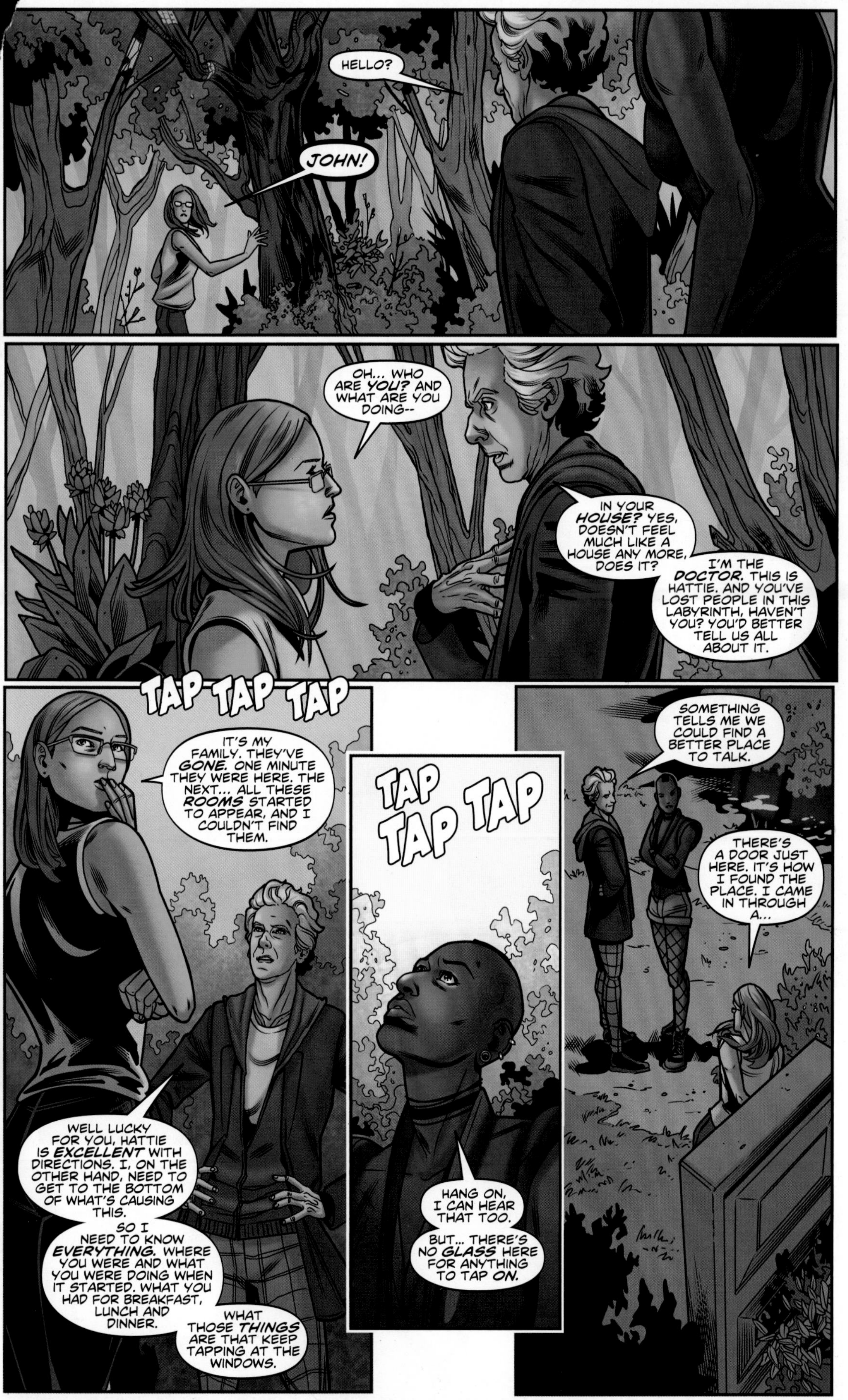
HELLO?
JOHN!
OH... WHO ARE YOU? AND WHAT ARE YOU DOING--
IN YOUR HOUSE? YES, DOESN'T FEEL MUCH LIKE A HOUSE ANY MORE, DOES IT?
I'M THE DOCTOR. THIS IS HATTIE. AND YOU'VE LOST PEOPLE IN THIS LABYRINTH, HAVEN'T YOU? YOU'D BETTER TELL US ALL ABOUT IT.
TAP TAP TAP
IT'S MY FAMILY. THEY'VE GONE. ONE MINUTE THEY WERE HERE. THE NEXT... ALL THESE ROOMS STARTED TO APPEAR, AND I COULDN'T FIND THEM.
WELL LUCKY FOR YOU, HATTIE IS EXCELLENT WITH DIRECTIONS. I, ON THE OTHER HAND, NEED TO GET TO THE BOTTOM OF WHAT'S CAUSING THIS.
SO I NEED TO KNOW EVERYTHING. WHERE YOU WERE AND WHAT YOU WERE DOING WHEN IT STARTED. WHAT YOU HAD FOR BREAKFAST, LUNCH AND DINNER.
WHAT THOSE THINGS ARE THAT KEEP TAPPING AT THE WINDOWS.
TAP TAP TAP
HANG ON, I CAN HEAR THAT TOO.
BUT... THERE'S NO GLASS HERE FOR ANYTHING TO TAP ON.
SOMETHING TELLS ME WE COULD FIND A BETTER PLACE TO TALK.
THERE'S A DOOR JUST HERE. IT'S HOW I FOUND THE PLACE. I CAME IN THROUGH A...

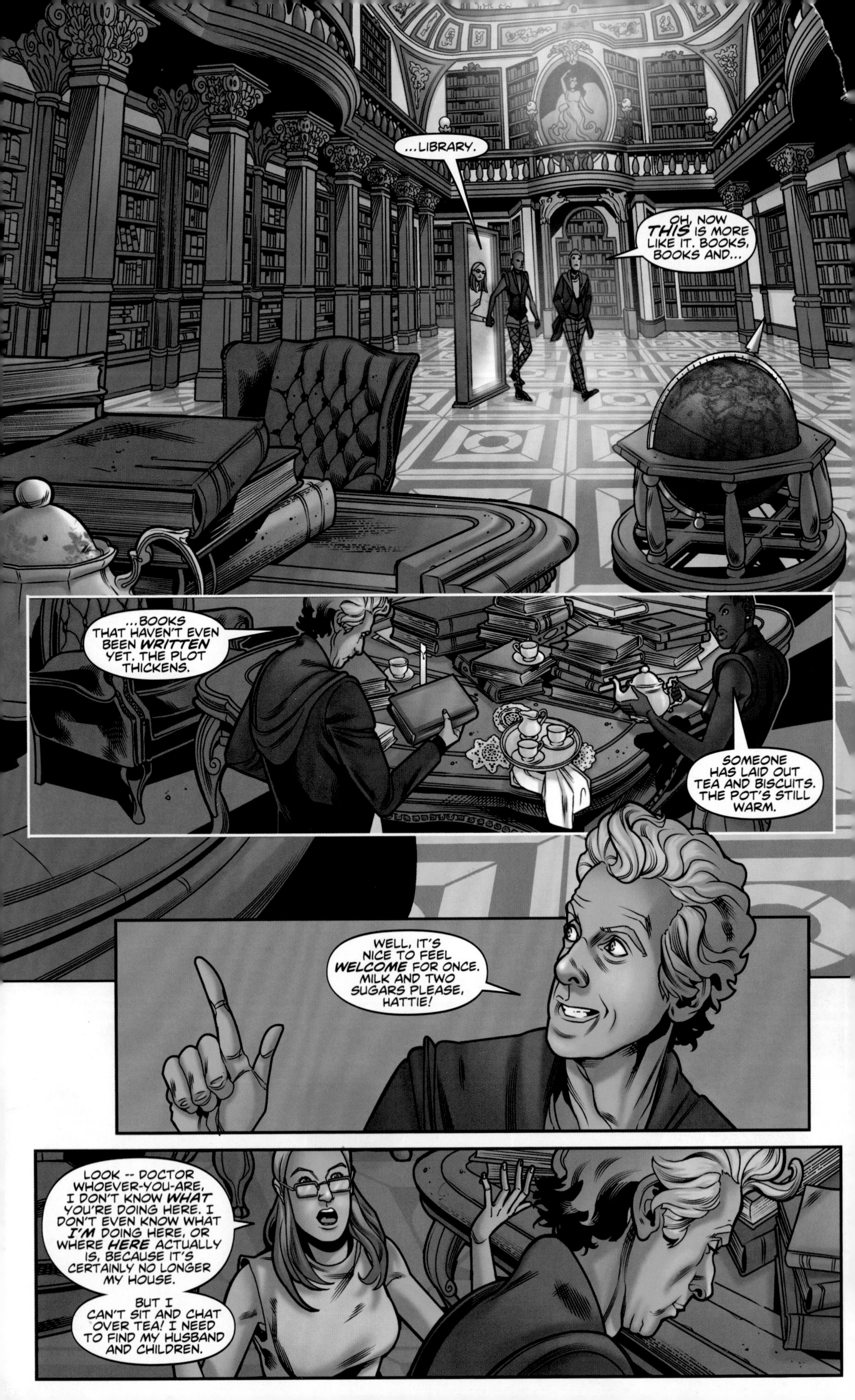
...LIBRARY.
OH, NOW THIS IS MORE LIKE IT. BOOKS, BOOKS AND...
...BOOKS THAT HAVEN'T EVEN BEEN WRITTEN YET. THE PLOT THICKENS.
SOMEONE HAS LAID OUT TEA AND BISCUITS. THE POT'S STILL WARM.
WELL, IT'S NICE TO FEEL WELCOME FOR ONCE. MILK AND TWO SUGARS PLEASE, HATTIE!
LOOK -- DOCTOR WHOEVER-YOU-ARE, I DON'T KNOW WHAT YOU'RE DOING HERE. I DON'T EVEN KNOW WHAT I'M DOING HERE, OR WHERE HERE ACTUALLY IS, BECAUSE IT'S CERTAINLY NO LONGER MY HOUSE.
BUT I CAN'T SIT AND CHAT OVER TEA! I NEED TO FIND MY HUSBAND AND CHILDREN.

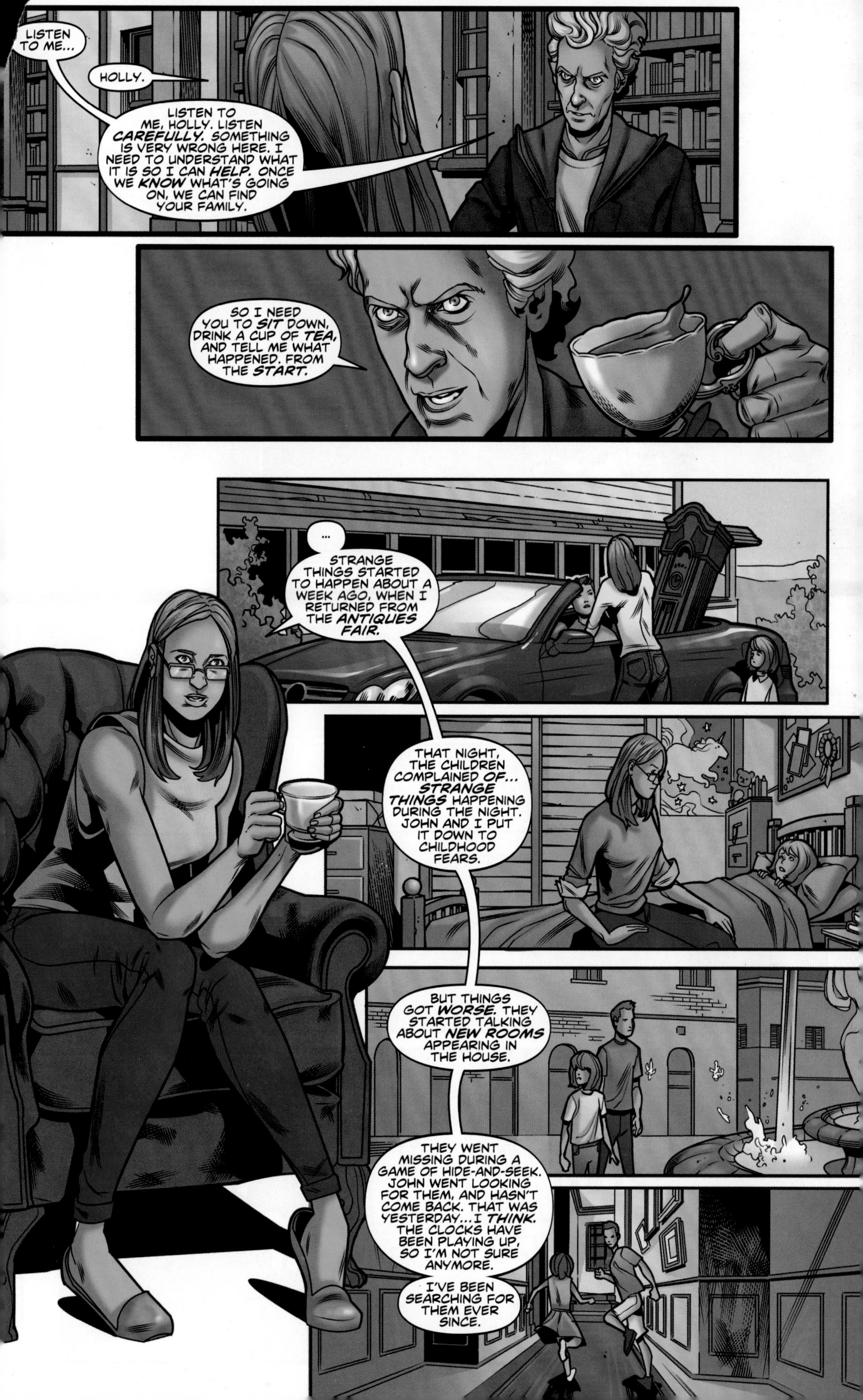
LISTEN TO ME...
HOLLY.
LISTEN TO ME, HOLLY. LISTEN CAREFULLY. SOMETHING IS VERY WRONG HERE. I NEED TO UNDERSTAND WHAT IT IS SO I CAN HELP. ONCE WE KNOW WHAT'S GOING ON, WE CAN FIND YOUR FAMILY.
SO I NEED YOU TO SIT DOWN, DRINK A CUP OF TEA, AND TELL ME WHAT HAPPENED. FROM THE START.
...
STRANGE THINGS STARTED TO HAPPEN ABOUT A WEEK AGO, WHEN I RETURNED FROM THE ANTIQUES FAIR.
THAT NIGHT, THE CHILDREN COMPLAINED OF... STRANGE THINGS HAPPENING DURING THE NIGHT. JOHN AND I PUT IT DOWN TO CHILDHOOD FEARS.
BUT THINGS GOT WORSE. THEY STARTED TALKING ABOUT NEW ROOMS APPEARING IN THE HOUSE.
THEY WENT MISSING DURING A GAME OF HIDE-AND-SEEK. JOHN WENT LOOKING FOR THEM, AND HASN'T COME BACK. THAT WAS YESTERDAY...I THINK. THE CLOCKS HAVE BEEN PLAYING UP, SO I'M NOT SURE ANYMORE.
I'VE BEEN SEARCHING FOR THEM EVER SINCE.

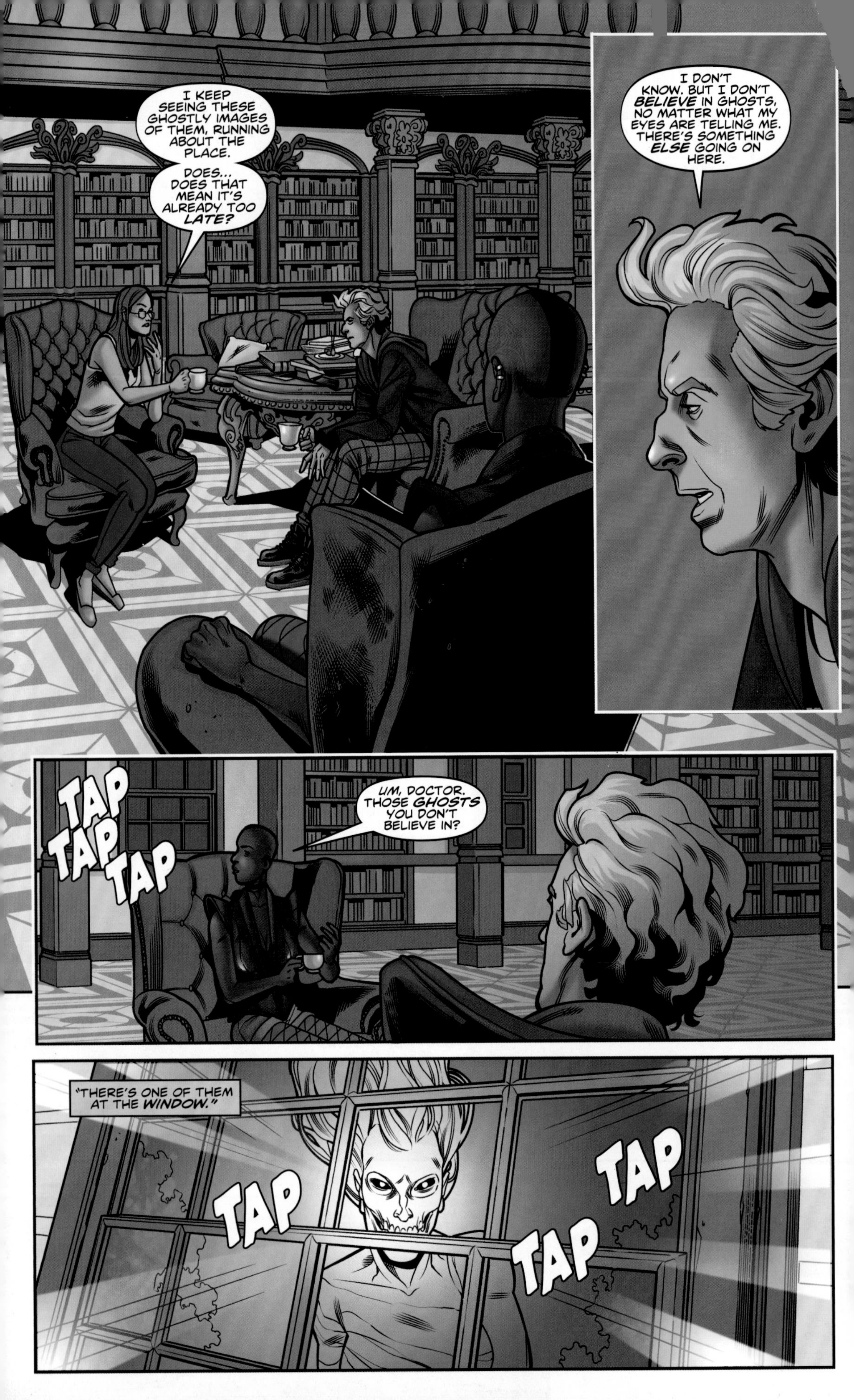
I KEEP SEEING THESE GHOSTLY IMAGES OF THEM, RUNNING ABOUT THE PLACE.
DOES... DOES THAT MEAN IT'S ALREADY TOO LATE?
I DON'T KNOW. BUT I DON'T BELIEVE IN GHOSTS, NO MATTER WHAT MY EYES ARE TELLING ME. THERE'S SOMETHING ELSE GOING ON HERE.
TAP TAP TAP
UM, DOCTOR. THOSE GHOSTS YOU DON'T BELIEVE IN?
"THERE'S ONE OF THEM AT THE WINDOW."
TAP
TAP
TAP

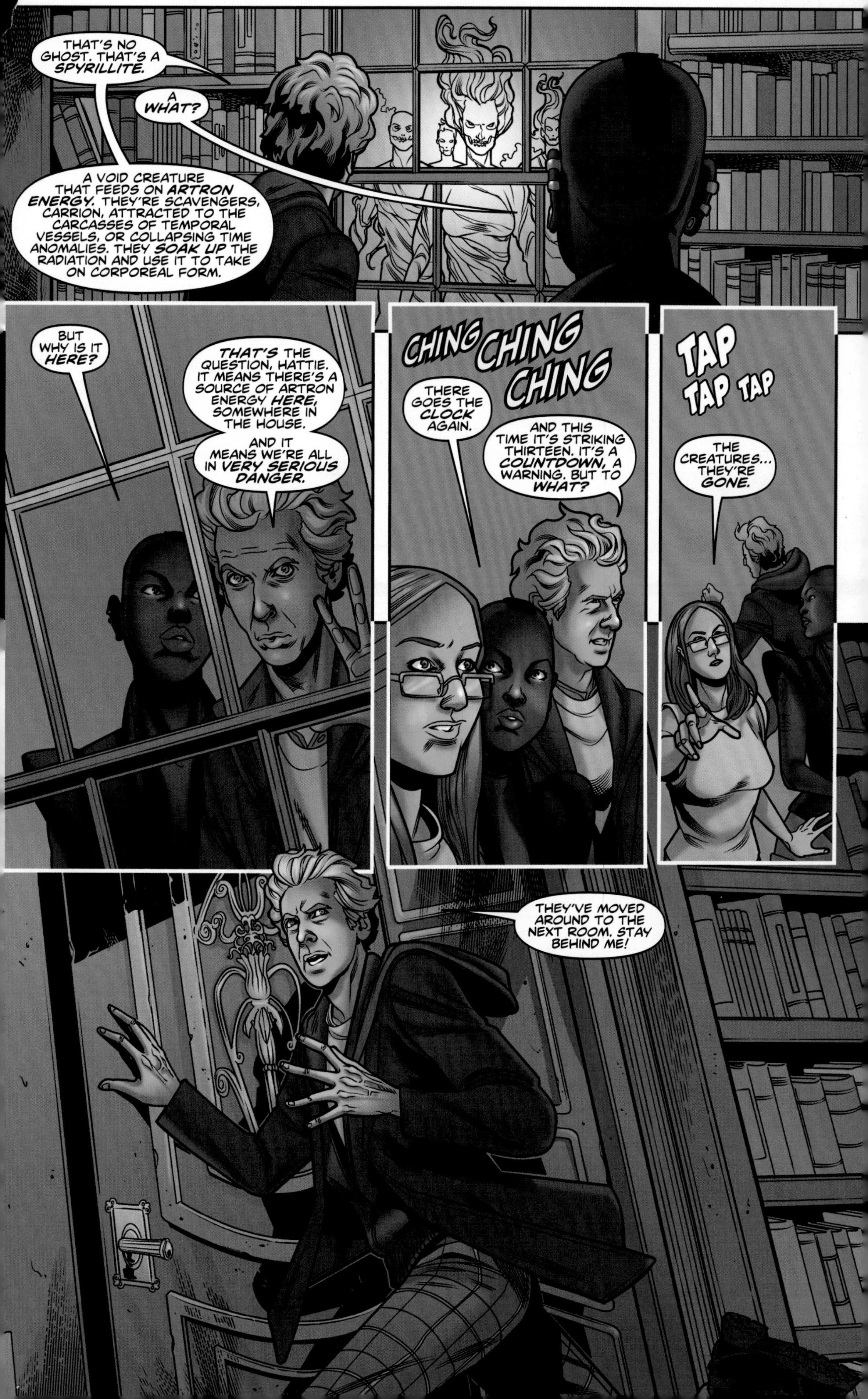

THAT'S NO GHOST. THAT'S A SPYRILLITE.
A WHAT?
A VOID CREATURE THAT FEEDS ON ARTRON ENERGY. THEY'RE SCAVENGERS, CARRION, ATTRACTED TO THE CARCASSES OF TEMPORAL VESSELS, OR COLLAPSING TIME ANOMALIES. THEY SOAK UP THE RADIATION AND USE IT TO TAKE ON CORPOREAL FORM.
BUT WHY IS IT HERE?
THAT'S THE QUESTION, HATTIE. IT MEANS THERE'S A SOURCE OF ARTRON ENERGY HERE, SOMEWHERE IN THE HOUSE.
AND IT MEANS WE'RE ALL IN VERY SERIOUS DANGER.
CHING CHING CHING
THERE GOES THE CLOCK AGAIN.
AND THIS TIME IT'S STRIKING THIRTEEN. IT'S A COUNTDOWN, A WARNING. BUT TO WHAT?
TAP TAP TAP
THE CREATURES... THEY'RE GONE.
THEY'VE MOVED AROUND TO THE NEXT ROOM. STAY BEHIND ME!

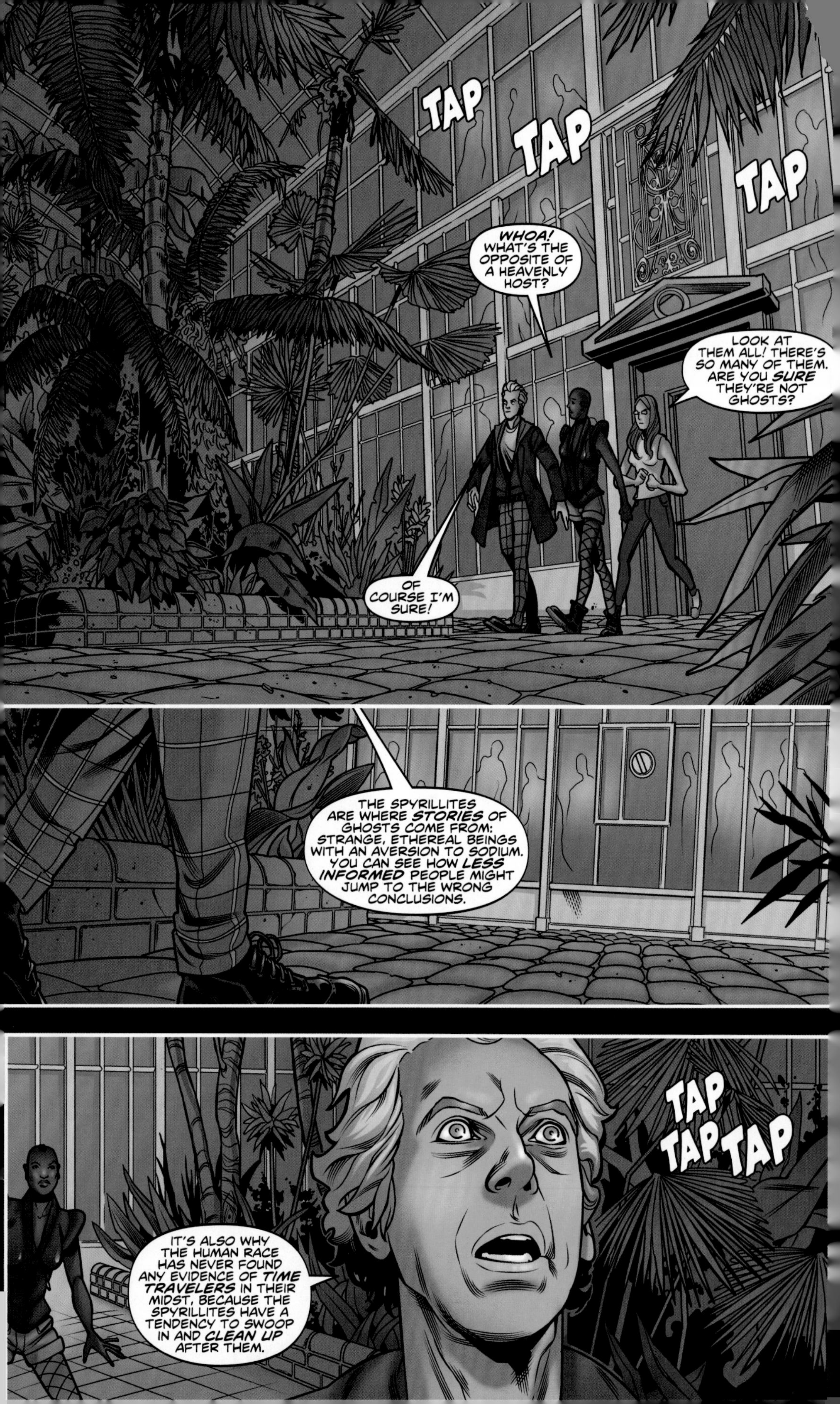
TAP
TAP
TAP
WHOA! WHAT'S THE OPPOSITE OF A HEAVENLY HOST?
LOOK AT THEM ALL! THERE'S SO MANY OF THEM. ARE YOU SURE THEY'RE NOT GHOSTS?
OF COURSE I'M SURE!
THE SPYRILLITES ARE WHERE STORIES OF GHOSTS COME FROM: STRANGE, ETHEREAL BEINGS WITH AN AVERSION TO SODIUM. YOU CAN SEE HOW LESS INFORMED PEOPLE MIGHT JUMP TO THE WRONG CONCLUSIONS.
TAP
TAP
TAP
IT'S ALSO WHY THE HUMAN RACE HAS NEVER FOUND ANY EVIDENCE OF TIME TRAVELERS IN THEIR MIDST, BECAUSE THE SPYRILLITES HAVE A TENDENCY TO SWOOP IN AND CLEAN UP AFTER THEM.

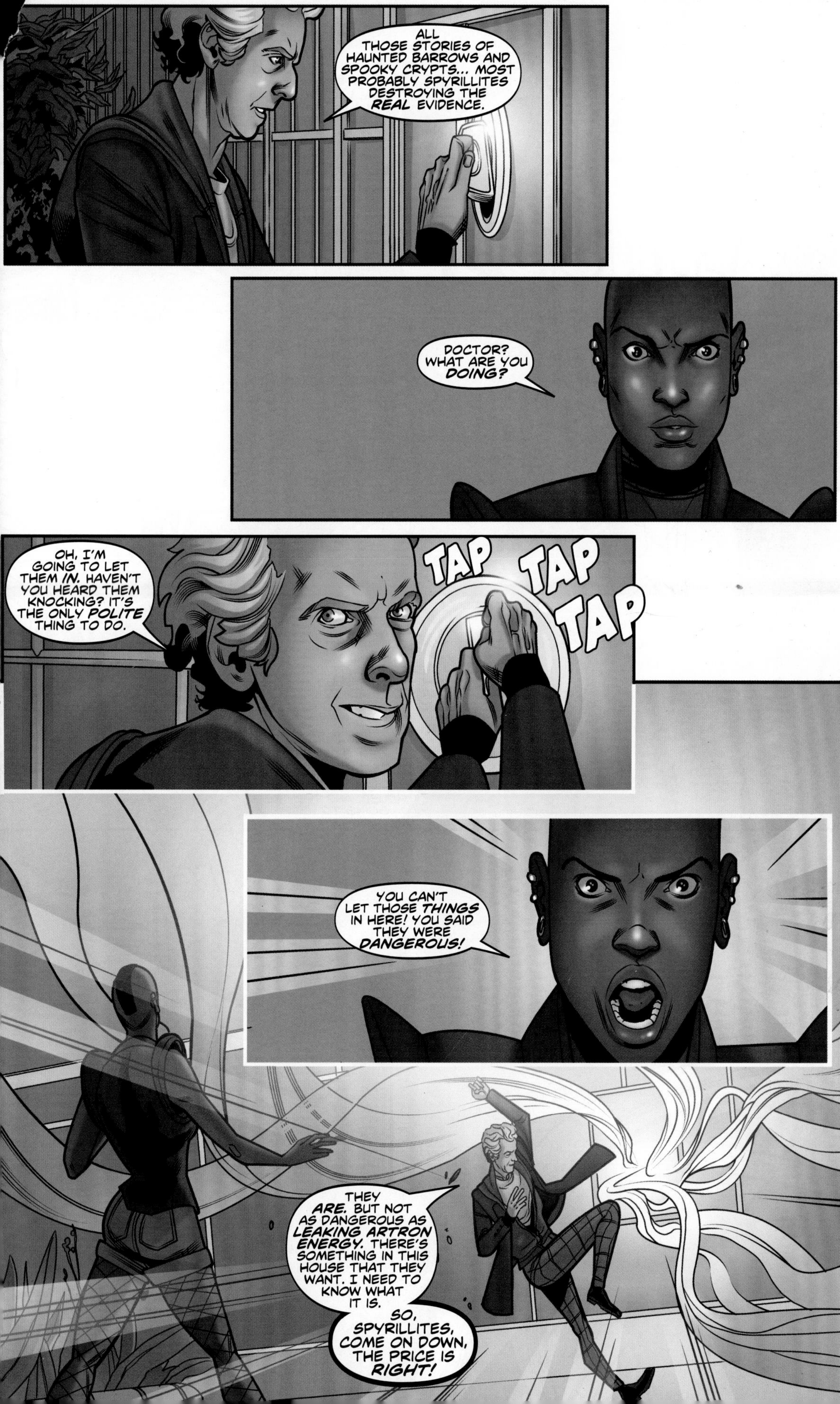
ALL THOSE STORIES OF HAUNTED BARROWS AND SPOOKY CRYPTS... MOST PROBABLY SPYRILLITES DESTROYING THE REAL EVIDENCE.
DOCTOR? WHAT ARE YOU DOING?
OH, I'M GOING TO LET THEM IN. HAVEN'T YOU HEARD THEM KNOCKING? IT'S THE ONLY POLITE THING TO DO.
TAP TAP TAP
YOU CAN'T LET THOSE THINGS IN HERE! YOU SAID THEY WERE DANGEROUS!
THEY ARE. BUT NOT AS DANGEROUS AS LEAKING ARTRON ENERGY. THERE'S SOMETHING IN THIS HOUSE THAT THEY WANT. I NEED TO KNOW WHAT IT IS.
SO, SPYRILLITES, COME ON DOWN, THE PRICE IS RIGHT!

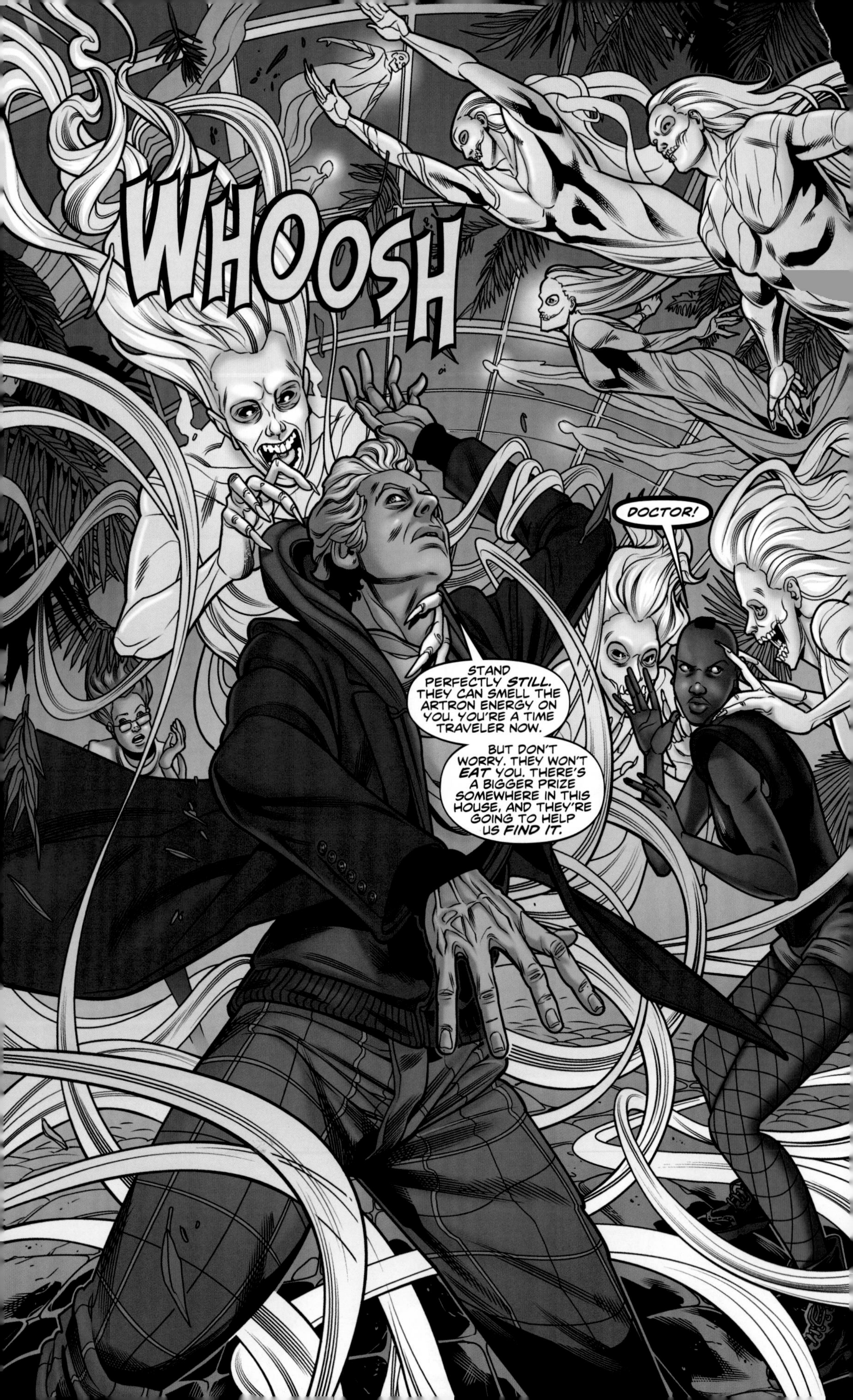
WHOOSH
DOCTOR!
STAND PERFECTLY STILL. THEY CAN SMELL THE ARTRON ENERGY ON YOU. YOU'RE A TIME TRAVELER NOW.
BUT DON'T WORRY. THEY WON'T EAT YOU. THERE'S A BIGGER PRIZE SOMEWHERE IN THIS HOUSE, AND THEY'RE GOING TO HELP US FIND IT.

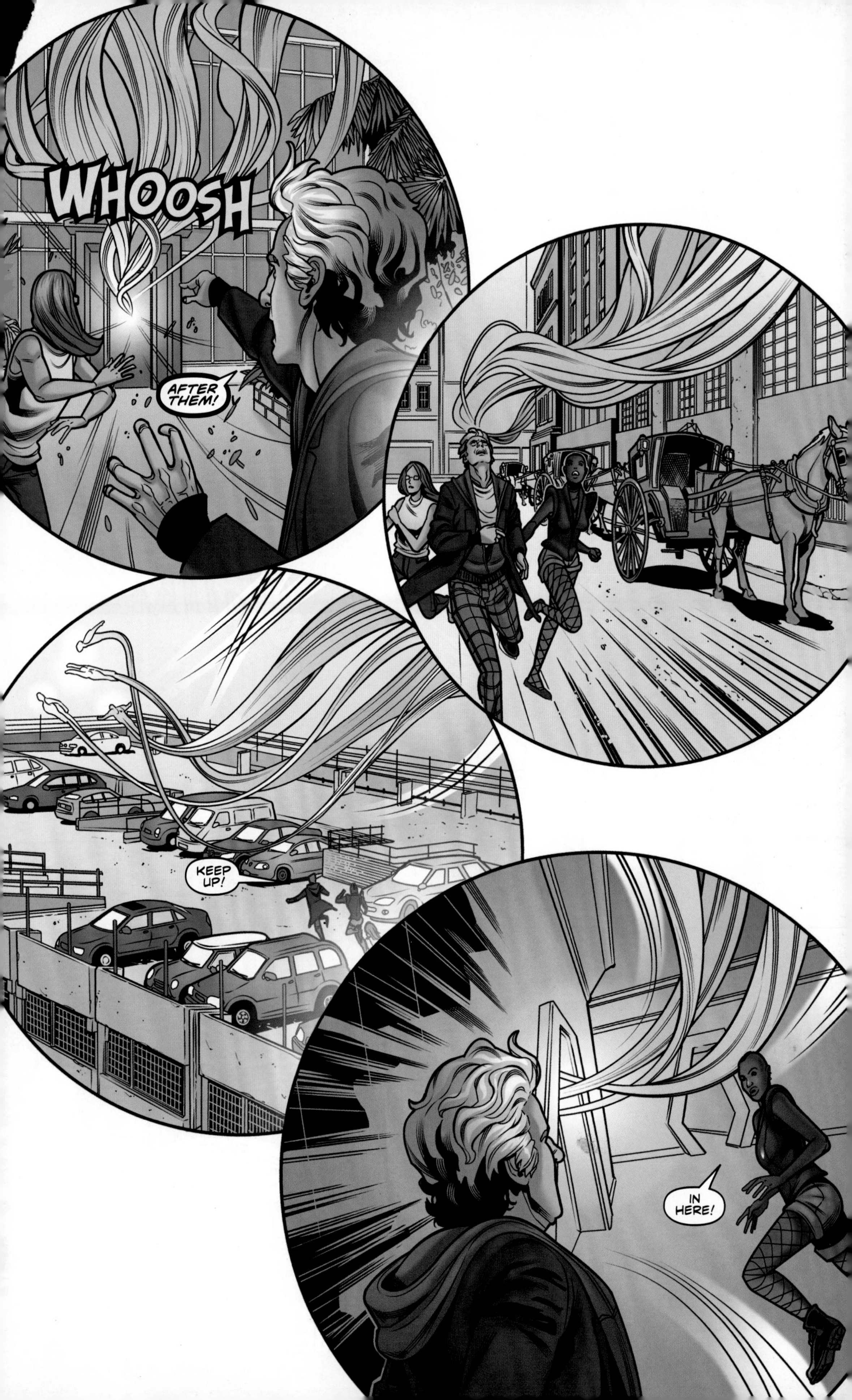
WHOOSH
AFTER THEM!
KEEP UP!
IN HERE!

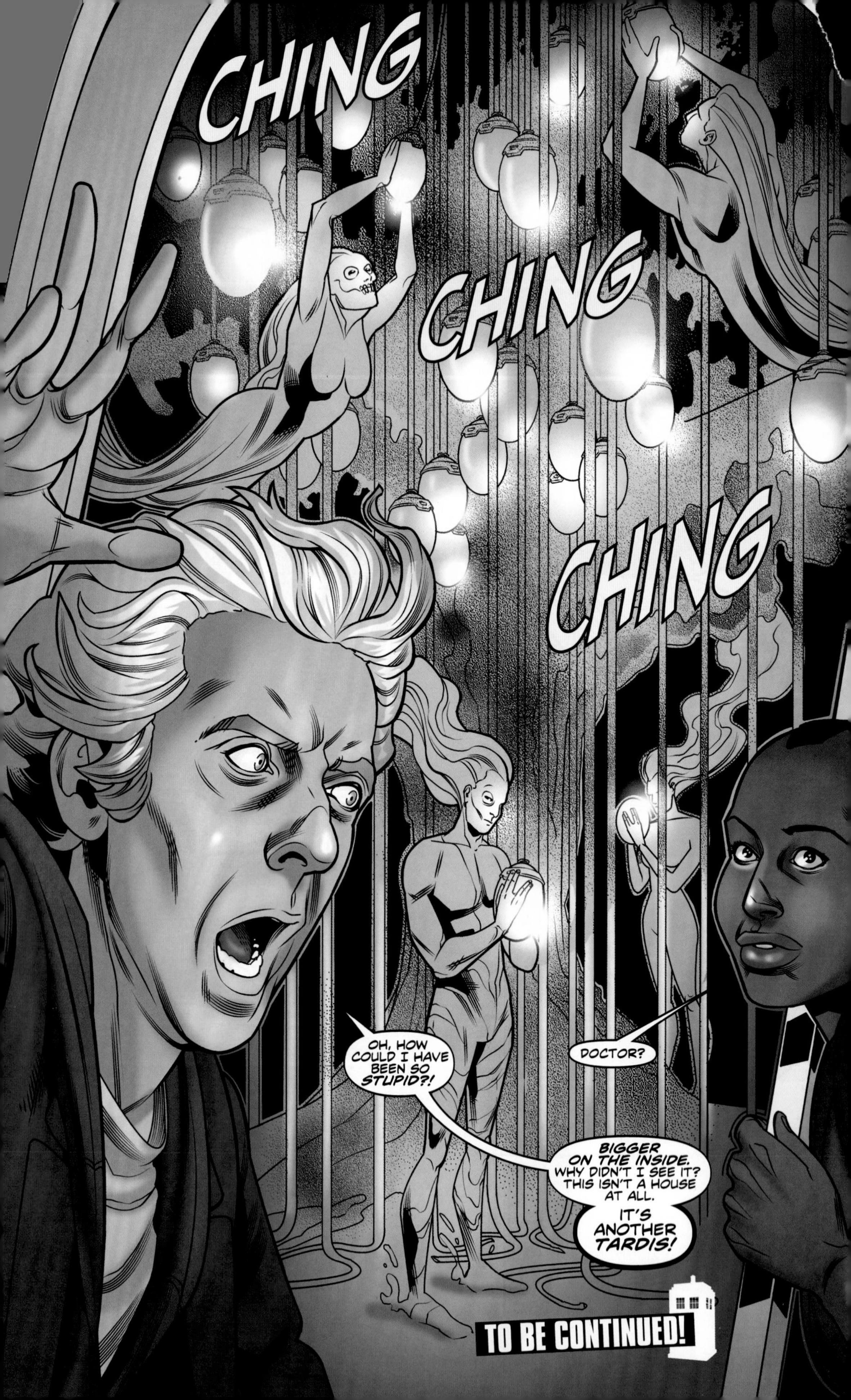
CHING
CHING
CHING
OH, HOW COULD I HAVE BEEN SO STUPID?!
DOCTOR?
BIGGER ON THE INSIDE. WHY DIDN'T I SEE IT? THIS ISN'T A HOUSE AT ALL.
IT'S ANOTHER TARDIS!
TO BE CONTINUED!

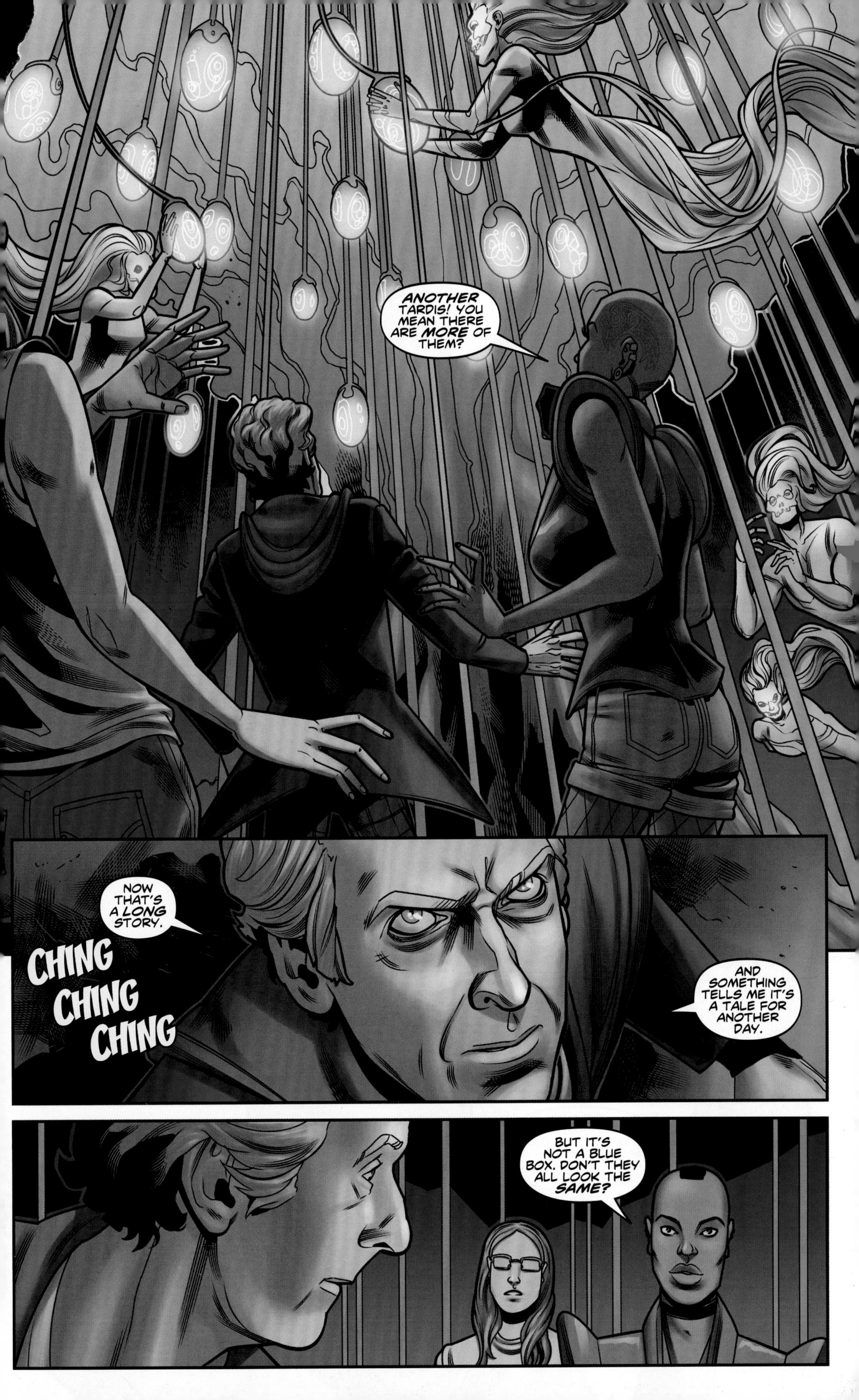
ANOTHER TARDIS! YOU MEAN THERE ARE MORE OF THEM?
NOW THAT'S A LONG STORY.
CHING CHING CHING
AND SOMETHING TELLS ME IT'S A TALE FOR ANOTHER DAY.
BUT IT'S NOT A BLUE BOX. DON'T THEY ALL LOOK THE SAME?

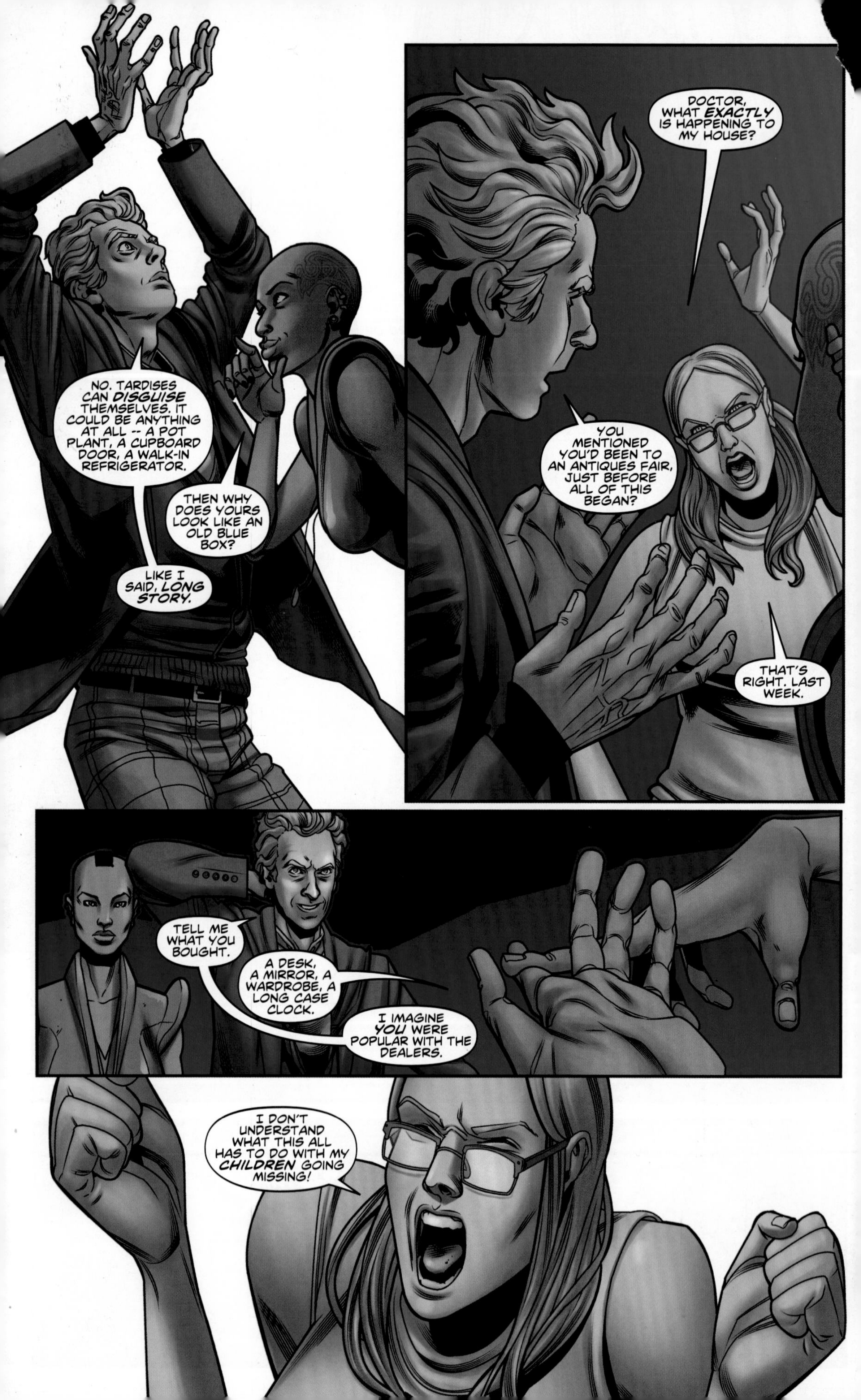
NO. TARDISES CAN DISGUISE THEMSELVES. IT COULD BE ANYTHING AT ALL -- A POT PLANT, A CUPBOARD DOOR, A WALK-IN REFRIGERATOR.
THEN WHY DOES YOURS LOOK LIKE AN OLD BLUE BOX?
LIKE I SAID, LONG STORY.
DOCTOR, WHAT EXACTLY IS HAPPENING TO MY HOUSE?
YOU MENTIONED YOU'D BEEN TO AN ANTIQUES FAIR, JUST BEFORE ALL OF THIS BEGAN?
THAT'S RIGHT. LAST WEEK.
TELL ME WHAT YOU BOUGHT.
A DESK, A MIRROR, A WARDROBE, A LONG CASE CLOCK.
I IMAGINE YOU WERE POPULAR WITH THE DEALERS.
I DON'T UNDERSTAND WHAT THIS ALL HAS TO DO WITH MY CHILDREN GOING MISSING!

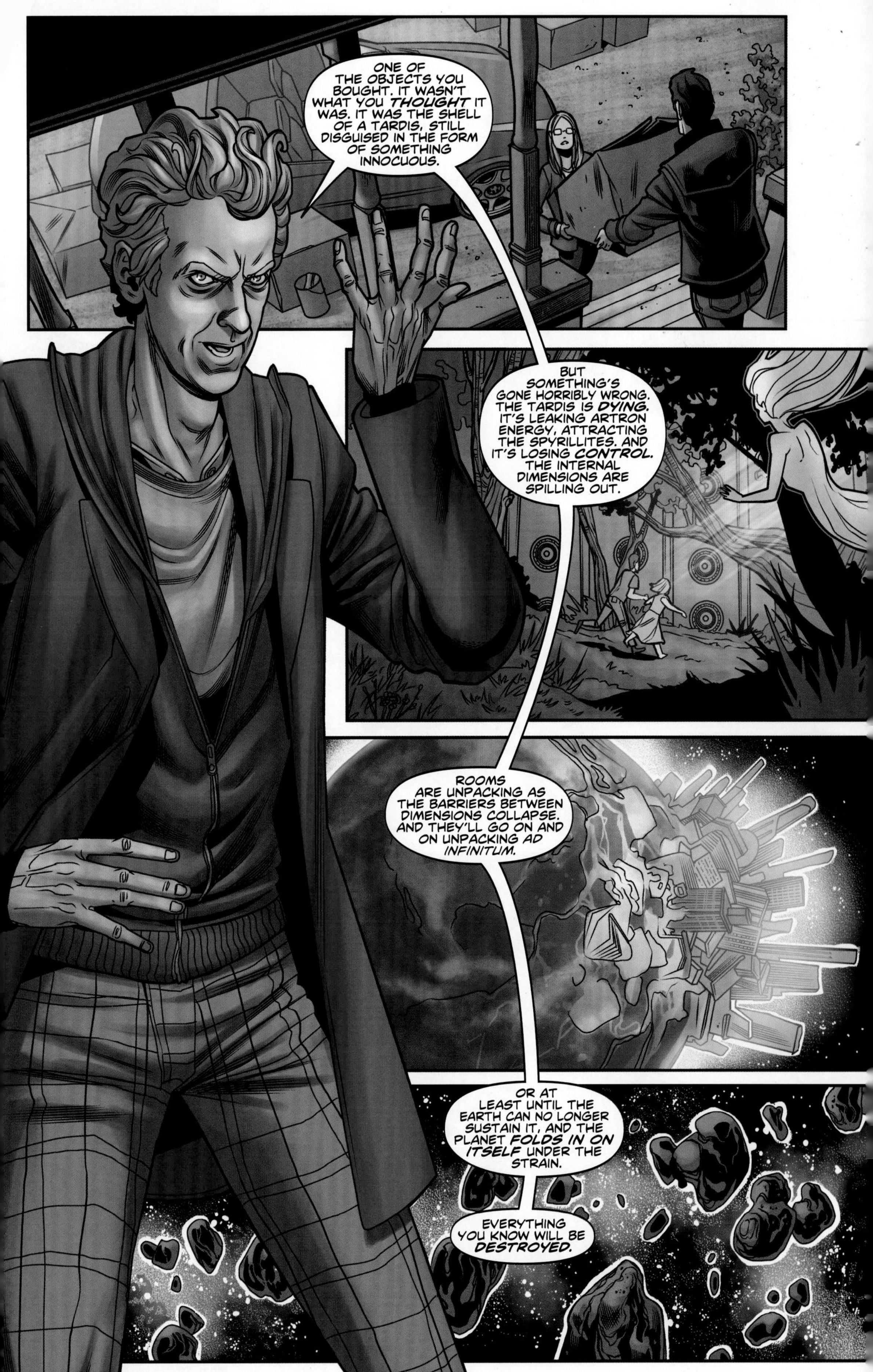
ONE OF THE OBJECTS YOU BOUGHT. IT WASN'T WHAT YOU *THOUGHT* IT WAS. IT WAS THE SHELL OF A TARDIS, STILL DISGUISED IN THE FORM OF SOMETHING INNOCUOUS.
BUT SOMETHING'S GONE HORRIBLY WRONG. THE TARDIS IS *DYING.* IT'S LEAKING ARTRON ENERGY, ATTRACTING THE SPYRILLITES. AND IT'S LOSING *CONTROL.* THE INTERNAL DIMENSIONS ARE SPILLING OUT.
ROOMS ARE UNPACKING AS THE BARRIERS BETWEEN DIMENSIONS COLLAPSE. AND THEY'LL GO ON AND ON UNPACKING AD *INFINITUM.*
OR AT LEAST UNTIL THE EARTH CAN NO LONGER SUSTAIN IT, AND THE PLANET *FOLDS IN ON ITSELF* UNDER THE STRAIN.
EVERYTHING YOU KNOW WILL BE *DESTROYED.*

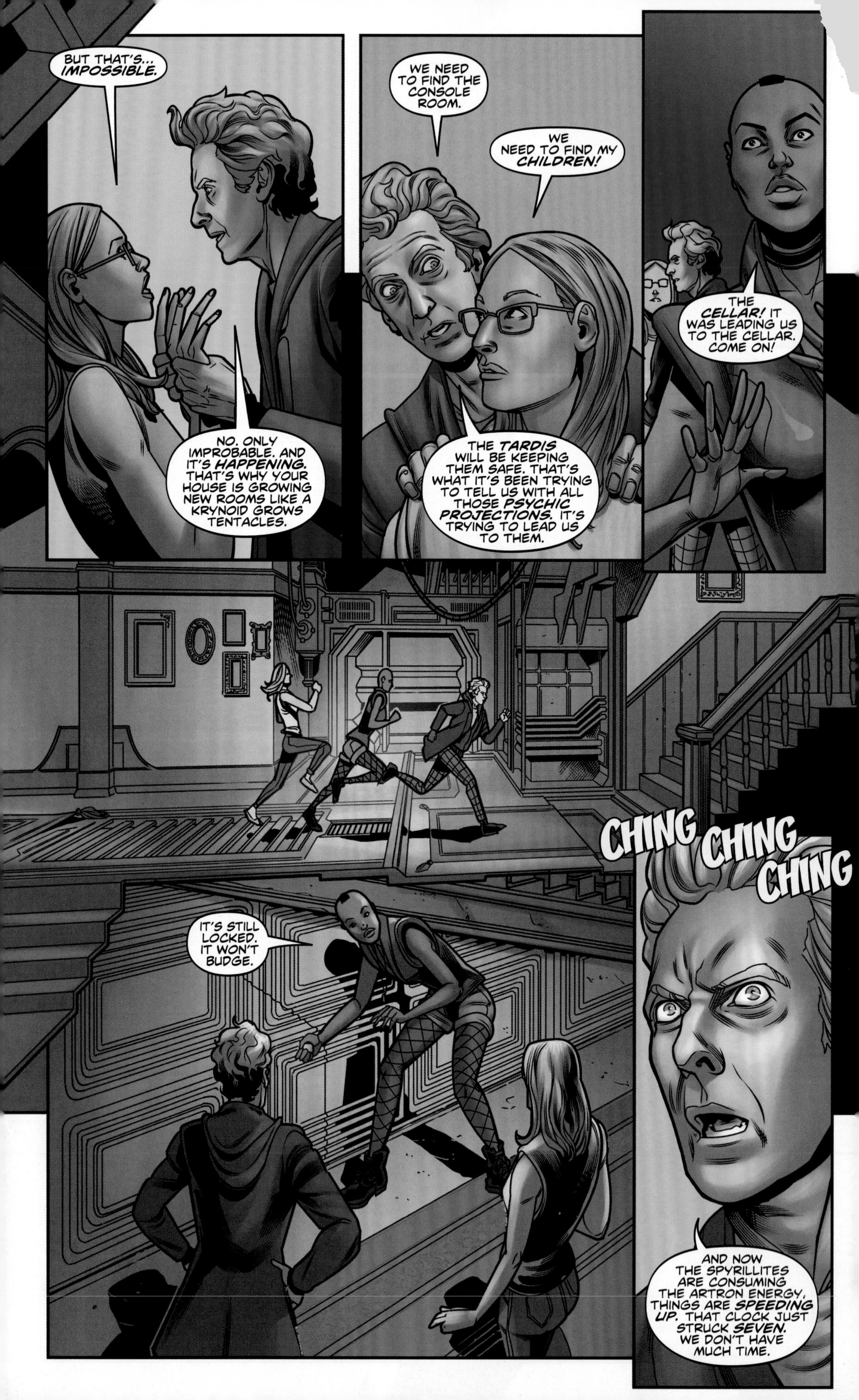
BUT THAT'S... IMPOSSIBLE.
NO. ONLY IMPROBABLE. AND IT'S HAPPENING. THAT'S WHY YOUR HOUSE IS GROWING NEW ROOMS LIKE A KRYNOID GROWS TENTACLES.
WE NEED TO FIND THE CONSOLE ROOM.
WE NEED TO FIND MY CHILDREN!
THE TARDIS WILL BE KEEPING THEM SAFE. THAT'S WHAT IT'S BEEN TRYING TO TELL US WITH ALL THOSE PSYCHIC PROJECTIONS. IT'S TRYING TO LEAD US TO THEM.
THE CELLAR! IT WAS LEADING US TO THE CELLAR. COME ON!
IT'S STILL LOCKED. IT WON'T BUDGE.
CHING CHING CHING
AND NOW THE SPYRILLITES ARE CONSUMING THE ARTRON ENERGY, THINGS ARE SPEEDING UP. THAT CLOCK JUST STRUCK SEVEN. WE DON'T HAVE MUCH TIME.

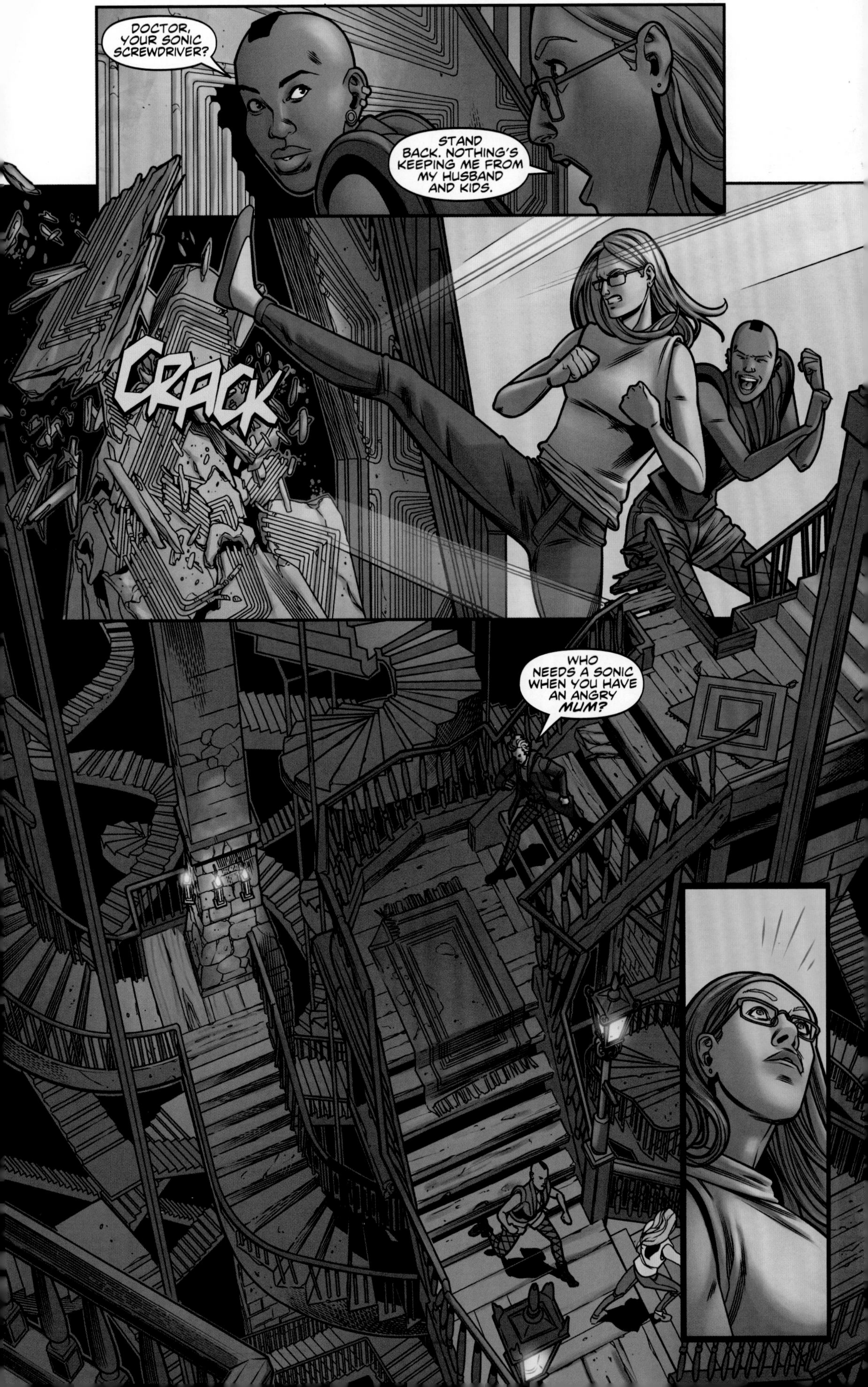
DOCTOR, YOUR SONIC SCREWDRIVER?
STAND BACK. NOTHING'S KEEPING ME FROM MY HUSBAND AND KIDS.
CRACK
WHO NEEDS A SONIC WHEN YOU HAVE AN ANGRY MUM?

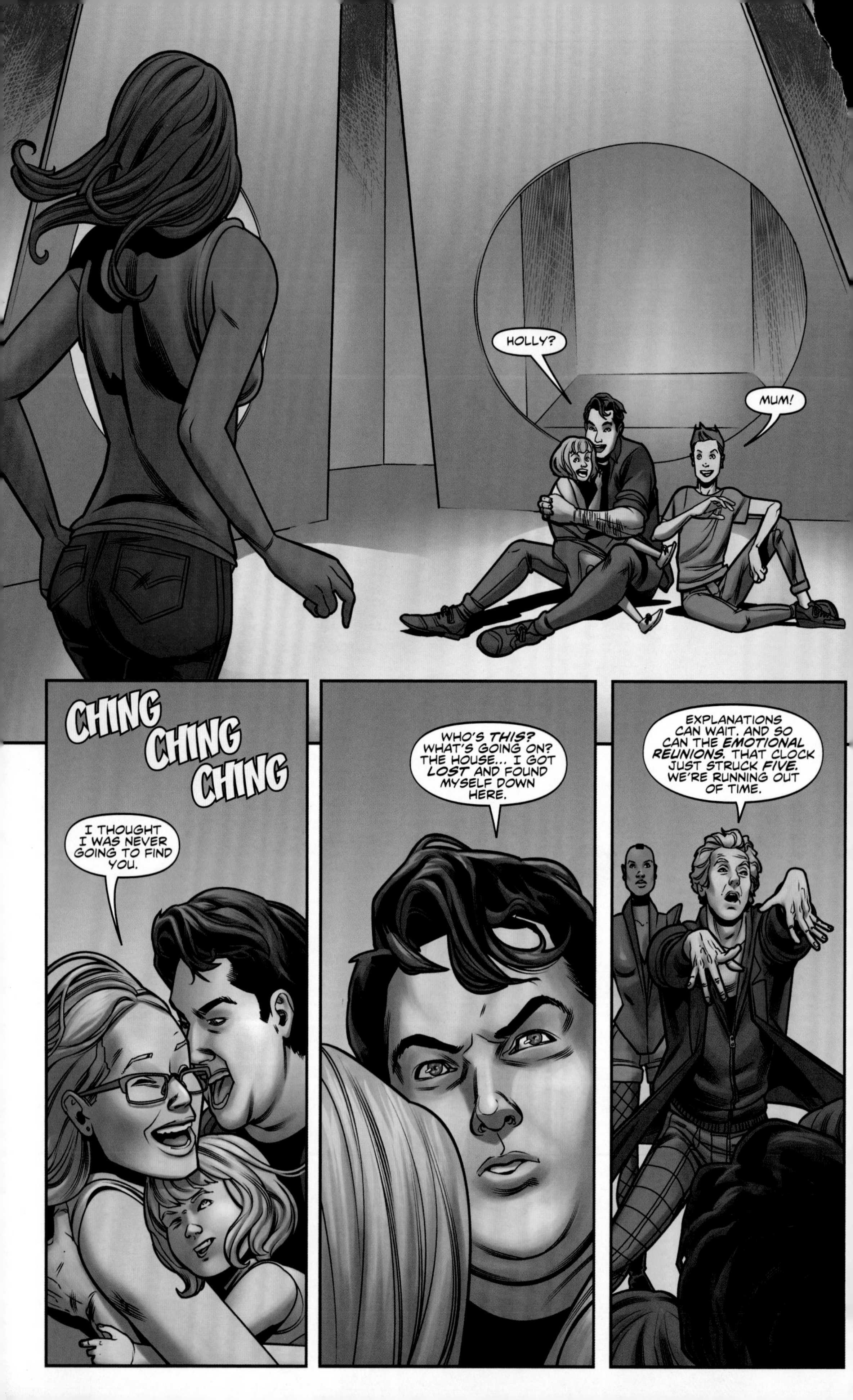
HOLLY?
MUM!
CHING CHING CHING
I THOUGHT I WAS NEVER GOING TO FIND YOU.
WHO'S THIS? WHAT'S GOING ON? THE HOUSE... I GOT LOST AND FOUND MYSELF DOWN HERE.
EXPLANATIONS CAN WAIT. AND SO CAN THE EMOTIONAL REUNIONS. THAT CLOCK JUST STRUCK FIVE. WE'RE RUNNING OUT OF TIME.

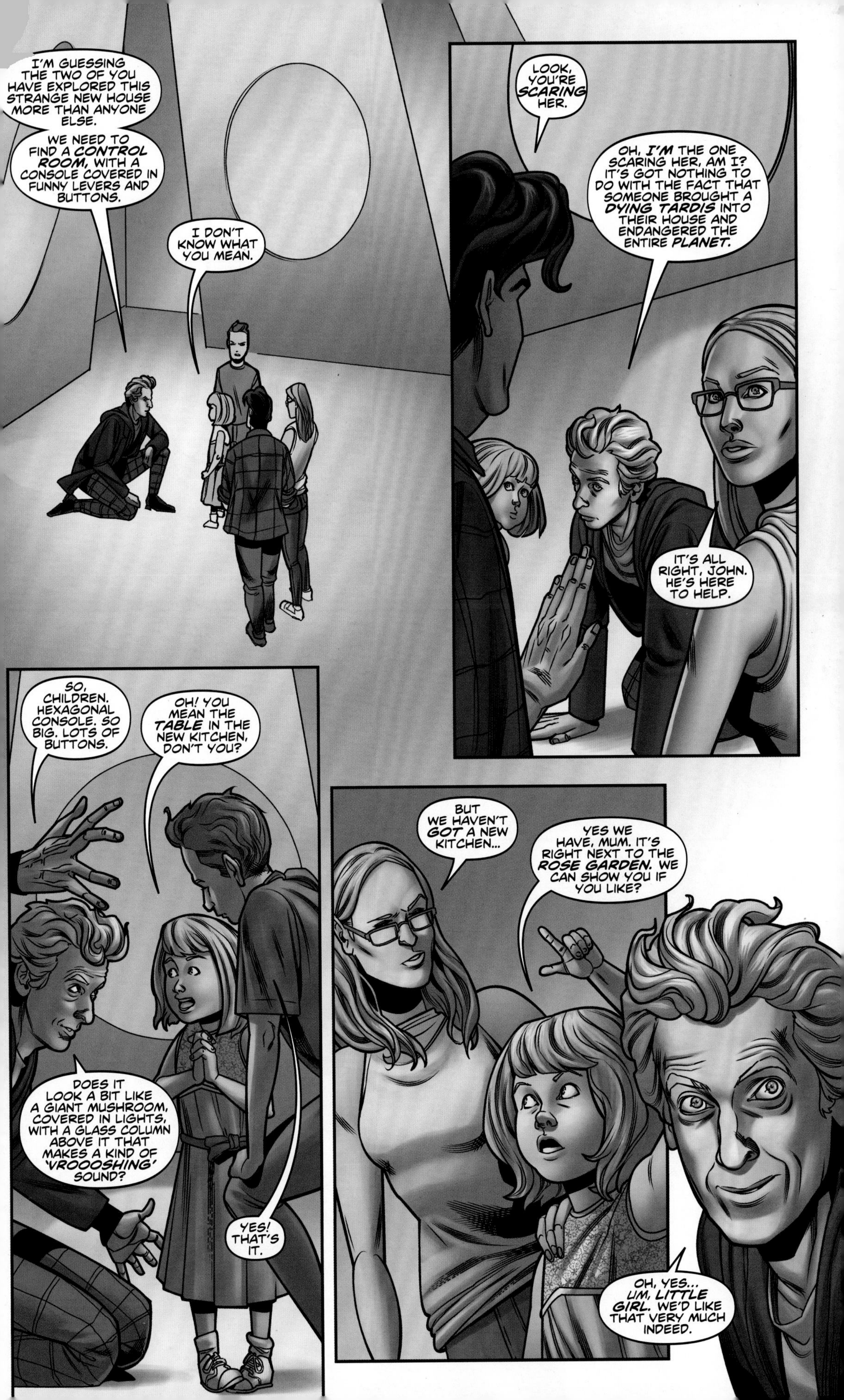
I'M GUESSING THE TWO OF YOU HAVE EXPLORED THIS STRANGE NEW HOUSE MORE THAN ANYONE ELSE.
WE NEED TO FIND A CONTROL ROOM, WITH A CONSOLE COVERED IN FUNNY LEVERS AND BUTTONS.
I DON'T KNOW WHAT YOU MEAN.
LOOK, YOU'RE SCARING HER.
OH, I'M THE ONE SCARING HER, AM I? IT'S GOT NOTHING TO DO WITH THE FACT THAT SOMEONE BROUGHT A DYING TARDIS INTO THEIR HOUSE AND ENDANGERED THE ENTIRE PLANET.
IT'S ALL RIGHT, JOHN. HE'S HERE TO HELP.
SO, CHILDREN. HEXAGONAL CONSOLE. SO BIG. LOTS OF BUTTONS.
OH! YOU MEAN THE TABLE IN THE NEW KITCHEN, DON'T YOU?
DOES IT LOOK A BIT LIKE A GIANT MUSHROOM, COVERED IN LIGHTS, WITH A GLASS COLUMN ABOVE IT THAT MAKES A KIND OF 'VROOOSHING' SOUND?
YES! THAT'S IT.
BUT WE HAVEN'T GOT A NEW KITCHEN...
YES WE HAVE, MUM. IT'S RIGHT NEXT TO THE ROSE GARDEN. WE CAN SHOW YOU IF YOU LIKE?
OH, YES... UM, LITTLE GIRL. WE'D LIKE THAT VERY MUCH INDEED.

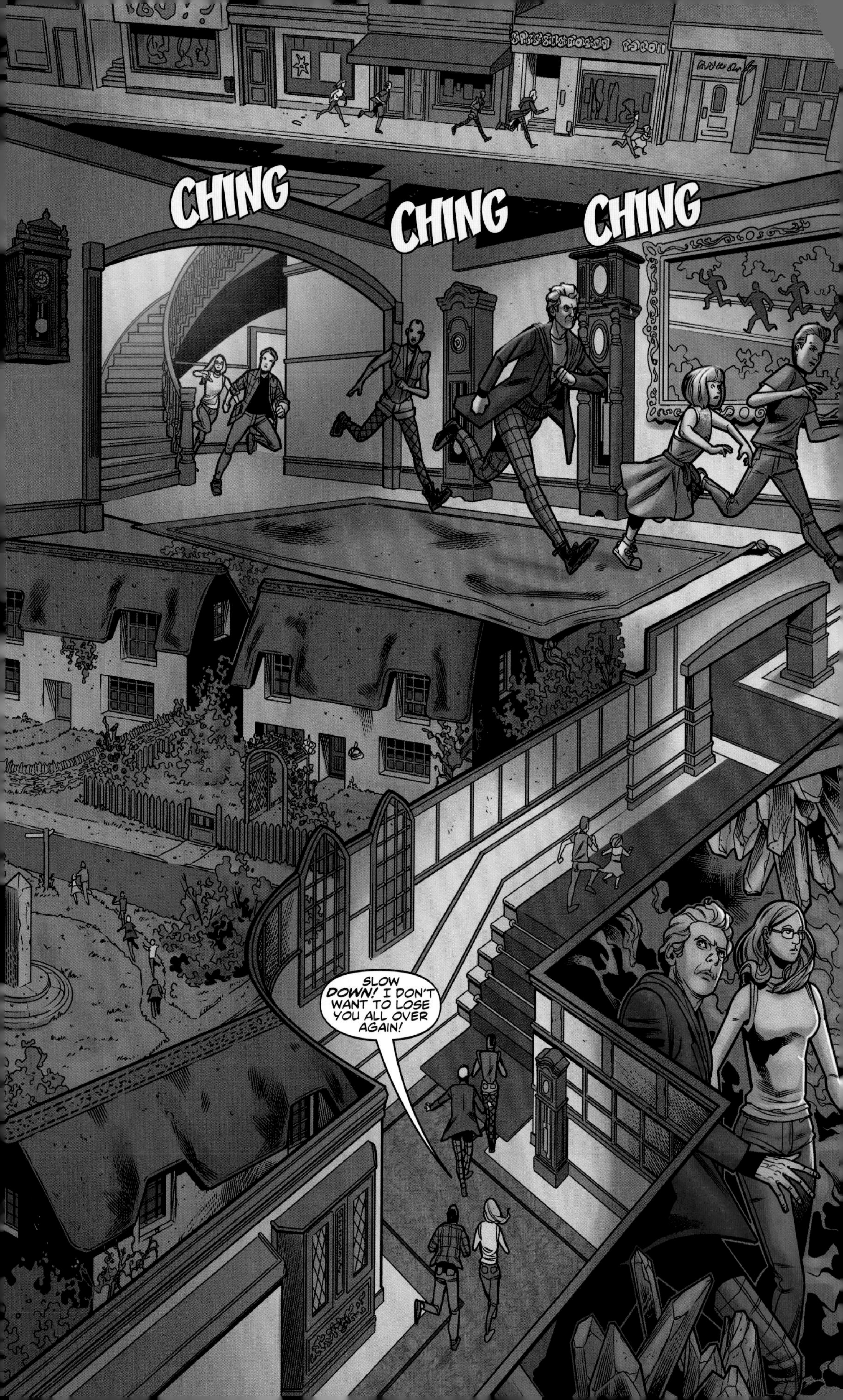
CHING
CHING
CHING
SLOW DOWN! I DON'T WANT TO LOSE YOU ALL OVER AGAIN!

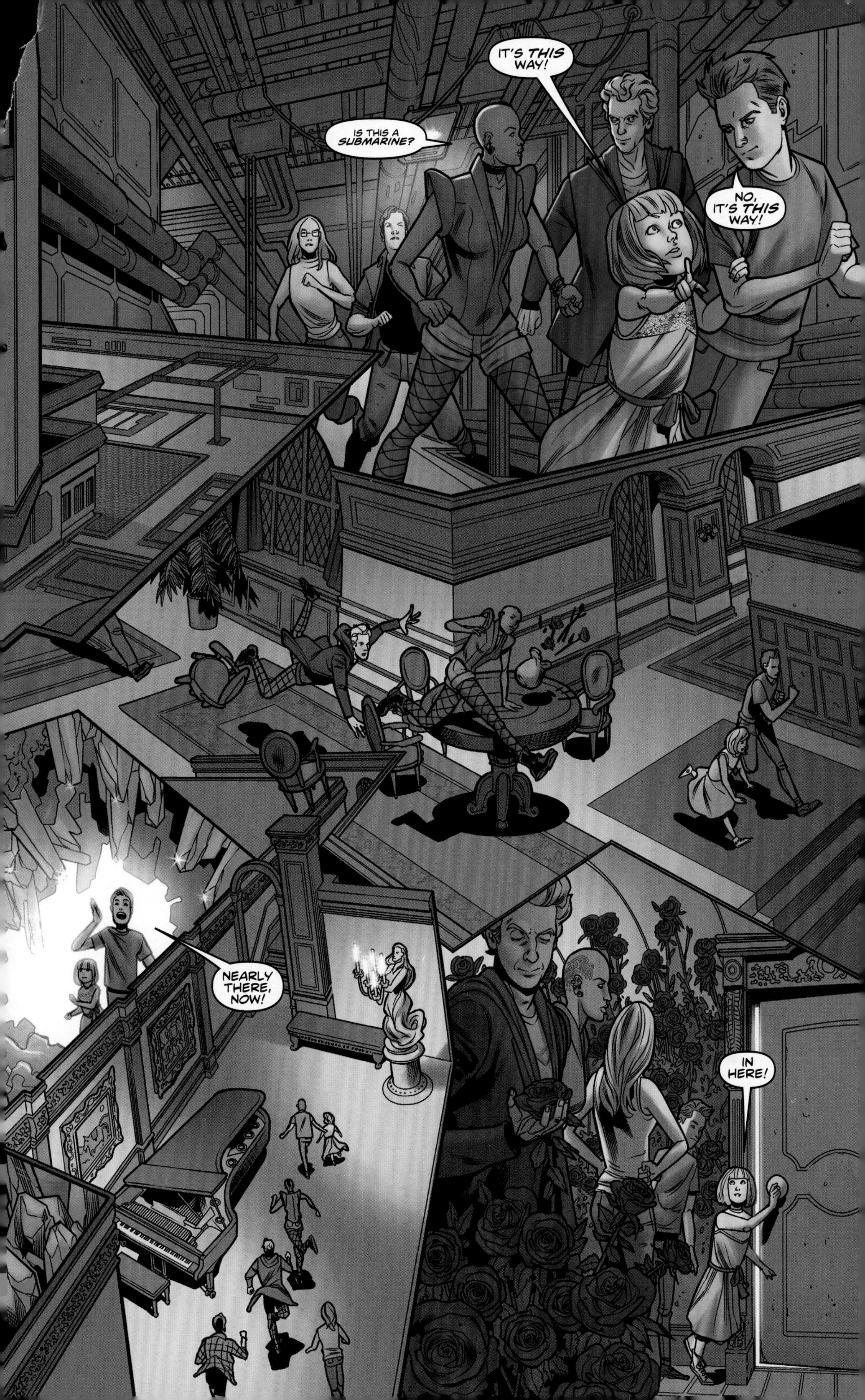
IS THIS A SUBMARINE?
IT'S THIS WAY!
NO, IT'S THIS WAY!
NEARLY THERE, NOW!
IN HERE!

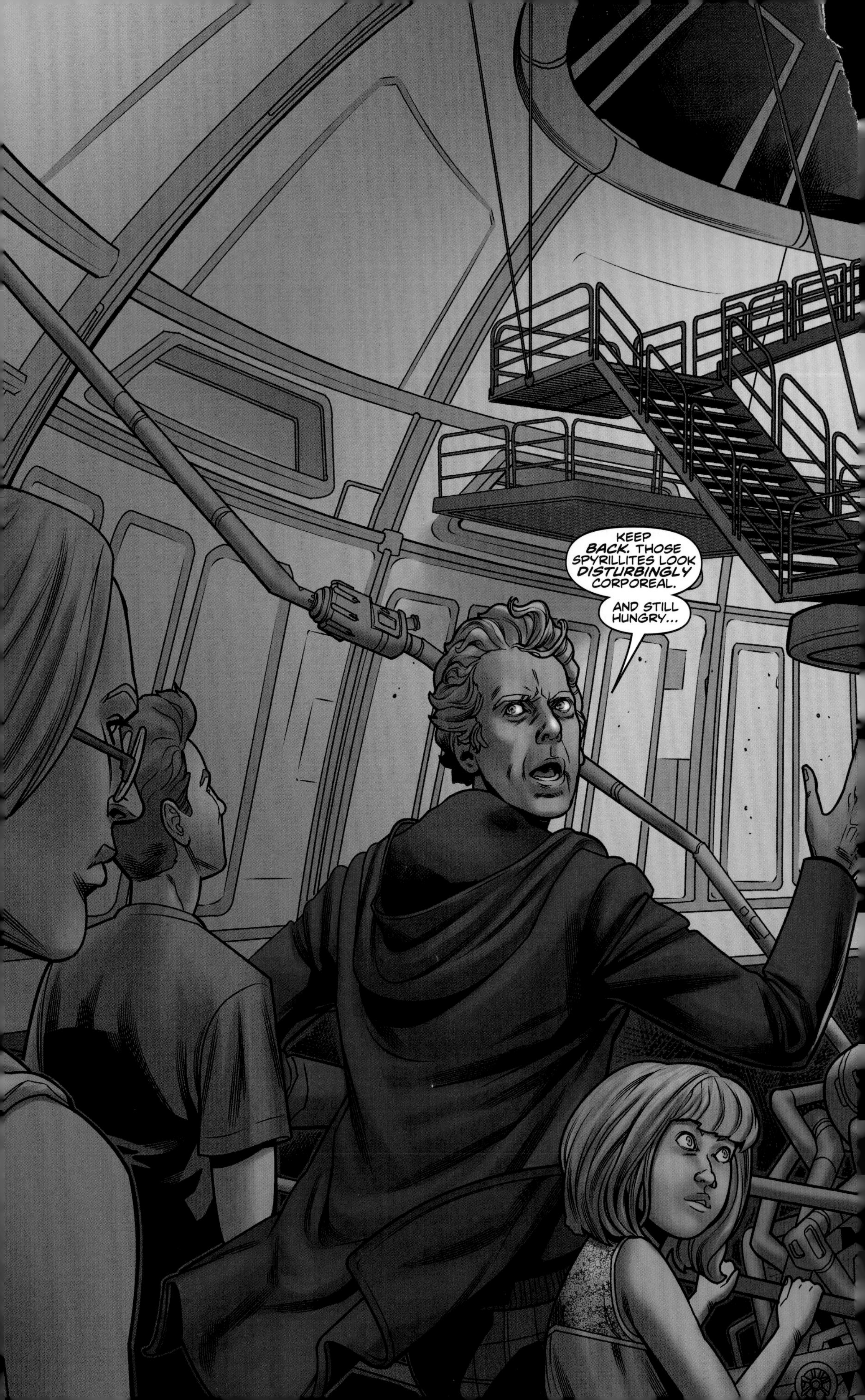
KEEP BACK. THOSE SPYRILLITES LOOK DISTURBINGLY CORPOREAL.
AND STILL HUNGRY...

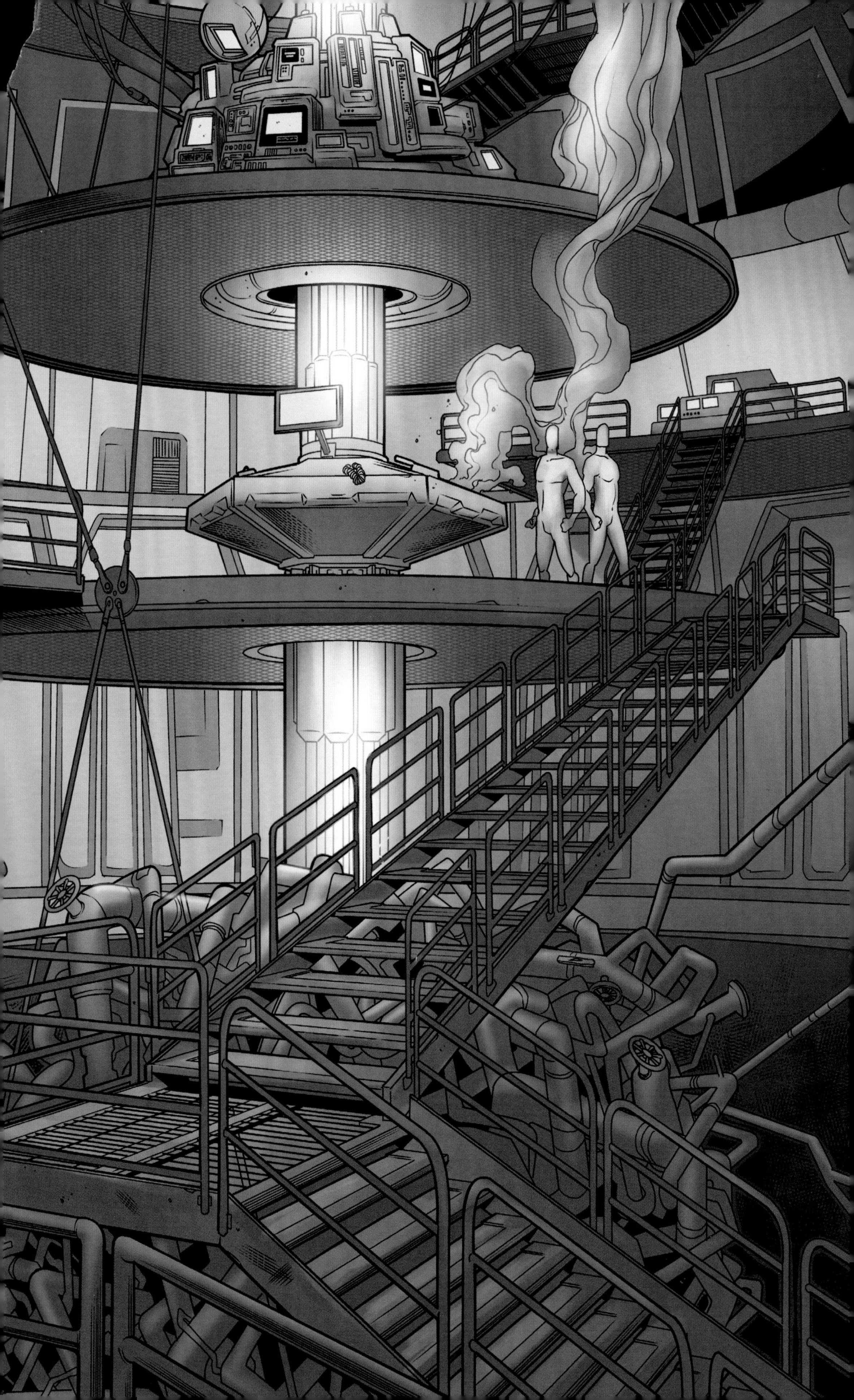

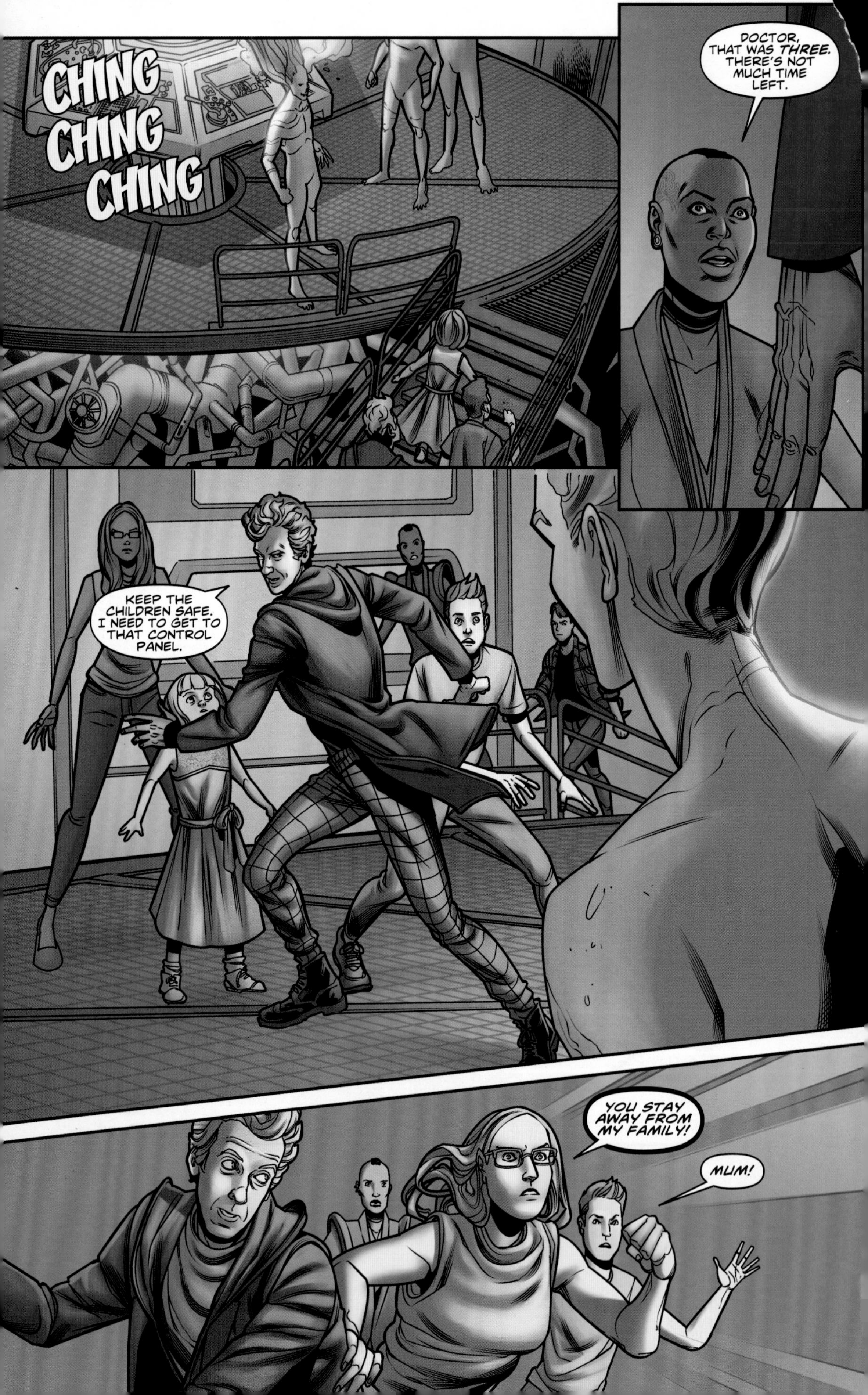
CHING CHING CHING
DOCTOR, THAT WAS THREE. THERE'S NOT MUCH TIME LEFT.
KEEP THE CHILDREN SAFE. I NEED TO GET TO THAT CONTROL PANEL.
YOU STAY AWAY FROM MY FAMILY!
MUM!

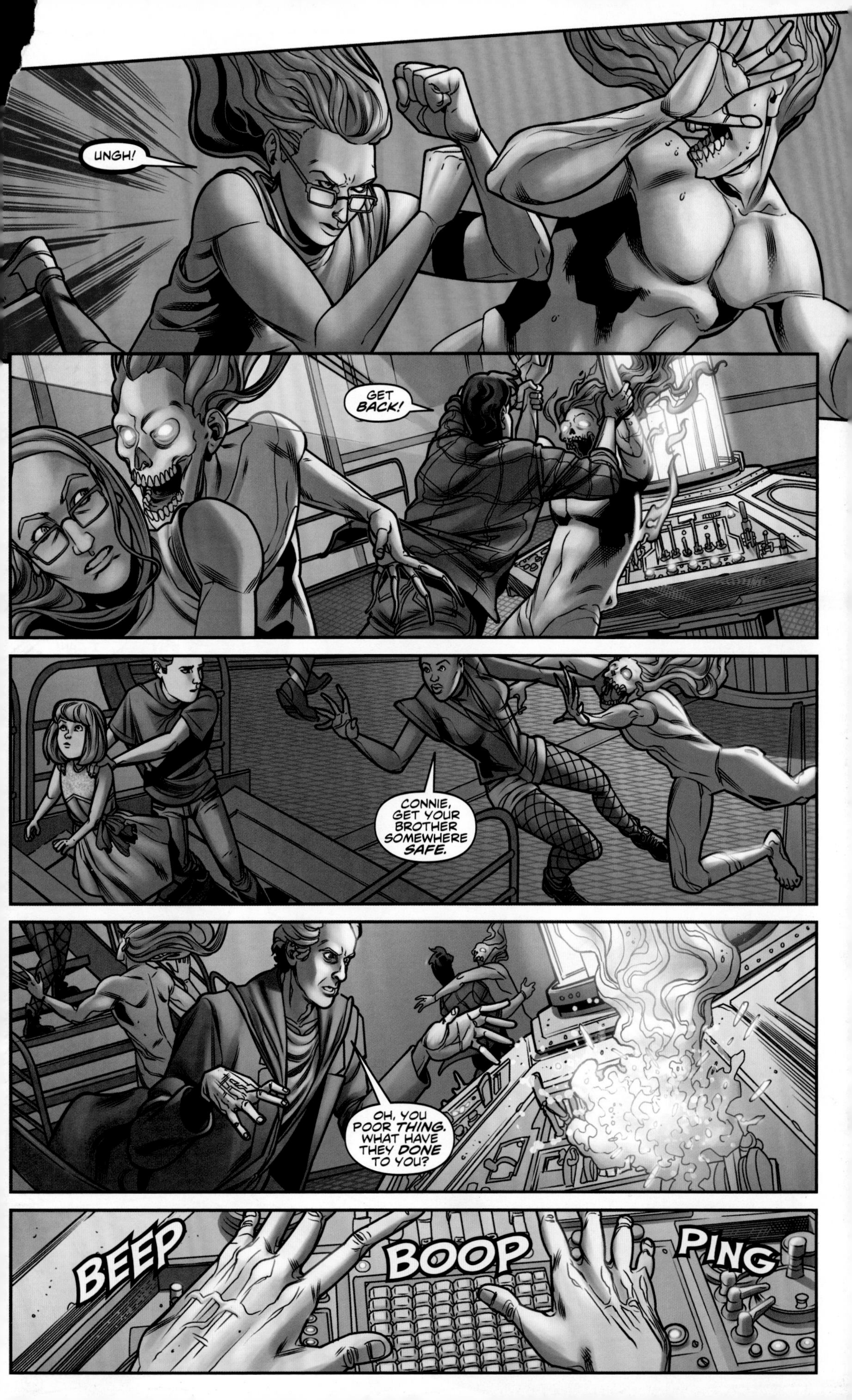
UNGH!
GET BACK!
CONNIE, GET YOUR BROTHER SOMEWHERE SAFE.
OH, YOU POOR THING. WHAT HAVE THEY DONE TO YOU?
BEEP
BOOP
PING

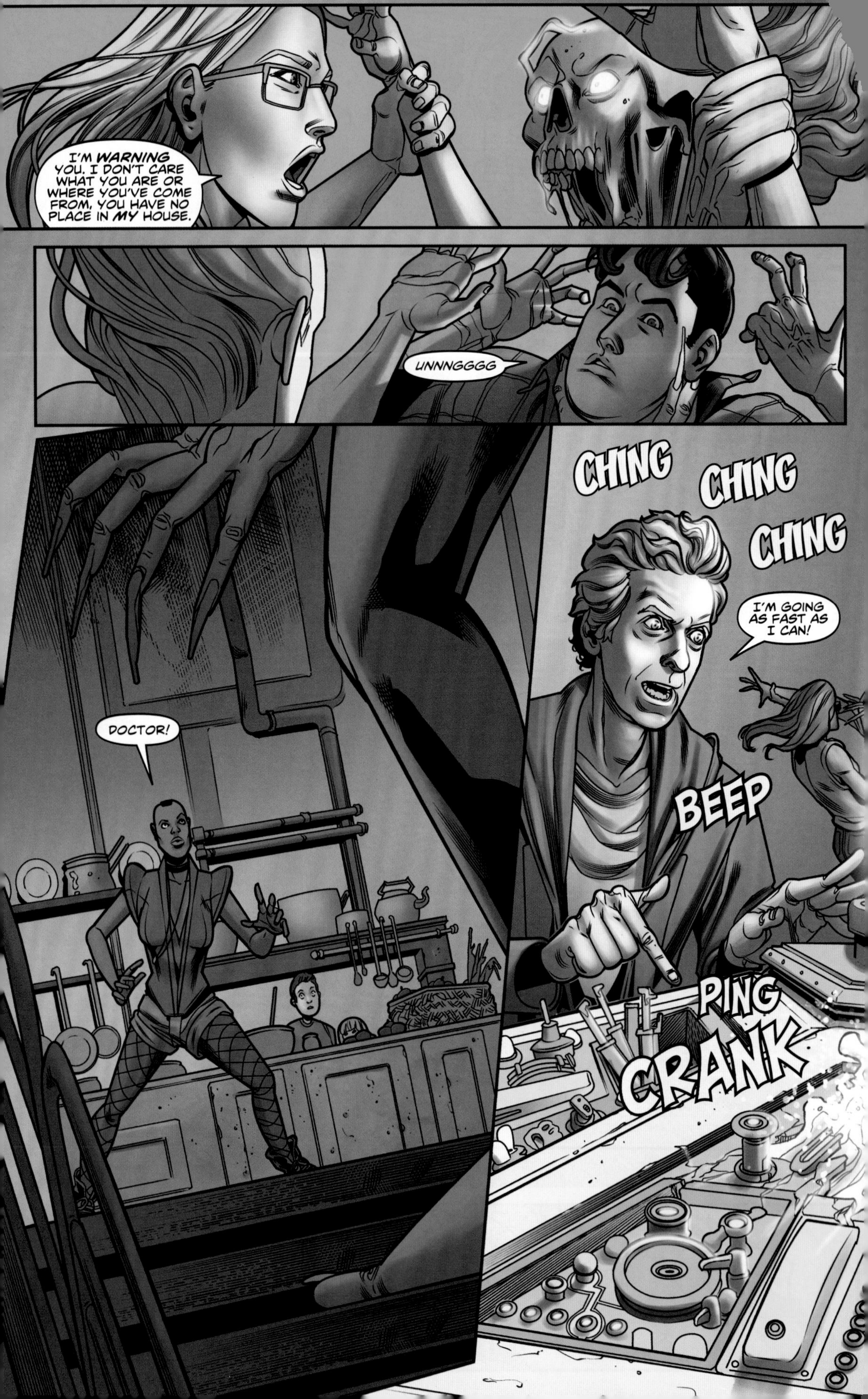
I'M WARNING YOU. I DON'T CARE WHAT YOU ARE OR WHERE YOU'VE COME FROM, YOU HAVE NO PLACE IN MY HOUSE.
UNNNGGGG
DOCTOR!
CHING
CHING
CHING
I'M GOING AS FAST AS I CAN!
BEEP
PING
CRANK

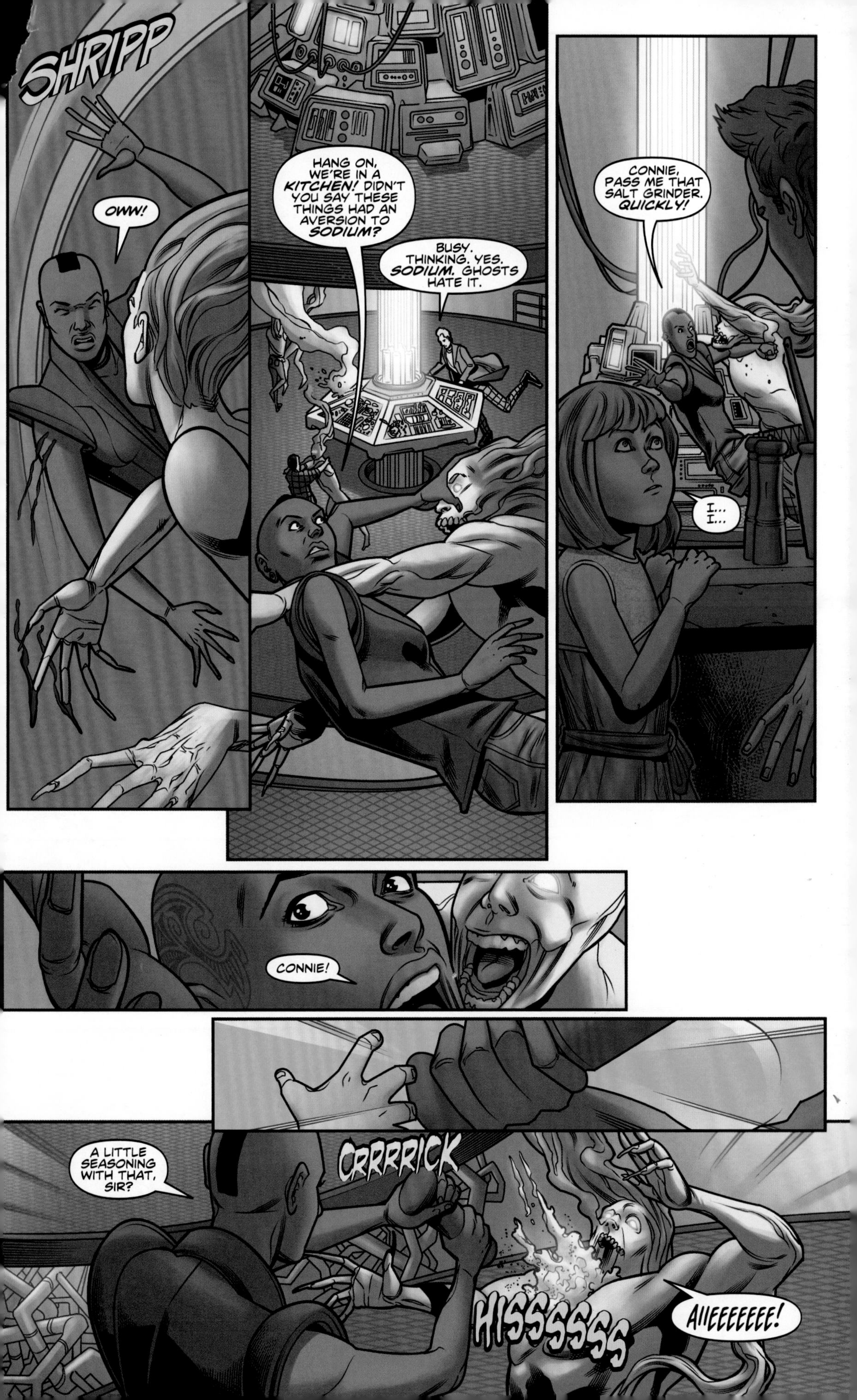
SHRIPP
OWW!
HANG ON, WE'RE IN A KITCHEN! DIDN'T YOU SAY THESE THINGS HAD AN AVERSION TO SODIUM?
BUSY. THINKING. YES. SODIUM. GHOSTS HATE IT.
CONNIE, PASS ME THAT SALT GRINDER. QUICKLY!
I... I...
CONNIE!
A LITTLE SEASONING WITH THAT, SIR?
CRRRRICK
HISSSSSS
AIIEEEEEEE!

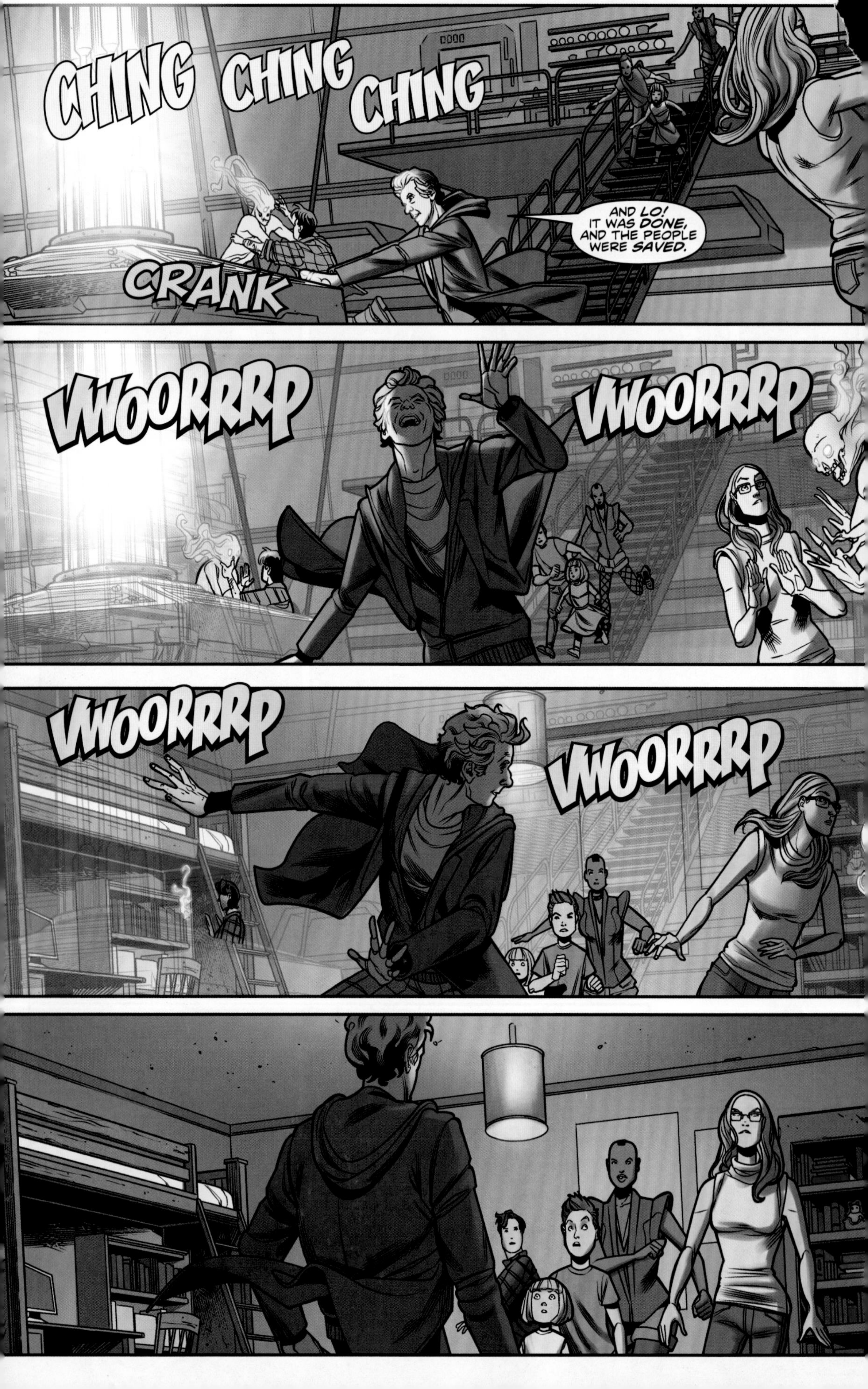
CHING CHING CHING
CRANK
AND LO! IT WAS DONE, AND THE PEOPLE WERE SAVED.
VWOORRRP
VWOORRRP
VWOORRRP
VWOORRRP

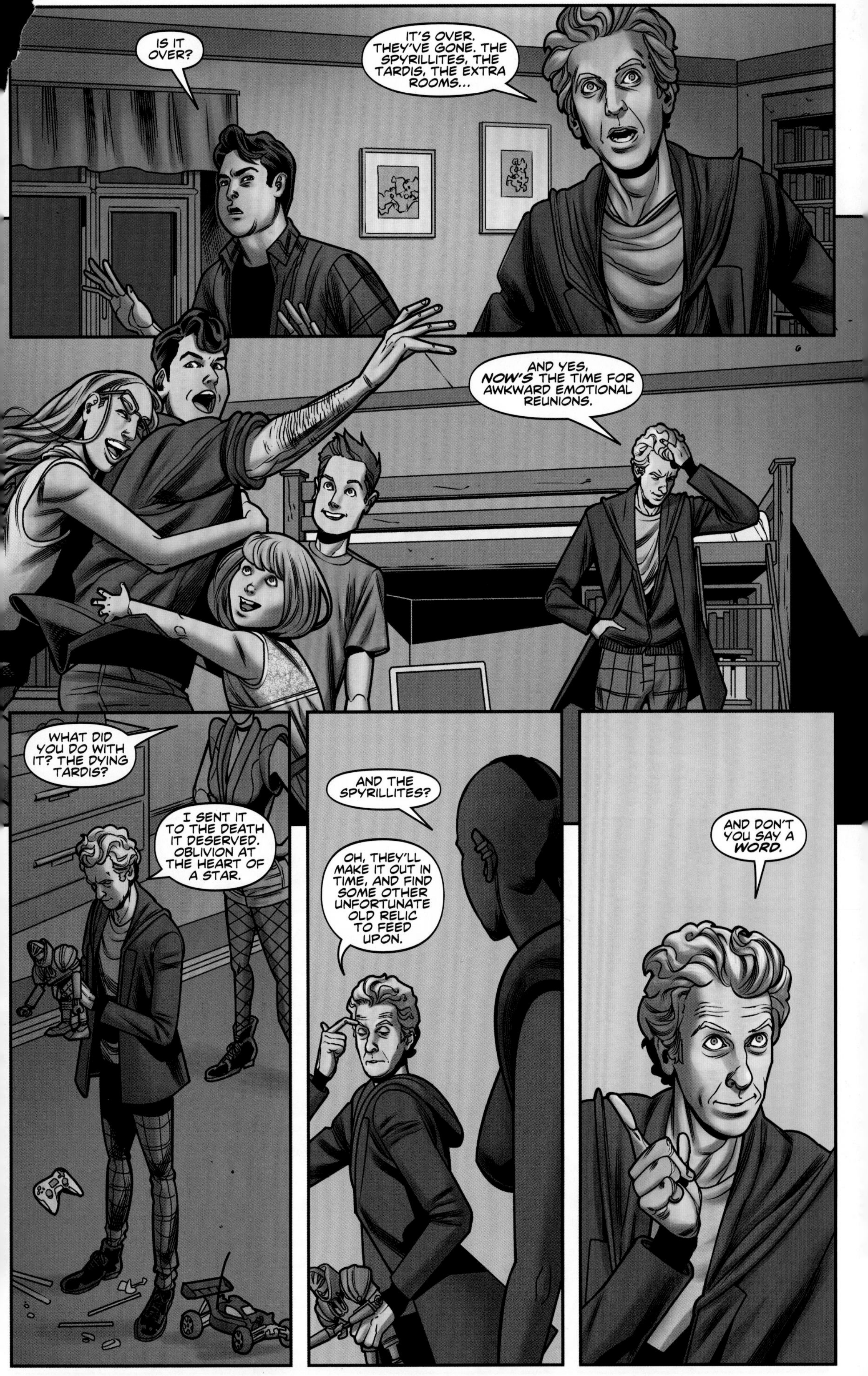
IS IT OVER?
IT'S OVER. THEY'VE GONE. THE SPYRILLITES, THE TARDIS, THE EXTRA ROOMS...
AND YES, *NOW'S* THE TIME FOR AWKWARD EMOTIONAL REUNIONS.
WHAT DID YOU DO WITH IT? THE DYING TARDIS?
I SENT IT TO THE DEATH IT DESERVED. OBLIVION AT THE HEART OF A STAR.
AND THE SPYRILLITES?
OH, THEY'LL MAKE IT OUT IN TIME, AND FIND SOME OTHER UNFORTUNATE OLD RELIC TO FEED UPON.
AND DON'T YOU SAY A **WORD.**

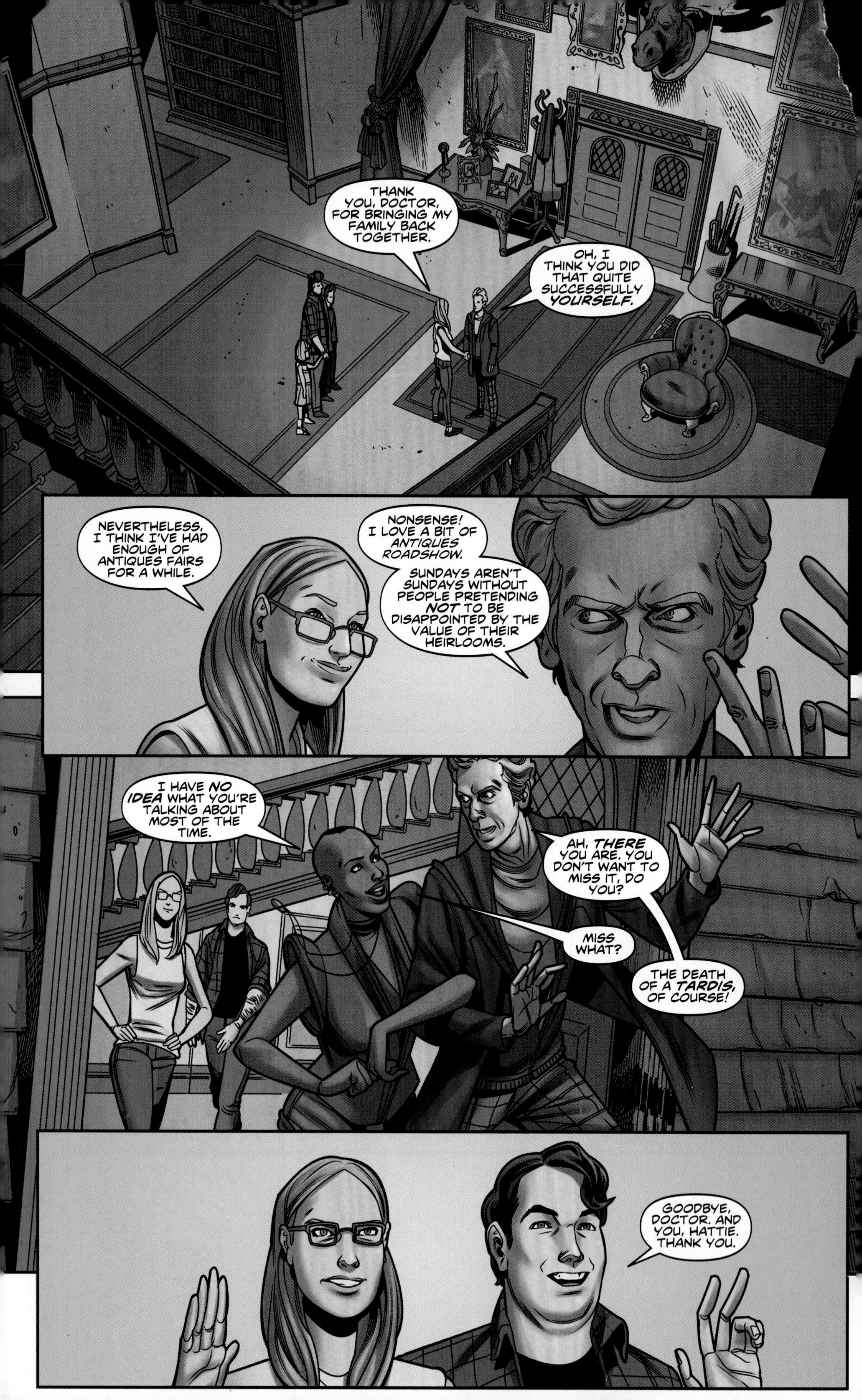
THANK YOU, DOCTOR, FOR BRINGING MY FAMILY BACK TOGETHER.
OH, I THINK YOU DID THAT QUITE SUCCESSFULLY *YOURSELF.*
NEVERTHELESS, I THINK I'VE HAD ENOUGH OF ANTIQUES FAIRS FOR A WHILE.
NONSENSE! I LOVE A BIT OF *ANTIQUES ROADSHOW.*
SUNDAYS AREN'T SUNDAYS WITHOUT PEOPLE PRETENDING ***NOT*** TO BE DISAPPOINTED BY THE VALUE OF THEIR HEIRLOOMS.
I HAVE ***NO IDEA*** WHAT YOU'RE TALKING ABOUT MOST OF THE TIME.
AH, ***THERE*** YOU ARE. YOU DON'T WANT TO MISS IT, DO YOU?
MISS WHAT?
THE DEATH OF A ***TARDIS,*** OF COURSE!
GOODBYE, DOCTOR. AND YOU, HATTIE. THANK YOU.

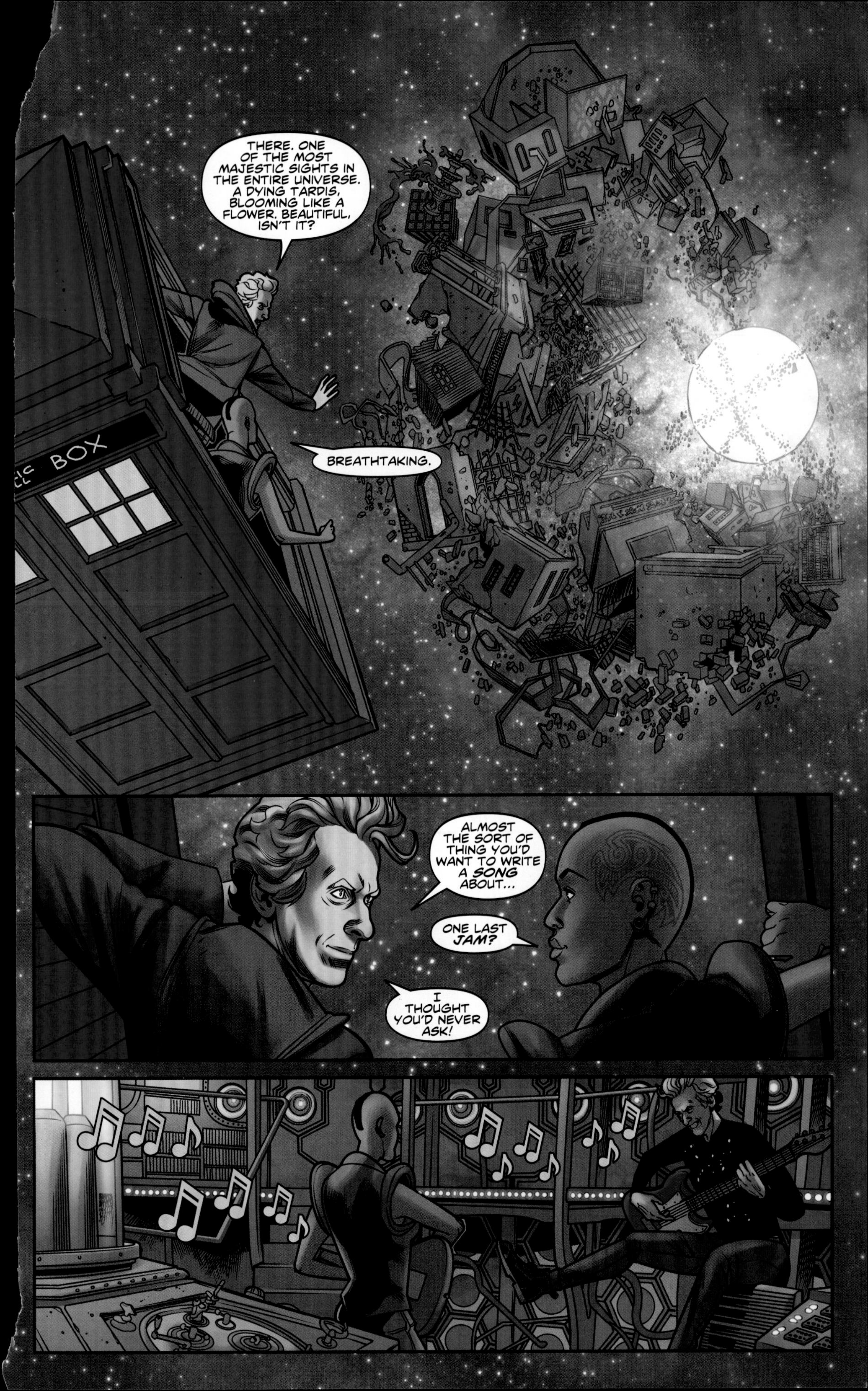
THERE. ONE OF THE MOST MAJESTIC SIGHTS IN THE ENTIRE UNIVERSE. A DYING TARDIS, BLOOMING LIKE A FLOWER. BEAUTIFUL, ISN'T IT?
BREATHTAKING.
BOX
ALMOST THE SORT OF THING YOU'D WANT TO WRITE A SONG ABOUT...
ONE LAST JAM?
I THOUGHT YOU'D NEVER ASK!

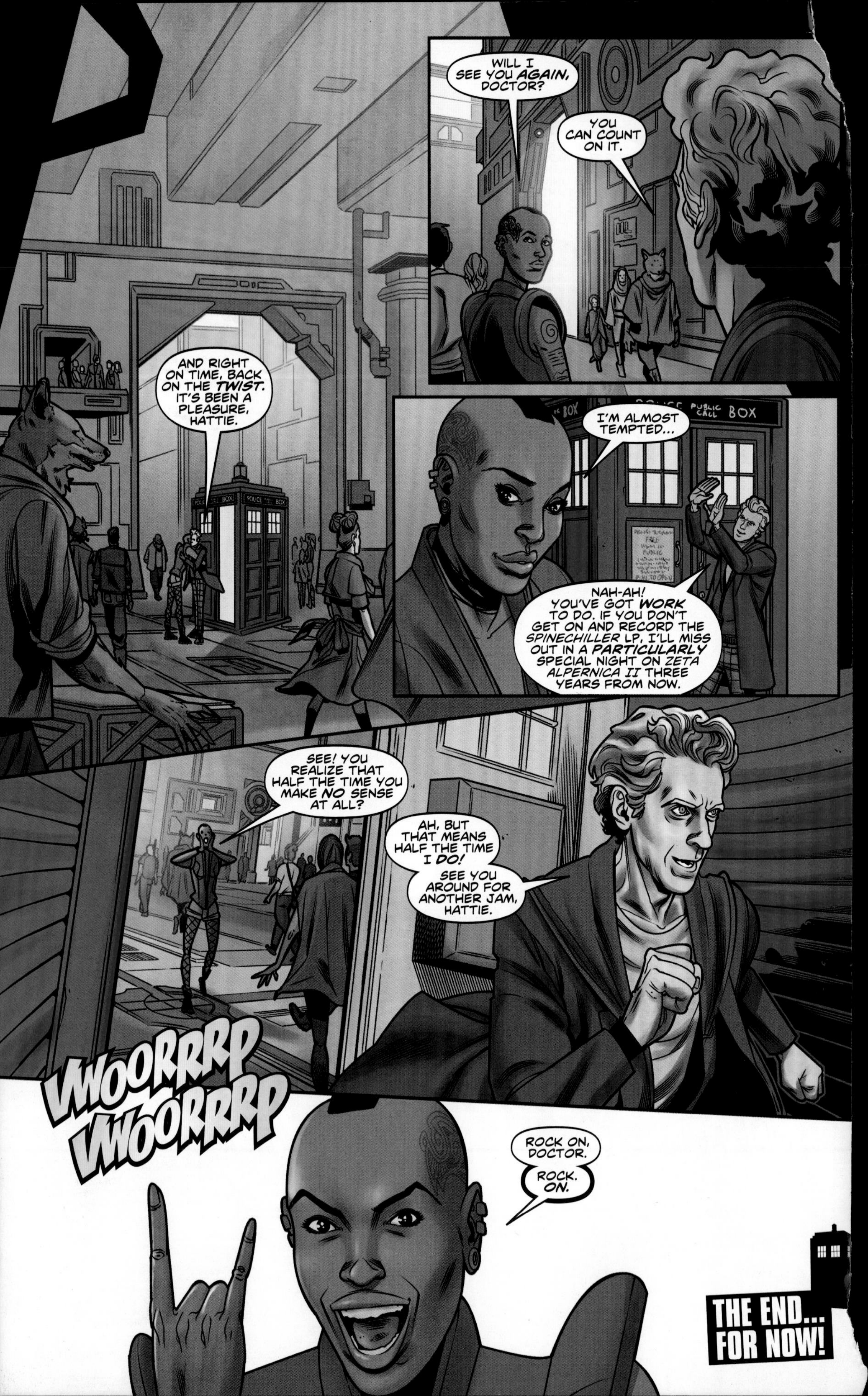
AND RIGHT ON TIME, BACK ON THE TWIST. IT'S BEEN A PLEASURE, HATTIE.
WILL I SEE YOU AGAIN, DOCTOR?
YOU CAN COUNT ON IT.
I'M ALMOST TEMPTED...
POLICE PUBLIC CALL BOX
NAH-AH! YOU'VE GOT WORK TO DO. IF YOU DON'T GET ON AND RECORD THE SPINECHILLER LP, I'LL MISS OUT IN A PARTICULARLY SPECIAL NIGHT ON ZETA ALPERNICA II THREE YEARS FROM NOW.
SEE! YOU REALIZE THAT HALF THE TIME YOU MAKE NO SENSE AT ALL?
AH, BUT THAT MEANS HALF THE TIME I DO!
SEE YOU AROUND FOR ANOTHER JAM, HATTIE.
VWOORRRP VWOORRRP
ROCK ON, DOCTOR.
ROCK. ON.
THE END... FOR NOW!

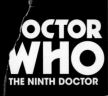

DOCTOR WHO
THE NINTH DOCTOR

COVER GALLERY

A

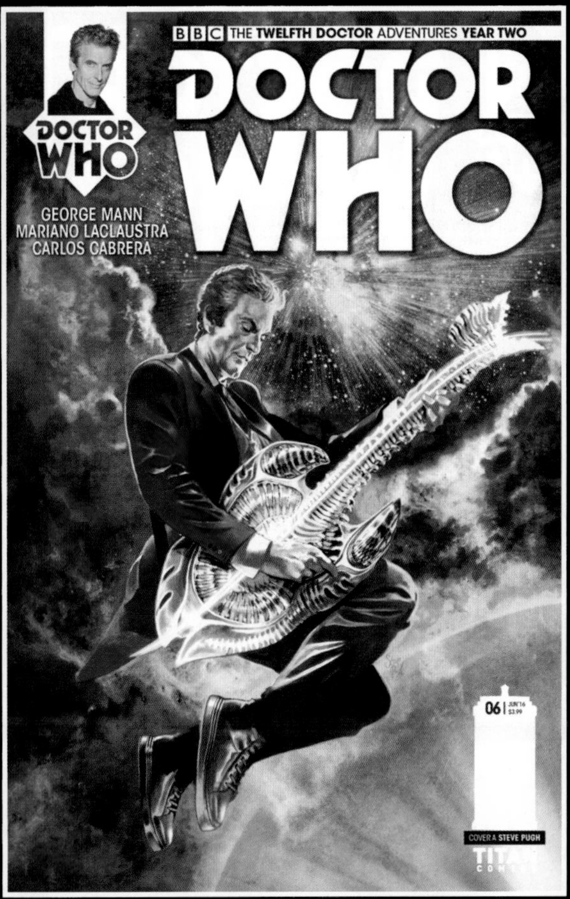

BBC THE TWELFTH DOCTOR ADVENTURES YEAR TWO
DOCTOR WHO
DOCTOR WHO
GEORGE MANN
MARIANO LACLAUSTRA
CARLOS CABRERA
06 | JUN'16 $3.99
COVER A STEVE PUGH

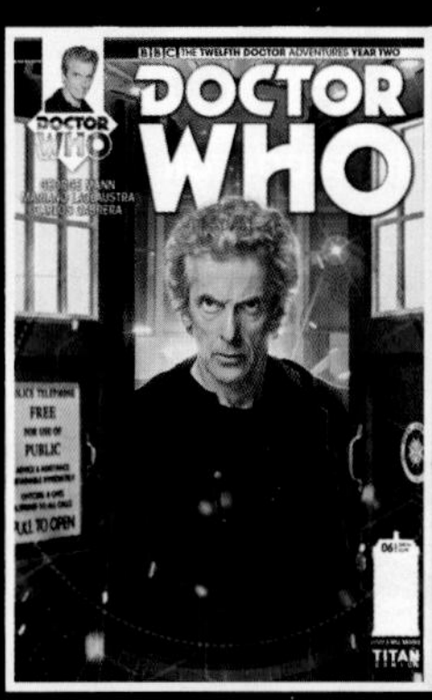

BBC THE TWELFTH DOCTOR ADVENTURES YEAR TWO
DOCTOR WHO
DOCTOR WHO
FREE
PUBLIC
PULL TO OPEN

B

C

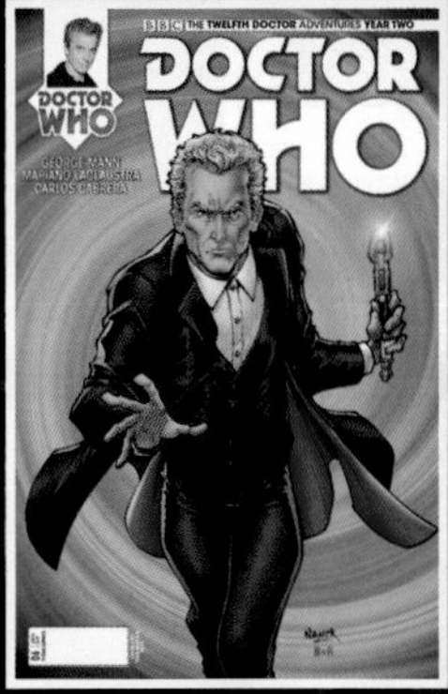

BBC THE TWELFTH DOCTOR ADVENTURES YEAR TWO
DOCTOR WHO
DOCTOR WHO

D

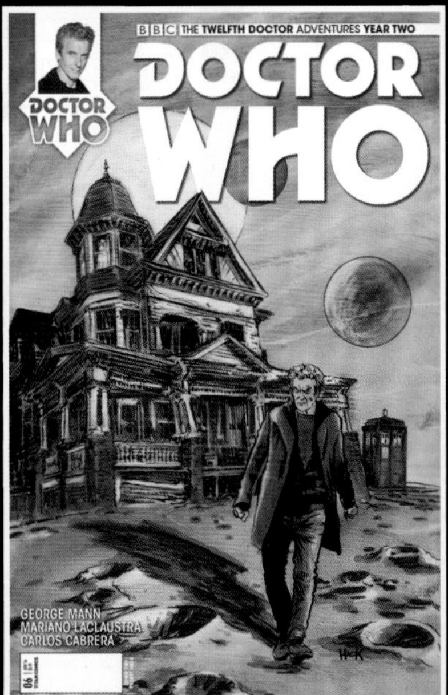

BBC THE TWELFTH DOCTOR ADVENTURES YEAR TWO
DOCTOR WHO
DOCTOR WHO
GEORGE MANN
MARIANO LACLAUSTRA
CARLOS CABRERA
HACK

E

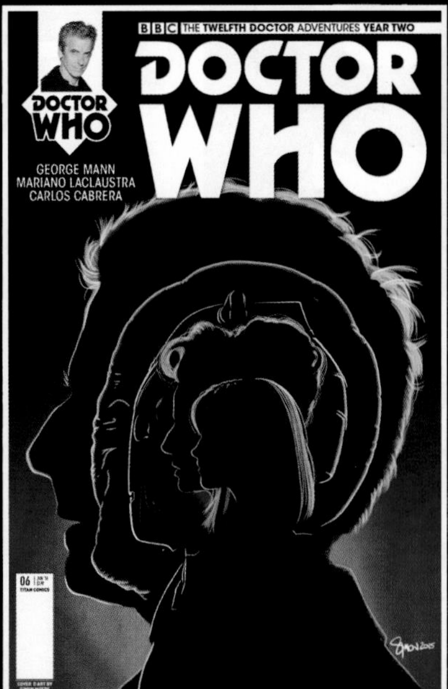

BBC THE TWELFTH DOCTOR ADVENTURES YEAR TWO
DOCTOR WHO
DOCTOR WHO
GEORGE MANN
MARIANO LACLAUSTRA
CARLOS CABRERA
TITAN COMICS

ISSUE #6

A. STEVE PUGH
B. PHOTO – WILL BROOKS
C. TODD NAUCK
D. ROBERT HACK
E. SIMON MYERS

COVER GALLERY

DOCTOR WHO
THE NINTH DOCTOR

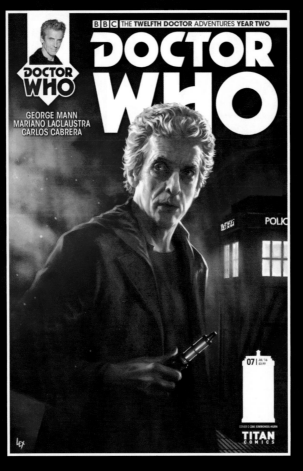

ISSUE #7

A. ALEX RONALD
B. PHOTO – WILL BROOKS
C. SIMON MYERS
D. ZAK SIMMONDS-HURN

A

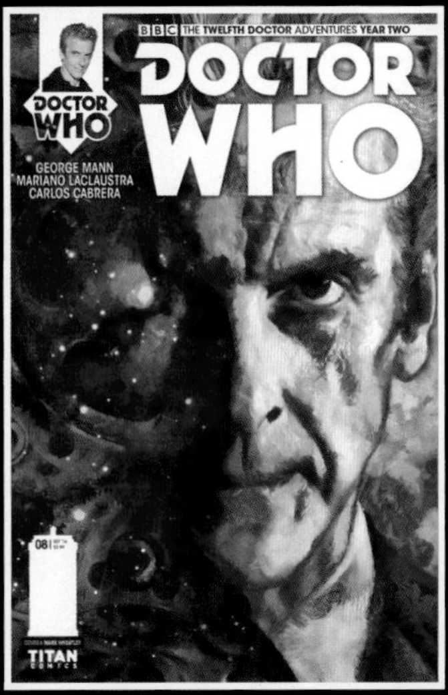
BBC THE TWELFTH DOCTOR ADVENTURES YEAR TWO
DOCTOR WHO
GEORGE MANN
MARIANO LACLAUSTRA
CARLOS CABRERA
TITAN COMICS

B

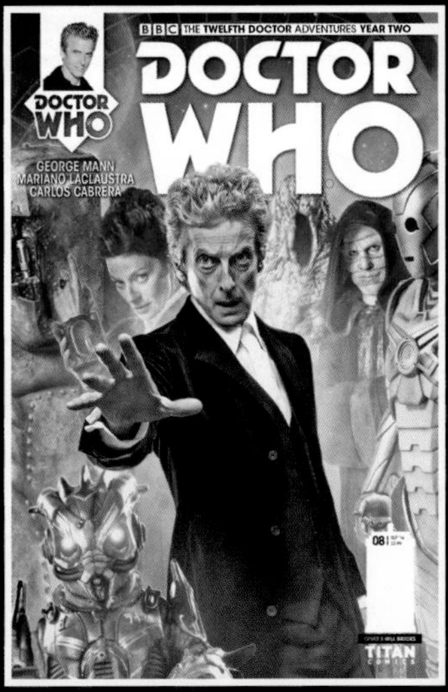
BBC THE TWELFTH DOCTOR ADVENTURES YEAR TWO
DOCTOR WHO
GEORGE MANN
MARIANO LACLAUSTRA
CARLOS CABRERA
TITAN COMICS

C

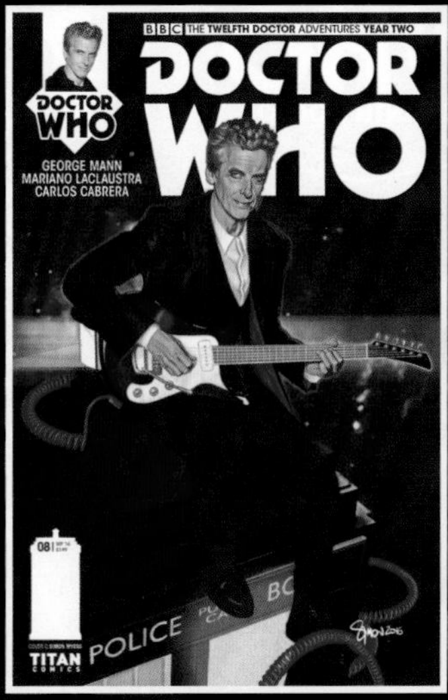
BBC THE TWELFTH DOCTOR ADVENTURES YEAR TWO
DOCTOR WHO
GEORGE MANN
MARIANO LACLAUSTRA
CARLOS CABRERA
POLICE
TITAN COMICS

ISSUE #8

A. MARK WHEATLEY
B. PHOTO – WILL BROOKS
C. SIMON MYERS

A

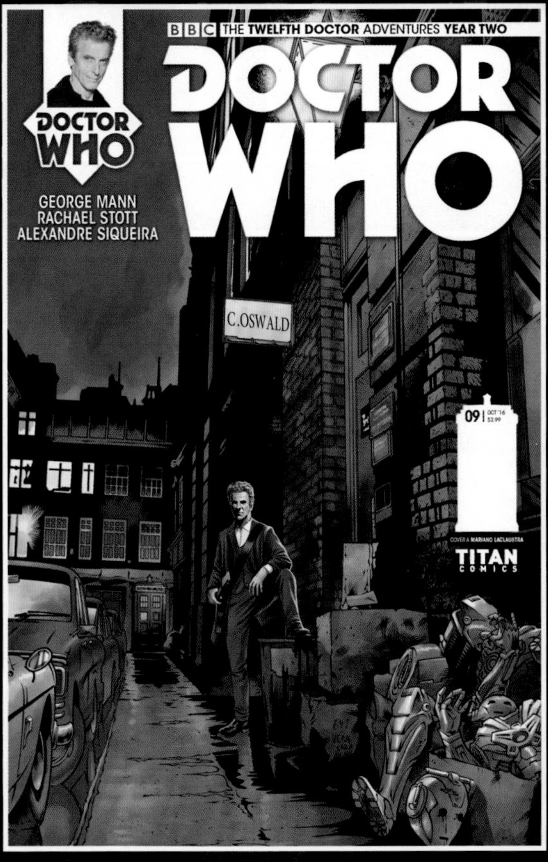
BBC THE TWELFTH DOCTOR ADVENTURES YEAR TWO
DOCTOR WHO
GEORGE MANN
RACHAEL STOTT
ALEXANDRE SIQUEIRA
C.OSWALD
09 OCT '16 $3.99
COVER A MARIANO LACLAUSTRA
TITAN COMICS

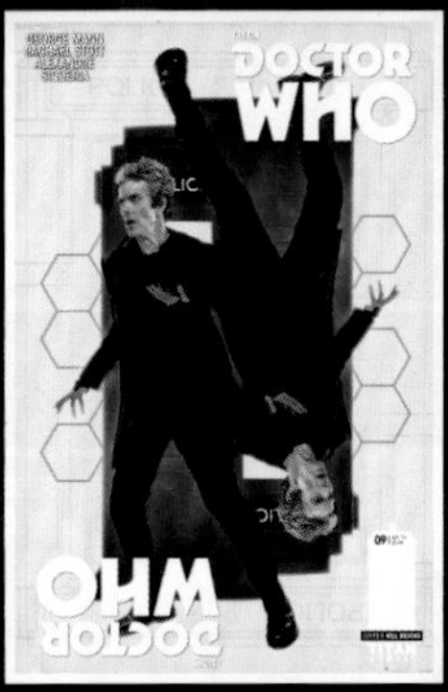
DOCTOR WHO

B

C

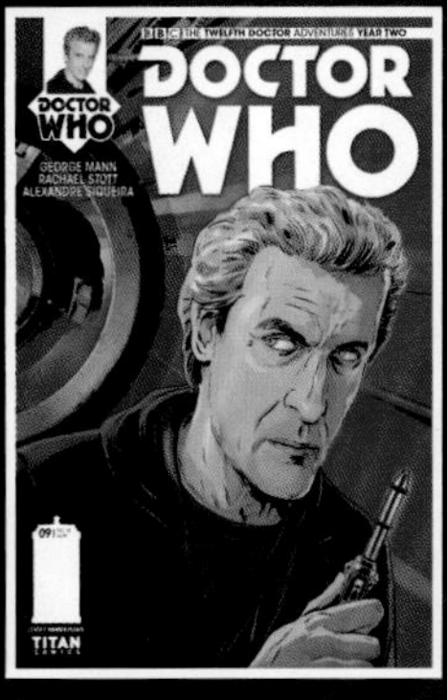
BBC THE TWELFTH DOCTOR ADVENTURES YEAR TWO
DOCTOR WHO
GEORGE MANN
RACHAEL STOTT
ALEXANDRE SIQUEIRA
TITAN COMICS

D

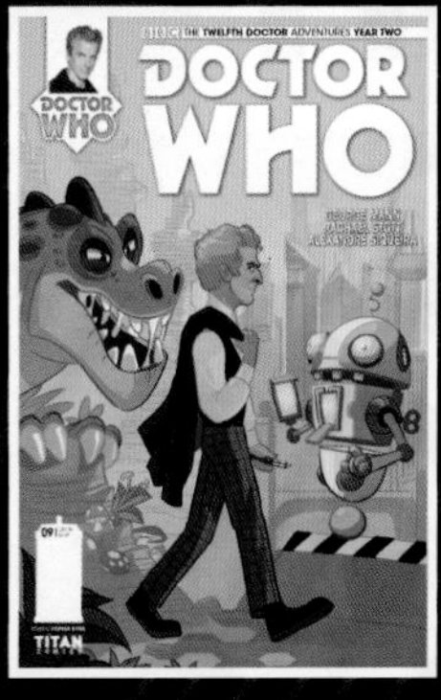
BBC THE TWELFTH DOCTOR ADVENTURES YEAR TWO
DOCTOR WHO

ISSUE #9

A. MARIANO LACLAUSTRA
B. PHOTO – WILL BROOKS
C. WARREN PLEECE

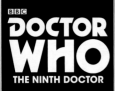

BBC
DOCTOR WHO
THE NINTH DOCTOR

COVER GALLERY

A

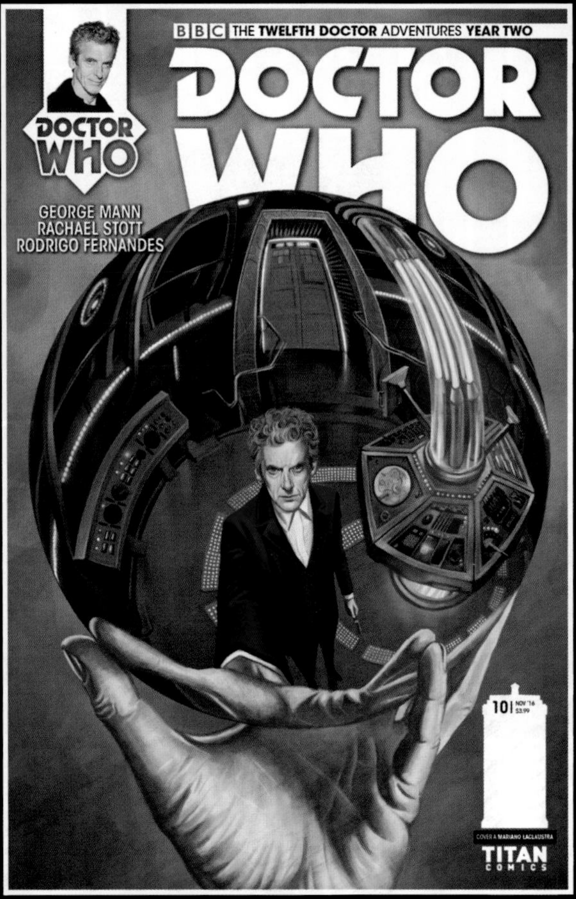
BBC THE TWELFTH DOCTOR ADVENTURES YEAR TWO
DOCTOR WHO
DOCTOR WHO
GEORGE MANN
RACHAEL STOTT
RODRIGO FERNANDES
10 NOV '16 $3.99
COVER A MARIANO LACLAUSTRA
TITAN COMICS

B

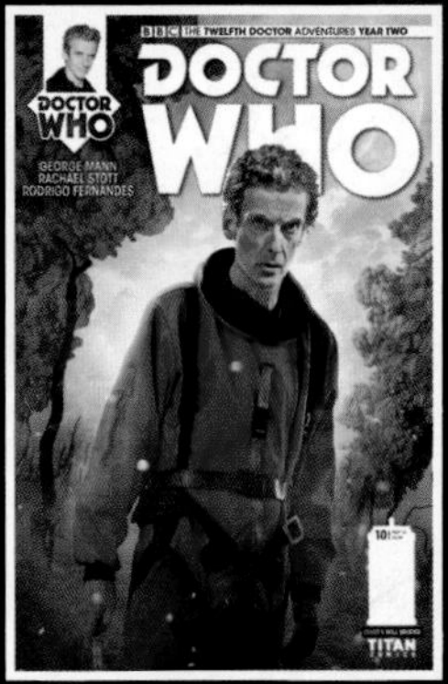
BBC THE TWELFTH DOCTOR ADVENTURES YEAR TWO
DOCTOR WHO
DOCTOR WHO
GEORGE MANN
RACHAEL STOTT
RODRIGO FERNANDES
TITAN

C

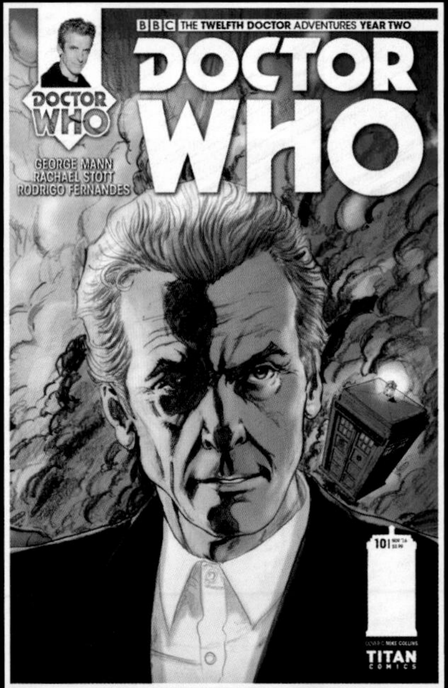
BBC THE TWELFTH DOCTOR ADVENTURES YEAR TWO
DOCTOR WHO
DOCTOR WHO
GEORGE MANN
RACHAEL STOTT
RODRIGO FERNANDES
10
TITAN COMICS

D

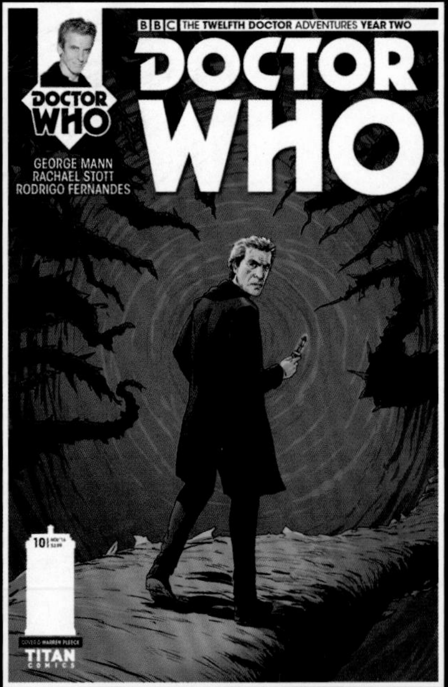
BBC THE TWELFTH DOCTOR ADVENTURES YEAR TWO
DOCTOR WHO
DOCTOR WHO
GEORGE MANN
RACHAEL STOTT
RODRIGO FERNANDES
10
TITAN COMICS

ISSUE #10

A. MARIANO LACLAUSTRA
B. PHOTO – WILL BROOKS
C. MIKE COLLINS
D. WARREN PLEECE

DOCTOR WHO

RACHAEL STOTT

TAKE A LOOK BEHIND THE SCENES AT SOME OF ARTIST
RACHAEL STOTT'S MOST INCREDIBLE INKED PAGES
FROM ISSUES #2.9 AND #2.10!

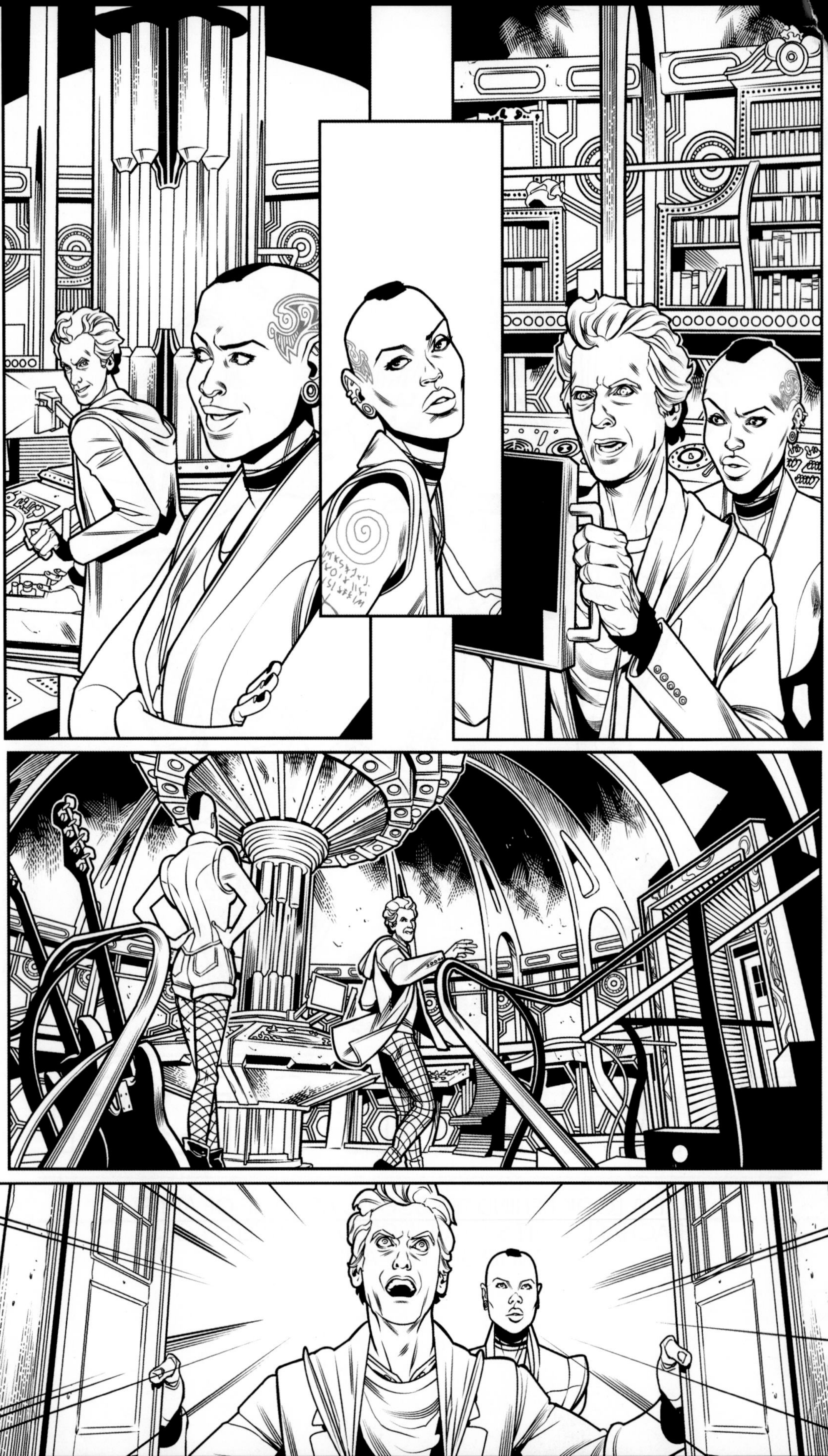

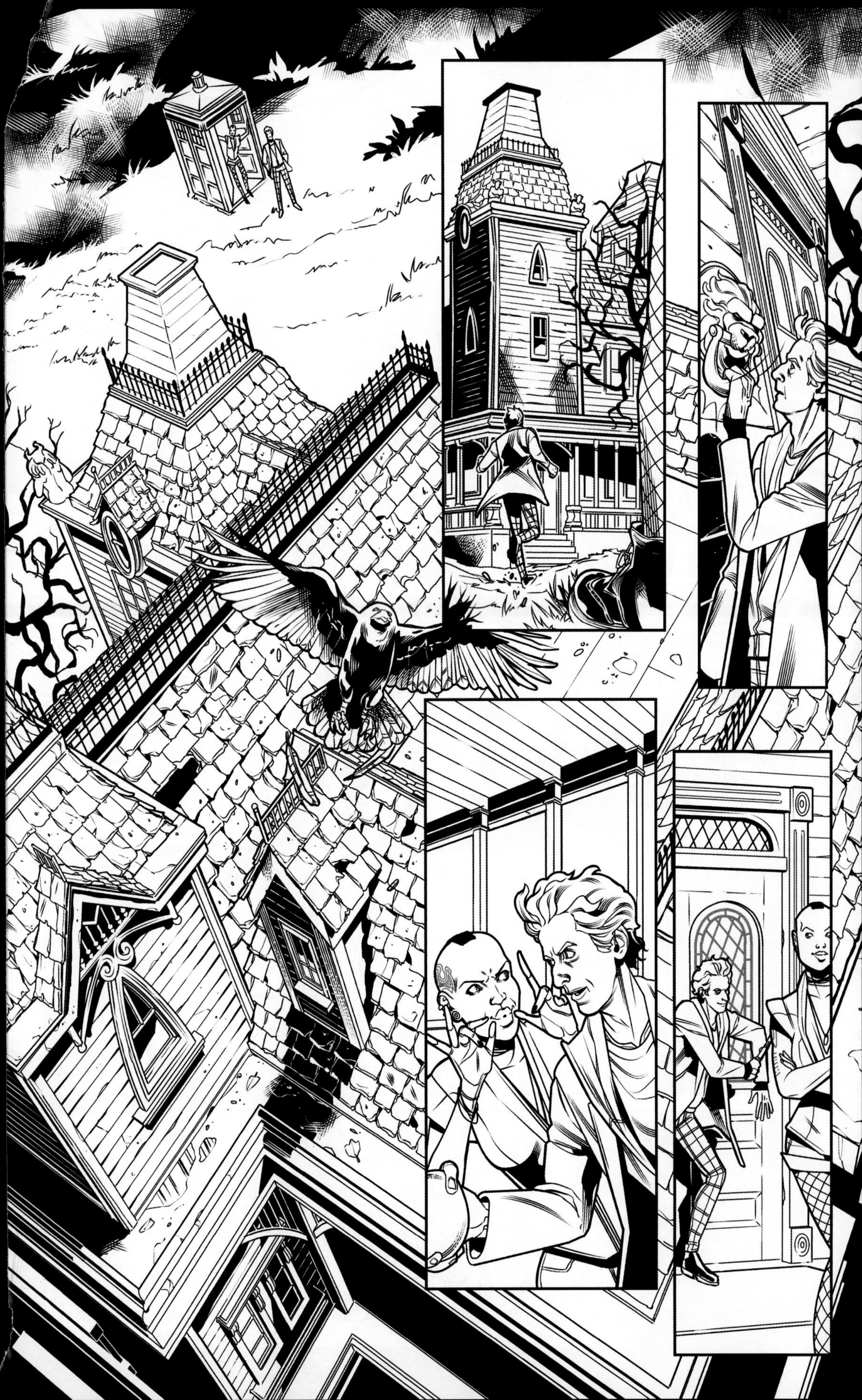

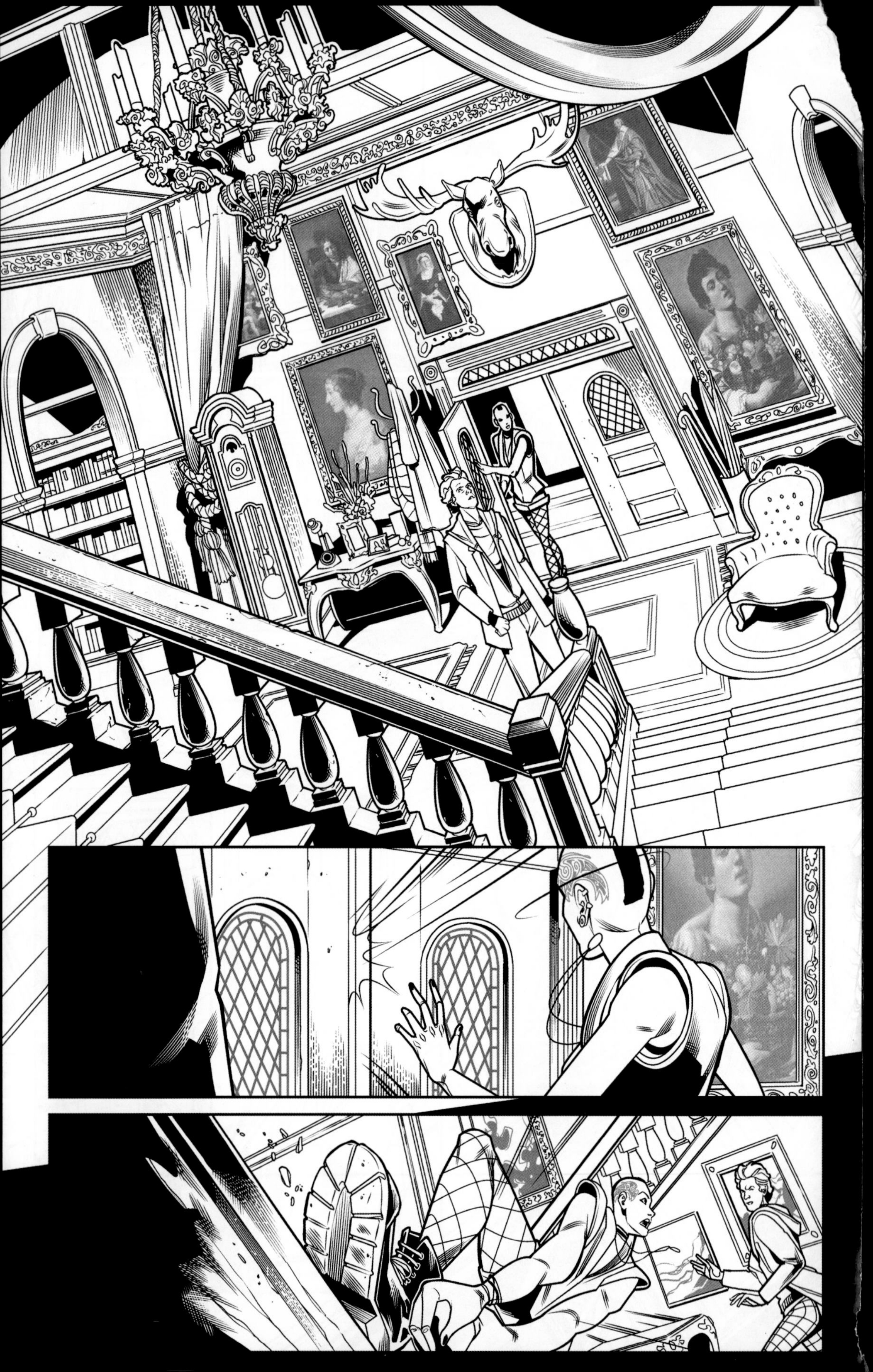

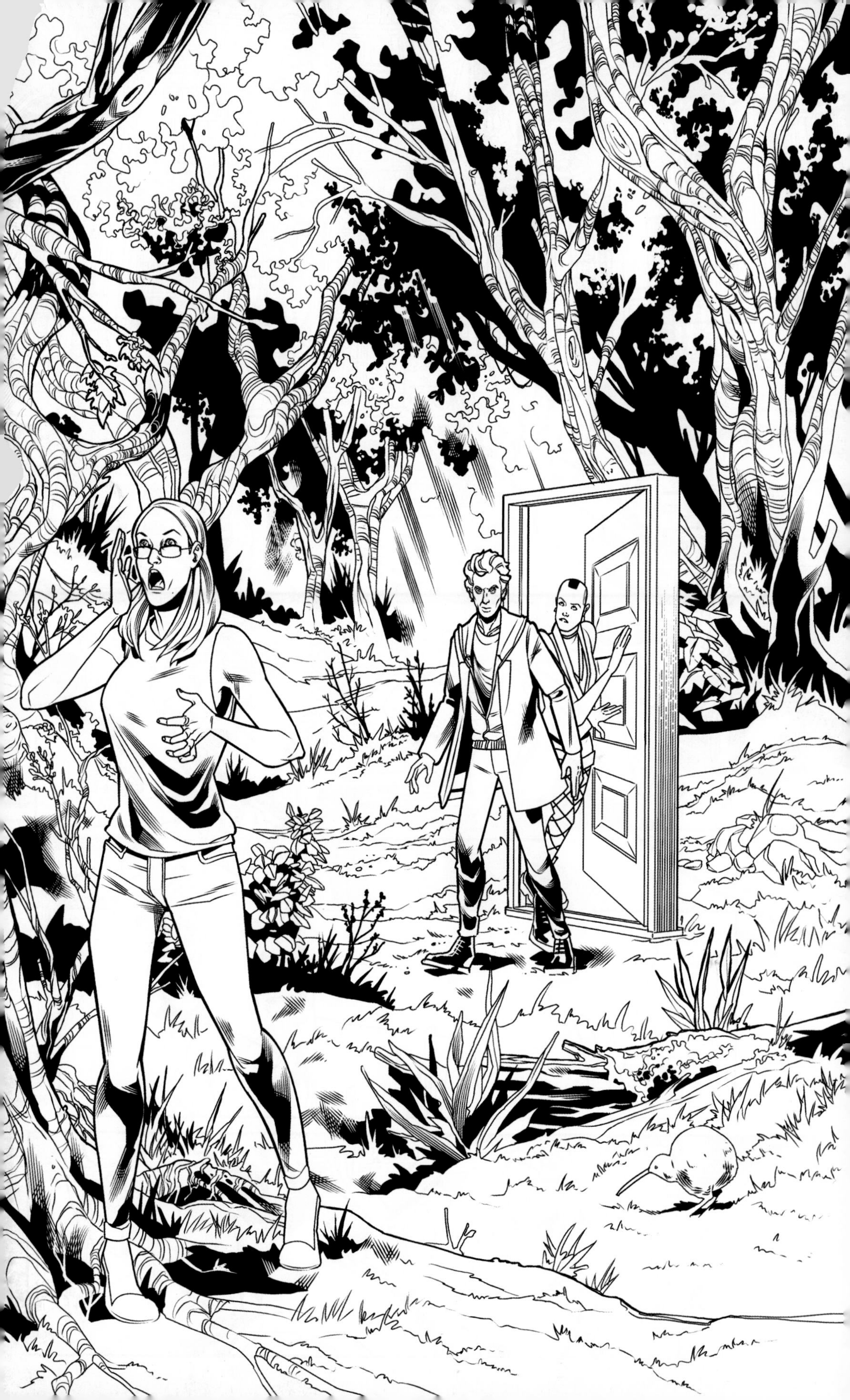

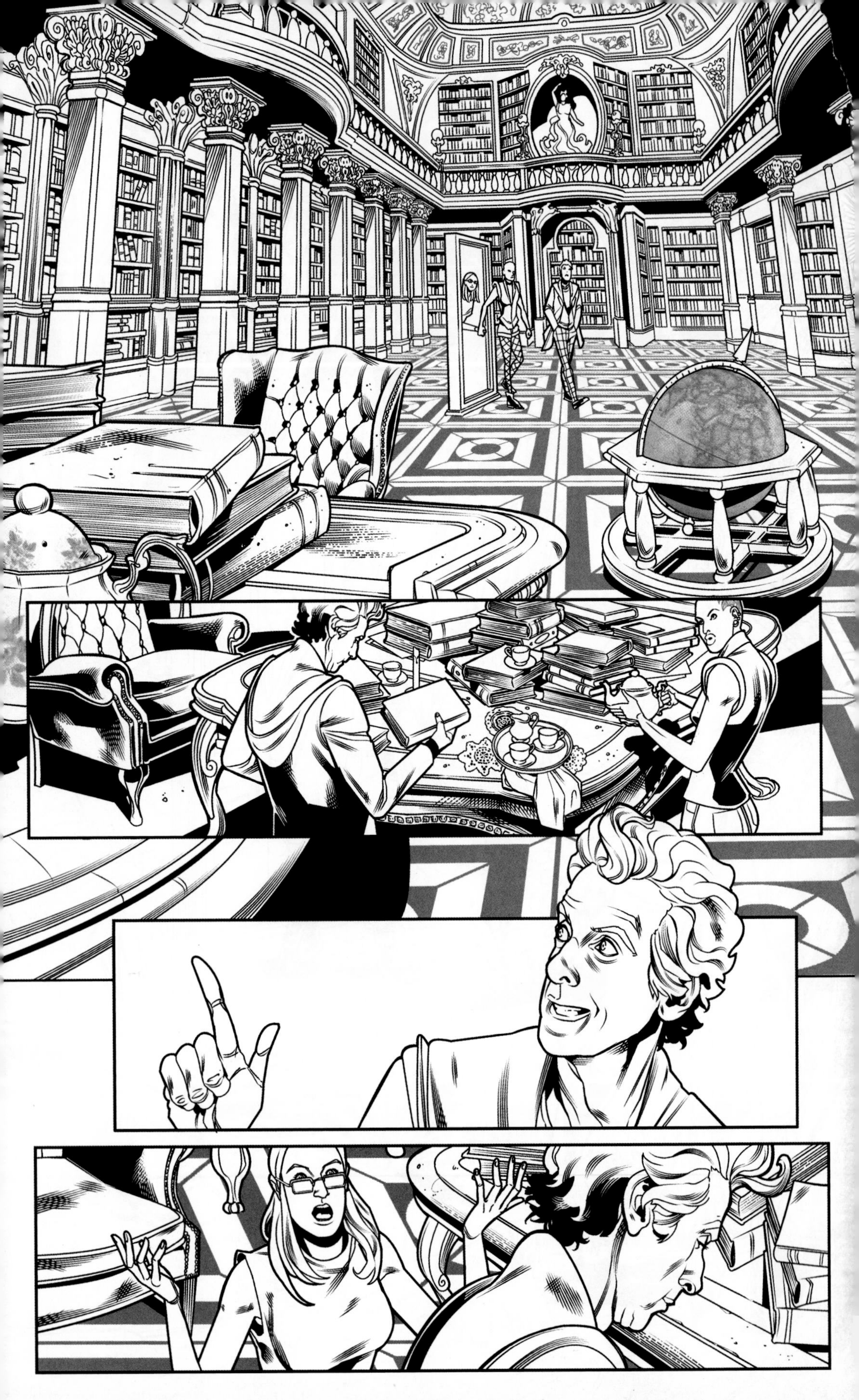

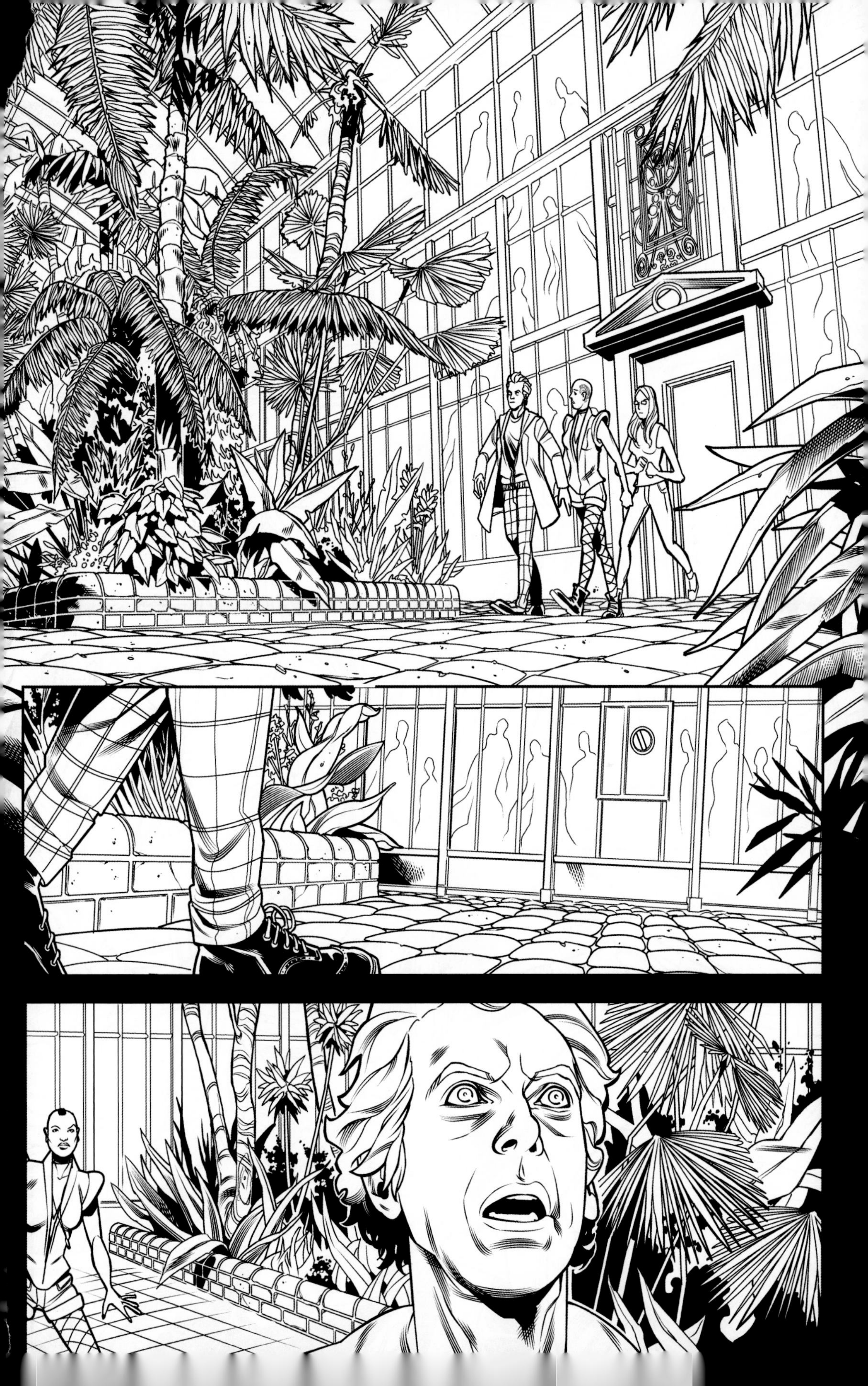

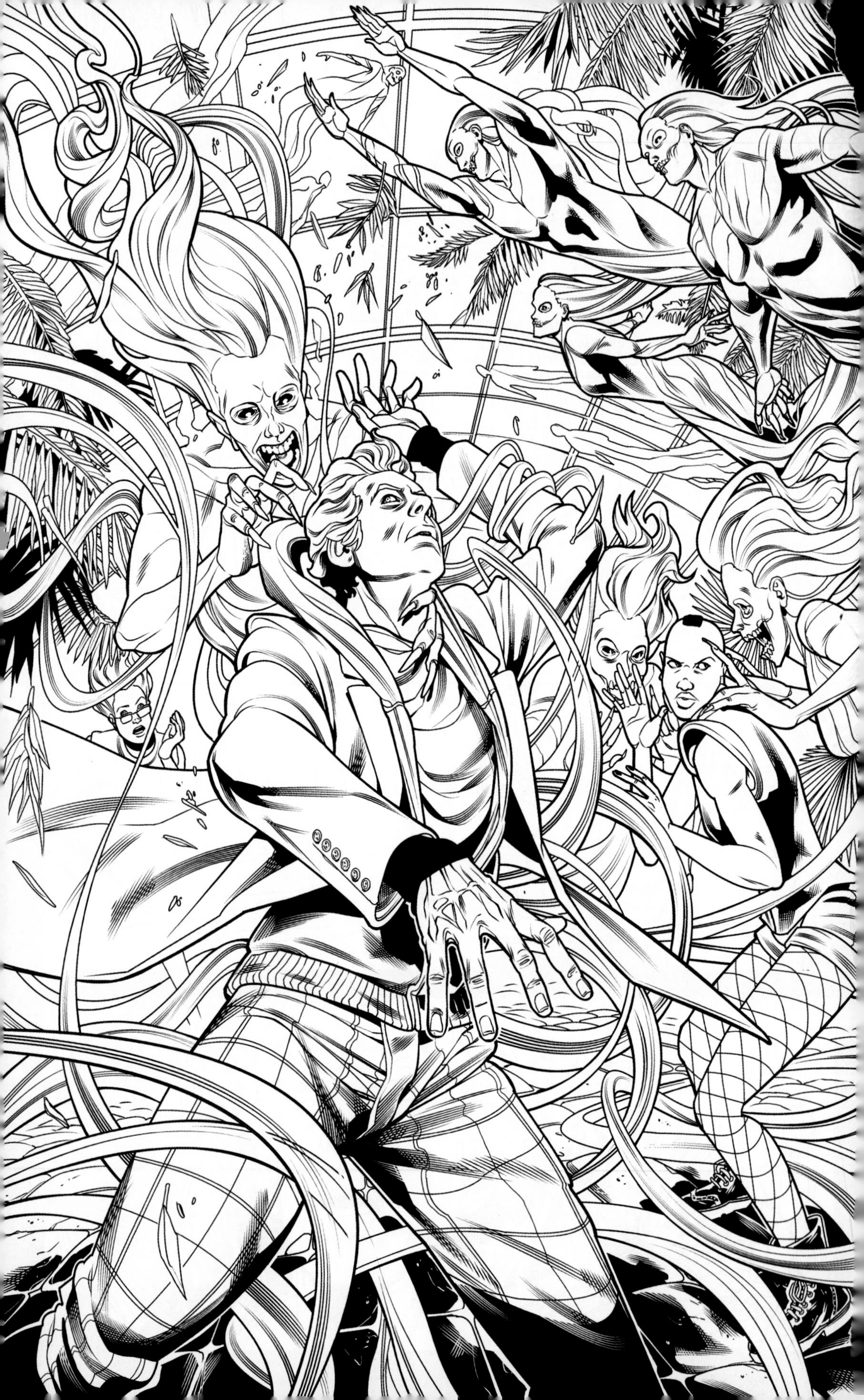

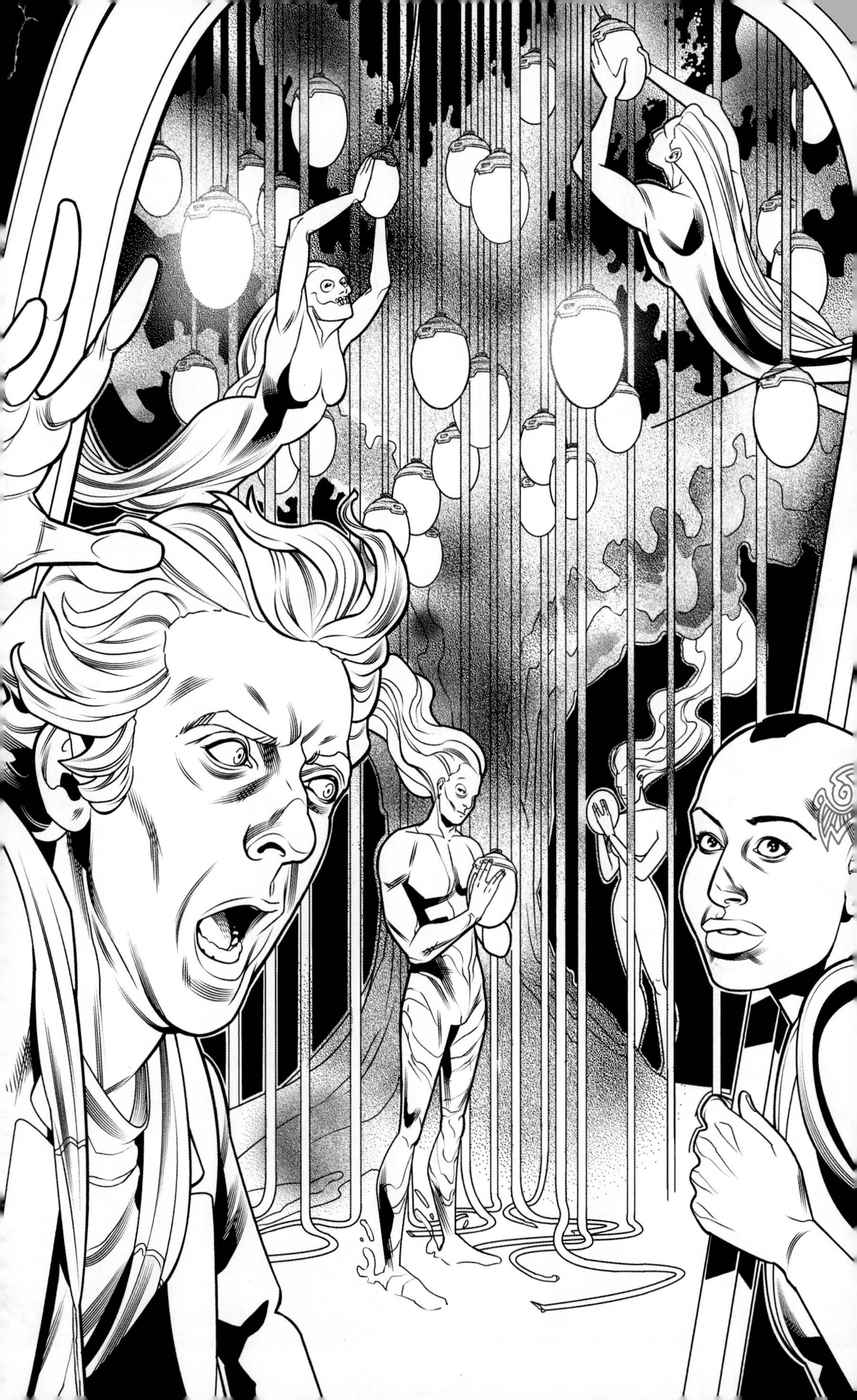

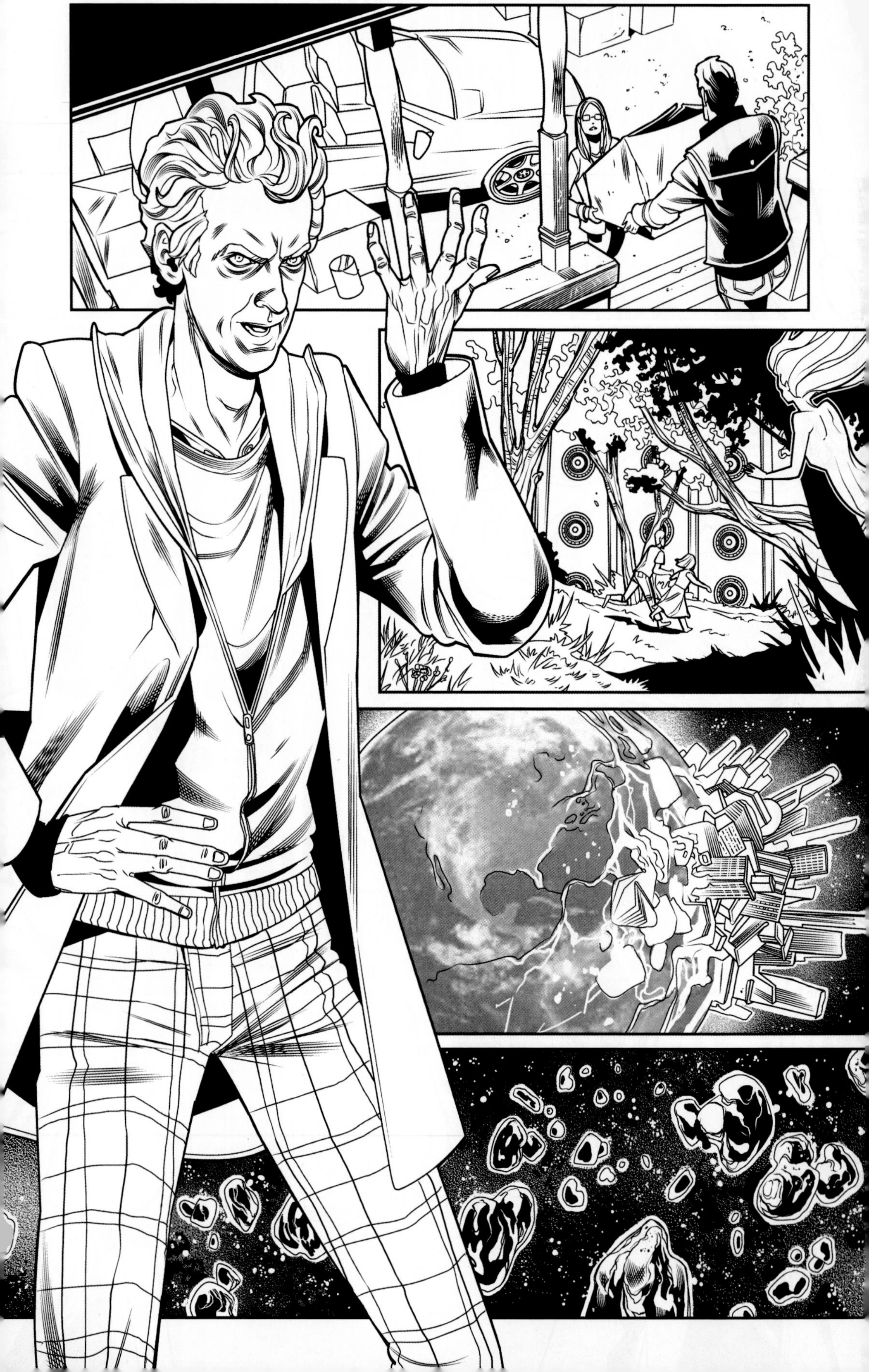

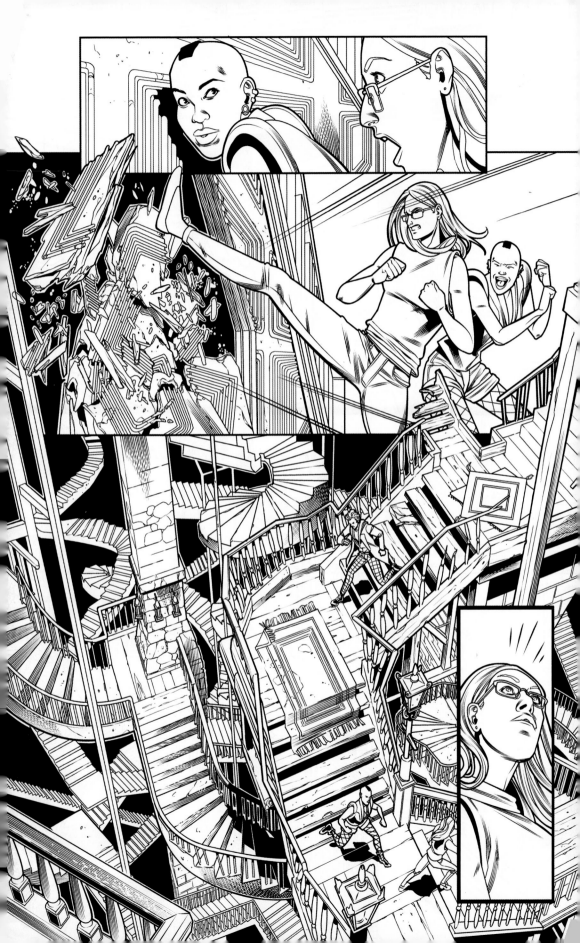

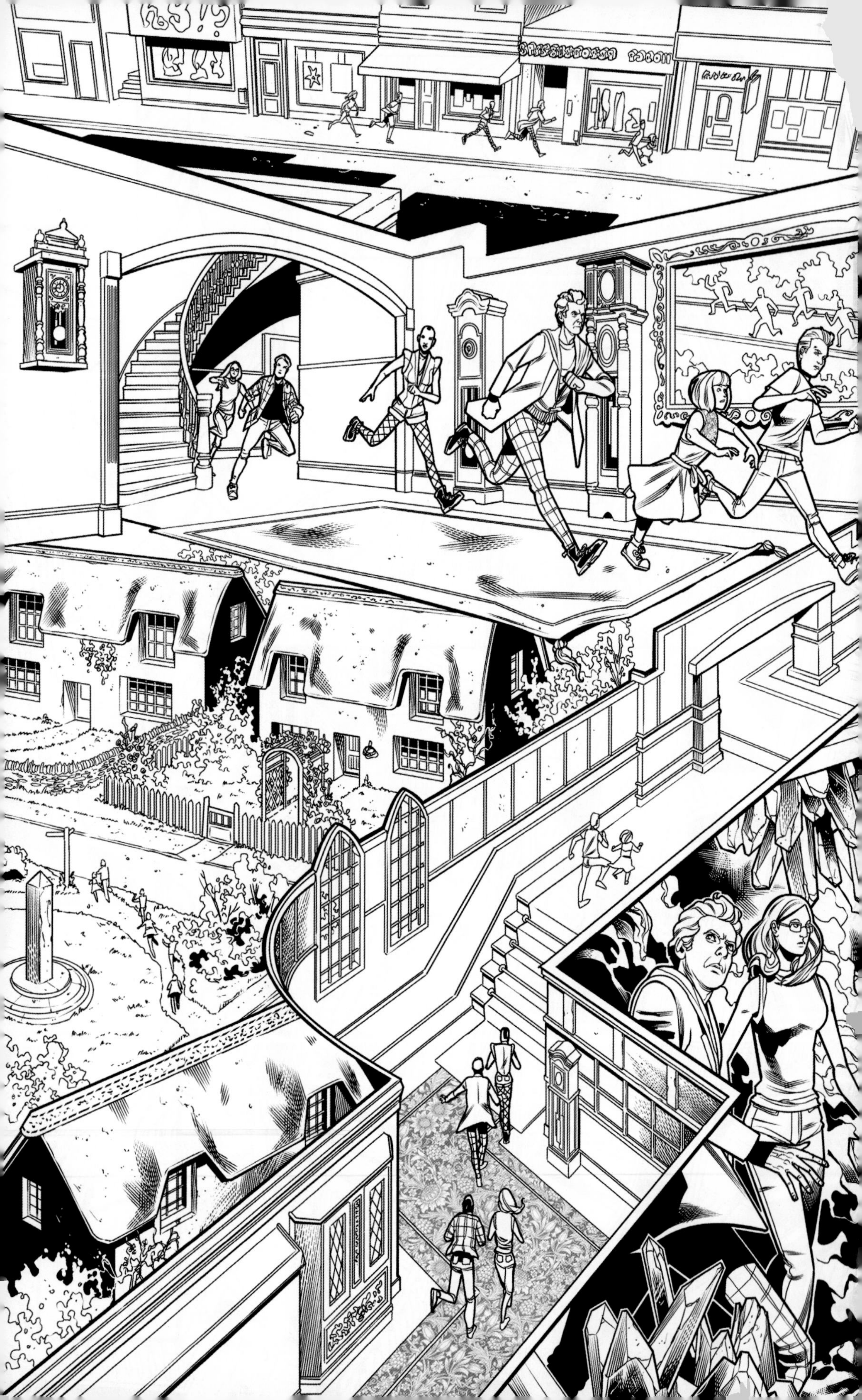

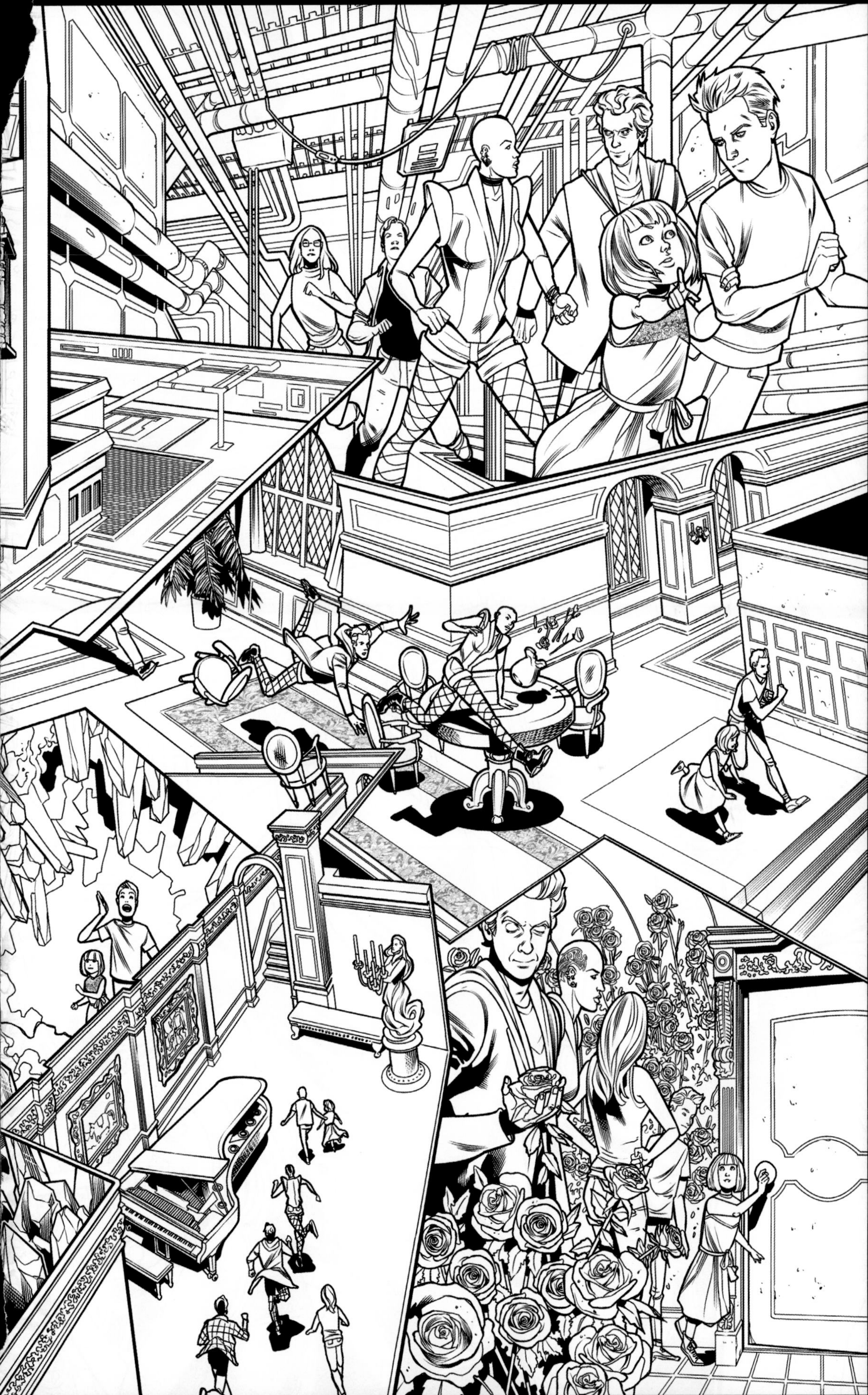

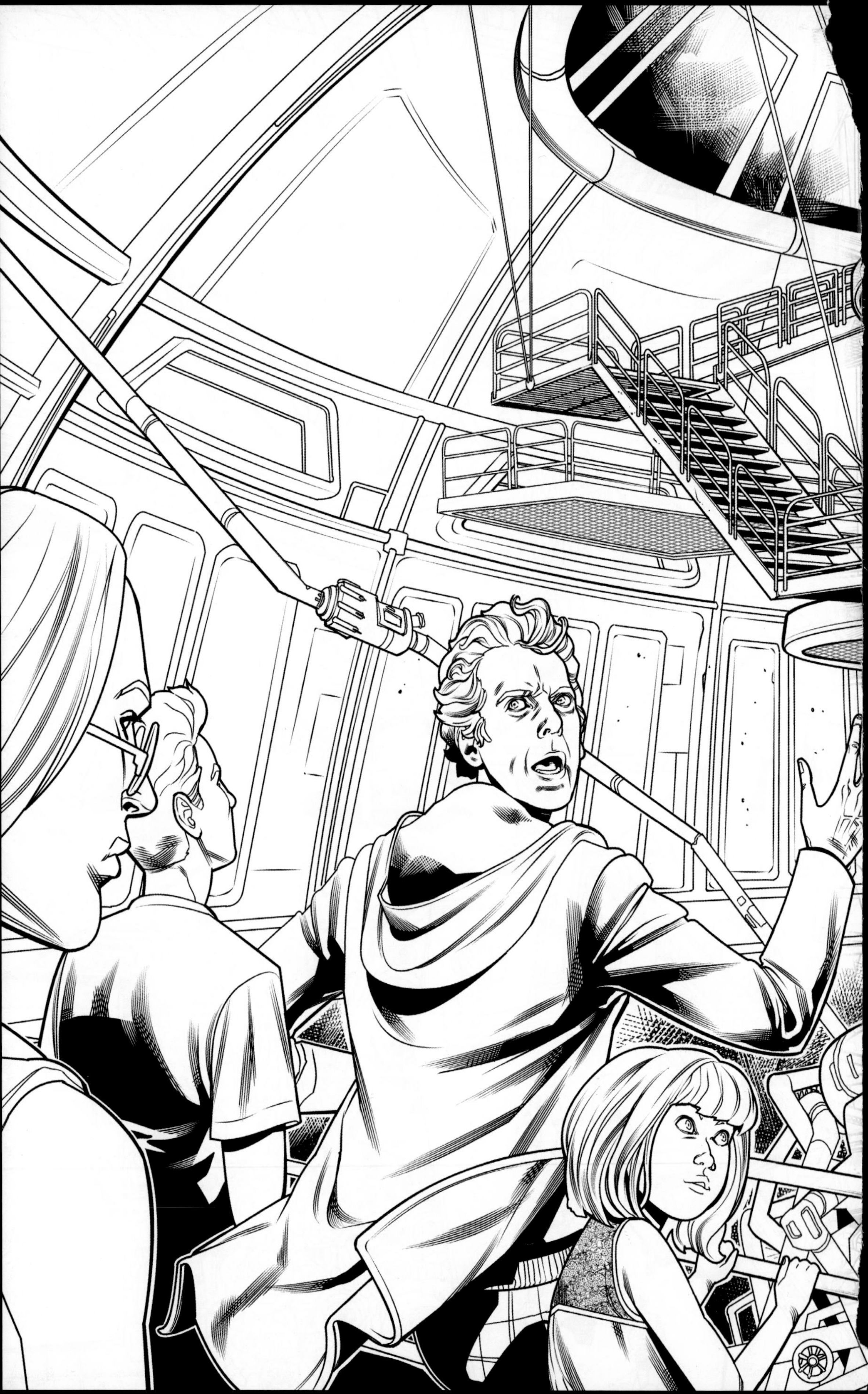

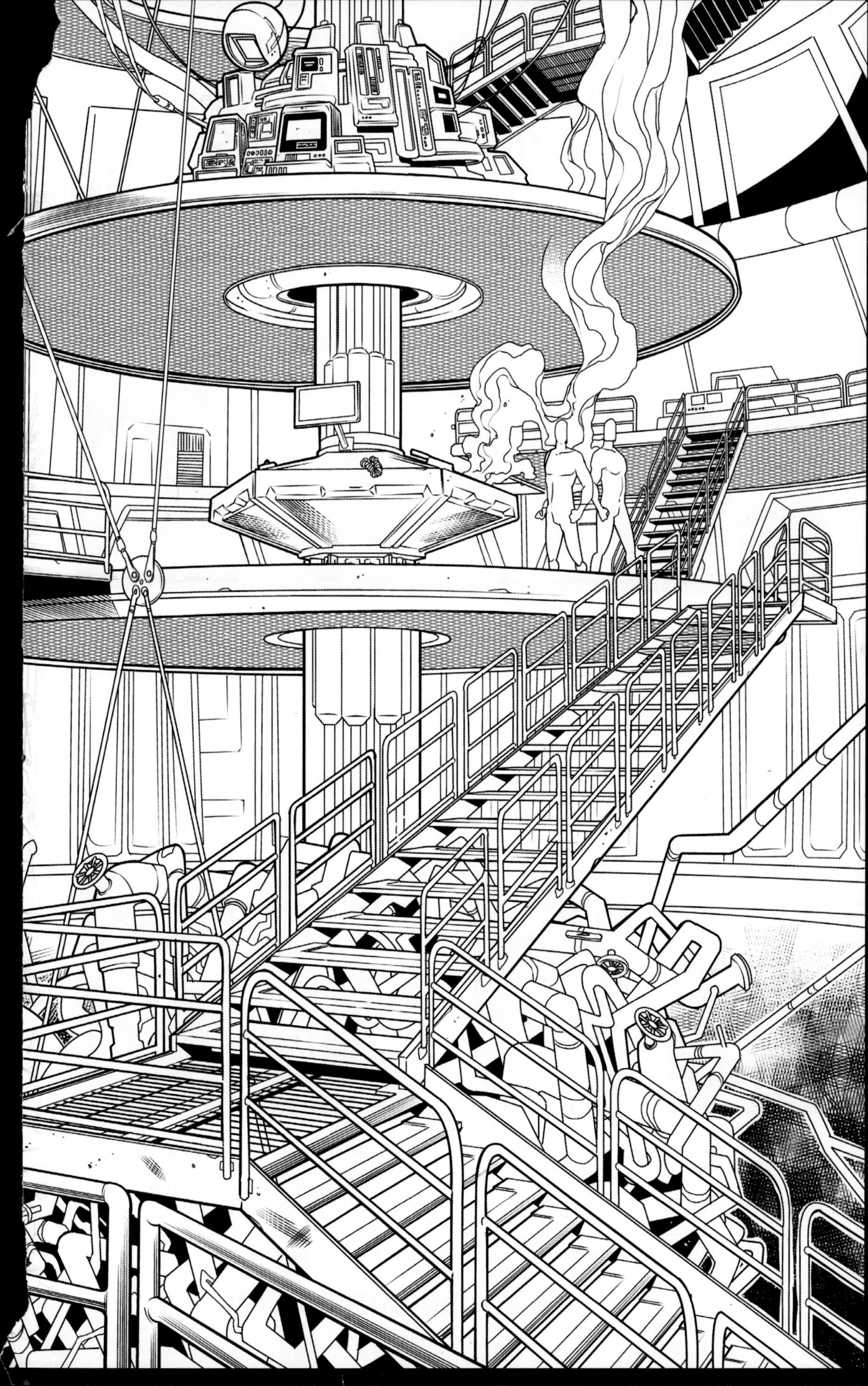

FOLLOW YOUR FAVORITE INCARNATIONS ACROSS THESE FANTASTIC COLLECTIONS!

DOCTOR WHO: THE TWELFTH DOCTOR VOL. 1:TERRORFORMER

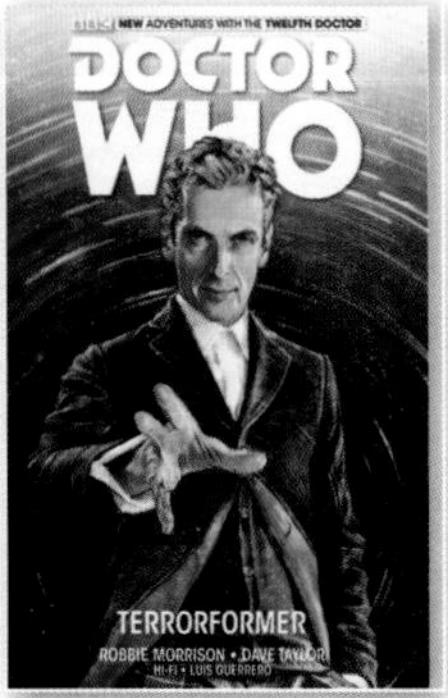
DOCTOR WHO
TERRORFORMER
ROBBIE MORRISON • DAVE TAYLOR

ISBN: 9781782761778
ON SALE NOW - $19.99 / $22.95 CAN / £10.99
(UK EDITION ISBN: 9781782763864)

DOCTOR WHO: THE TWELFTH DOCTOR VOL. 2: FRACTURES

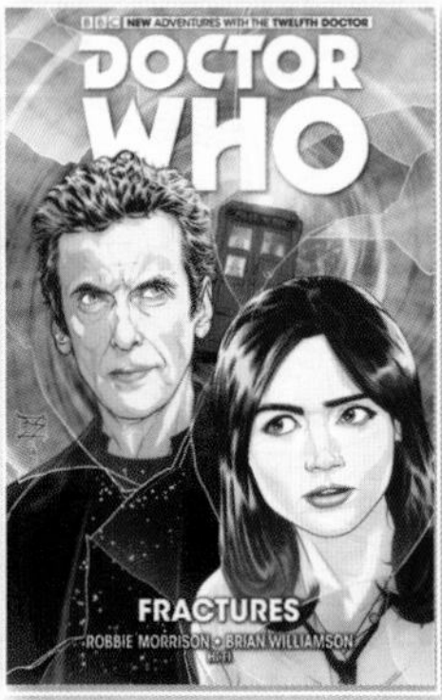
NEW ADVENTURES WITH THE TWELFTH DOCTOR
DOCTOR WHO
FRACTURES
ROBBIE MORRISON • BRIAN WILLIAMSON

ISBN: 9781782763017
ON SALE NOW - $19.99 / $25.99 CAN / £10.99
(UK EDITION ISBN: 9781782766599)

DOCTOR WHO: THE TWELFTH DOCTOR VOL. 3: HYPERION

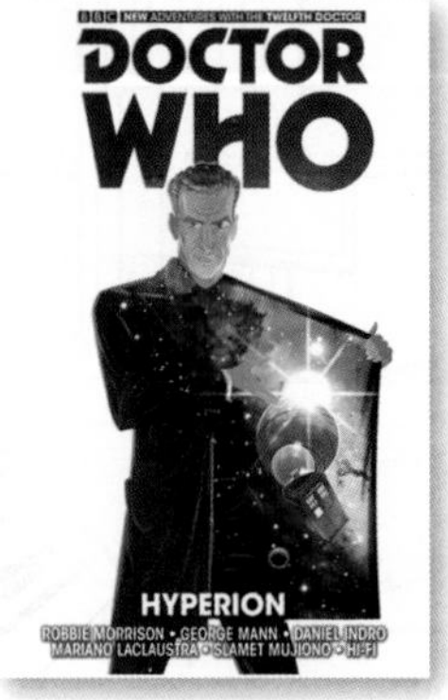
NEW ADVENTURES WITH THE TWELFTH DOCTOR
DOCTOR WHO
HYPERION
ROBBIE MORRISON • GEORGE MANN • DANIEL INDRO
MARIANO LACLAUSTRA • SLAMET MUJIONO • HI-FI

ISBN: 9781782767473
ON SALE NOW- $19.99 / $25.99 CAN / £10.99
(UK EDITION ISBN: 97817827674442)

DOCTOR WHO: THE TWELFTH DOCTOR VOL. 4: THE SCHOOL OF DEATH

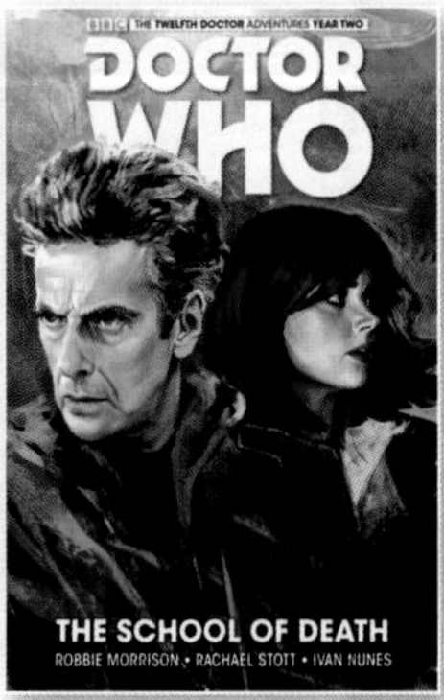
THE TWELFTH DOCTOR ADVENTURES YEAR TWO
DOCTOR WHO
THE SCHOOL OF DEATH
ROBBIE MORRISON • RACHAEL STOTT • IVAN NUNES

ISBN: 9781785851087
COMING SOON - $19.99 / $25.99 CAN / £10.99
(UK EDITION ISBN: 9781785851070)

DOCTOR WHO: THE ELEVENTH DOCTOR VOL. 1: AFTER LIFE

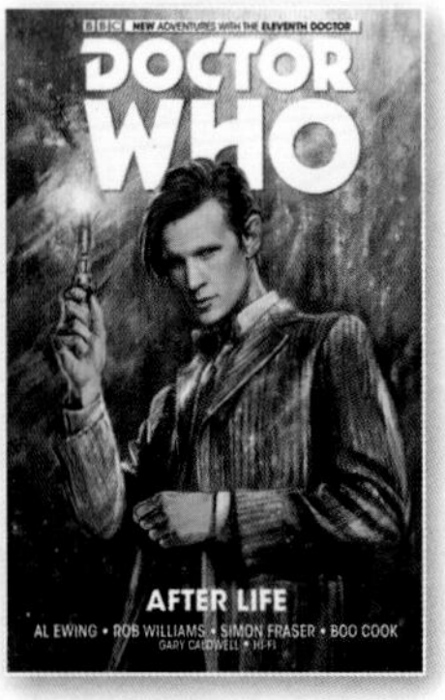
NEW ADVENTURES WITH THE ELEVENTH DOCTOR
DOCTOR WHO
AFTER LIFE
AL EWING • ROB WILLIAMS • SIMON FRASER • BOO COOK

ISBN: 9781782761747
ON SALE NOW - $19.99 / $22.95 CAN / £10.99
(UK EDITION ISBN: 9781782763857)

DOCTOR WHO: THE ELEVENTH DOCTOR VOL. 2: SERVE YOU

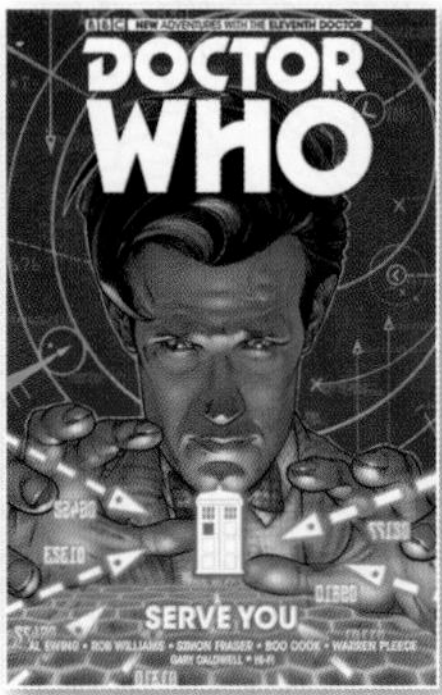
NEW ADVENTURES WITH THE ELEVENTH DOCTOR
DOCTOR WHO
SERVE YOU

ISBN: 9781782761754
ON SALE NOW - $19.99 / $25.99 CAN / £10.99
(UK EDITION ISBN: 9781782766582)

DOCTOR WHO: THE ELEVENTH DOCTOR VOL. 3: CONVERSION

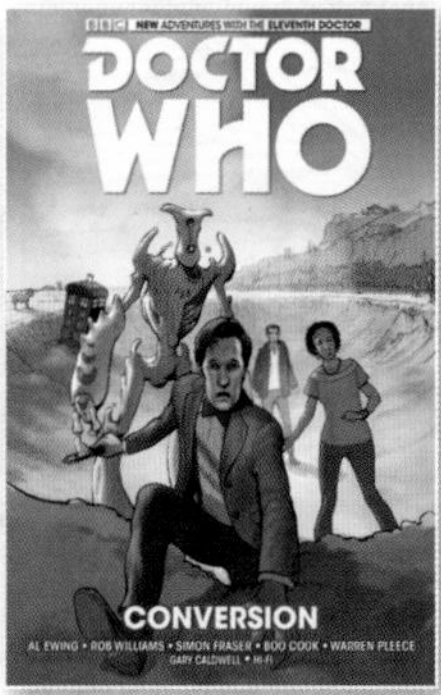
NEW ADVENTURES WITH THE ELEVENTH DOCTOR
DOCTOR WHO
CONVERSION

ISBN: 9781782763024
ON SALE NOW - $19.99 / $25.99 CAN / £10.99
(UK EDITION ISBN: 9781782767435)

DOCTOR WHO: THE ELEVENTH DOCTOR VOL. 4:THE THEN AND THE NOW

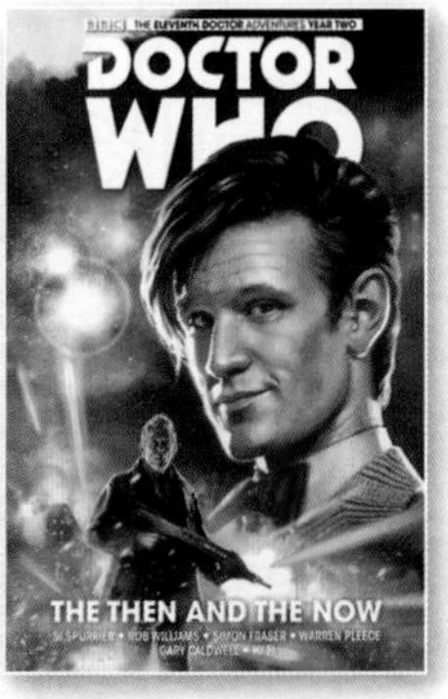
THE ELEVENTH DOCTOR ADVENTURES YEAR TWO
DOCTOR WHO
THE THEN AND THE NOW

ISBN: 9781782767466
ON SALE NOW - $19.99 / $25.99 CAN / £10.99
(UK EDITION ISBN: 9781722767428)

For information on how to subscribe to our great Doctor Who titles, or to purchase them digitally for your favorite device, visit:

WWW.TITAN-COMICS.COM

TITAN COMICS

COMPLETE YOUR COLLECTION!

DOCTOR WHO: THE TENTH DOCTOR VOL. 1: REVOLUTIONS OF TERROR

ISBN: 9781782761747
ON SALE NOW - $19.99 / $22.95 CAN / £10.99
(UK EDITION ISBN: 9781782763840)

DOCTOR WHO: THE TENTH DOCTOR VOL. 2: THE WEEPING ANGELS OF MONS

ISBN: 9781782761754
ON SALE NOW - $19.99 / $25.99 CAN / £10.99
(UK EDITION ISBN: 9781782766575)

DOCTOR WHO: THE TENTH DOCTOR VOL. 3: THE FOUNTAINS OF FOREVER

ISBN: 9781782763024
ON SALE NOW - $19.99 / $25.99 CAN / £10.99
(UK EDITION ISBN: 9781782767435)

DOCTOR WHO: THE TENTH DOCTOR VOL. 4: THE ENDLESS SONG

ISBN: 9781785854286
ON SALE NOW - $19.99 / $25.99 CAN / £10.99
(SC ISBN: 9781785853227)

DOCTOR WHO: THE NINTH DOCTOR VOL. 1: WEAPONS OF PAST DESTRUCTION

ISBN: 9781782763369
ON SALE NOW - $19.99 / $25.99 CAN / £10.99
(UK EDITION ISBN: 9781782761056)

DOCTOR WHO EVENT 2015 FOUR DOCTORS

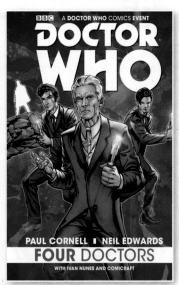

ISBN: 9781782765967
ON SALE NOW - $19.99 / $25.99 CAN / £10.99
(UK EDITION ISBN: 9781785851063)

AVAILABLE IN ALL GOOD COMIC STORES, BOOK STORES, AND DIGITAL PROVIDERS!

BIOGRAPHIES

George Mann is the author of *Dark Souls, The Affinity Bridge, The Osiris Ritual* and *Ghosts of Manhattan*, as well as numerous short stories, novellas and an original *Doctor Who* audiobook. He has edited a number of anthologies, including a retrospective collection of *Sexton Blake* stories, *Sexton Blake, Detective*. He lives near Grantham, UK, with his wife and children.

Mariano Laclaustra is a creator with a background in the Fine Arts. A freelance artist based in Argentina, he has worked with publishers across Europe and the United States, including for *Dark Horse Presents*. In between drawing and coloring comics, he teaches oil painting.

Rachael Stott is a talented illustrator and winner of the Best Newcomer Artist at the British Comic Awards 2015. She has worked on *Planet of the Apes, Star Trek, Doctor Who,* and *Ghostbusters International*.

Carlos Cabrera is an up and coming colorist with many diverse projects to his name, such as *Invincible Iron Man, Agents of Atlas* and *Doctor Who*.

Alexandre Siqueira is a fresh coloring talent who has worked on *Doctor Who*.

Rodrigo Fernandes is a colorist whose beautiful work can be seen on titles such as *Vikings, Independence Day* and *Doctor Who*.

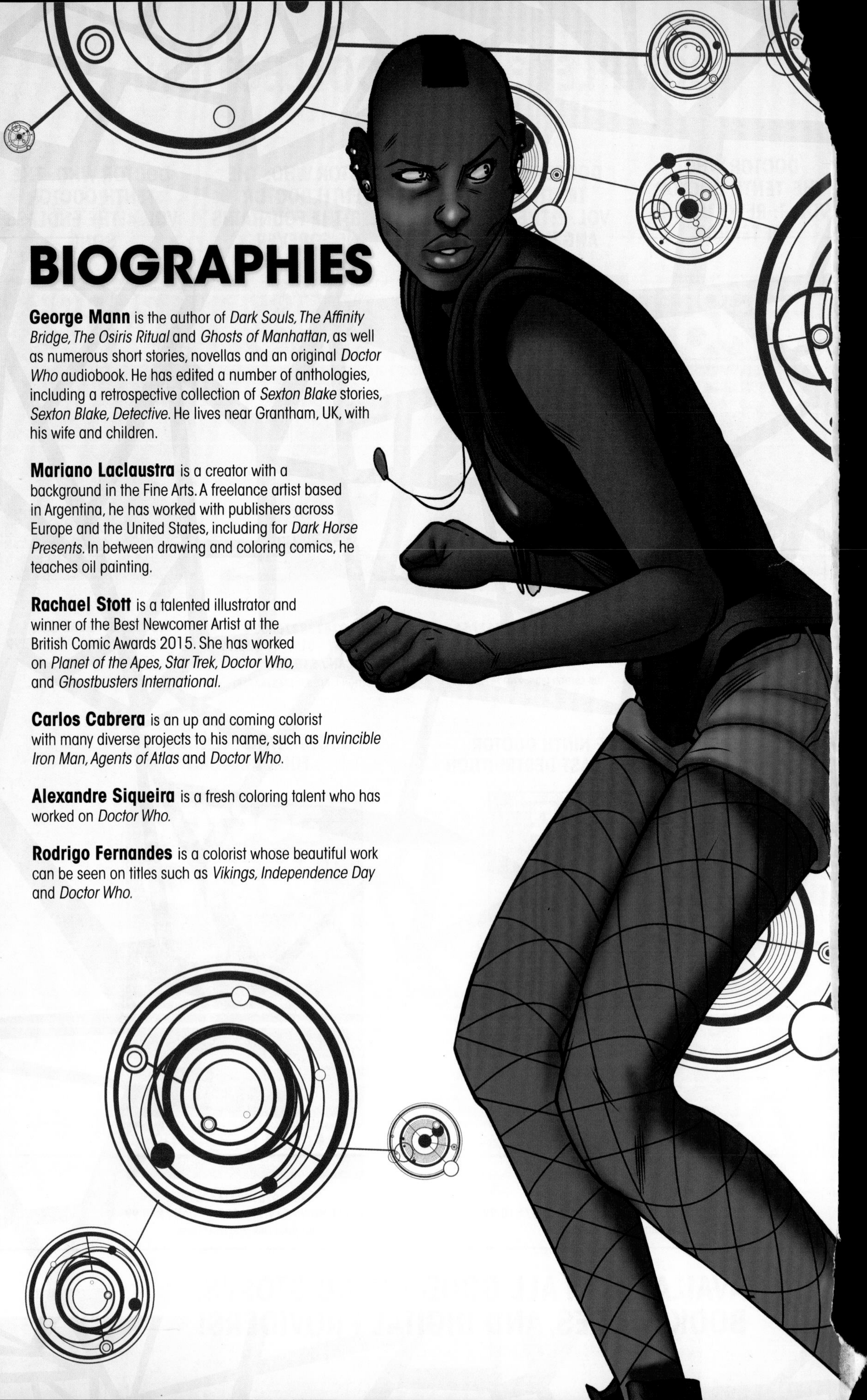